This book takes up iconoclasm, t
ordinary people entered into "l
towns of the 1520s. It seeks to recover the agency of ordinary people in Reformation and to discern their theology in their acts. In
part, its purpose is to suggest ways of excavating the meaning of
the acts of those who did not have access to more protected and
fixed forms of communication – that is, printed texts and images.
In part, it illuminates the meaning of images for ordinary Christians in the sixteenth century.

Voracious Idols and Violent Hands posits a vision of "Reformation"
as a dialogue in which different persons "spoke" through different forms, according to their education and social and political
place. Each brought his or her vision of true Christianity to that
dialogue, and articulated that vision in the cultural form he or she
found most accessible: theologians in sermons and treatises, magistrates in laws and their enforcement, and ordinary people – the
focus of this volume – in acts.

Voracious idols and violent hands

Voracious idols and violent hands

Iconoclasm in Reformation Zurich, Strasbourg, and Basel

LEE PALMER WANDEL

Yale University

CAMBRIDGE
UNIVERSITY PRESS

PUBLISHED BY THE PRESS SYNDICATE OF THE UNIVERSITY OF CAMBRIDGE
The Pitt Building, Trumpington Street, Cambridge

CAMBRIDGE UNIVERSITY PRESS
The Edinburgh Building, Cambridge CB2 2RU, UK www.cup.cam.ac.uk
40 West 20th Street, New York, NY 10011-4211, USA www.cup.org
10 Stamford Road, Oakleigh, Melbourne 3166, Australia
Ruiz de Alarcón 13, 28014 Madrid, Spain

© Cambridge University Press 1994

First published 1994
First paperback edition 1999

Printed in the United States of America

Typeface New Baskerville 11/13 pt. *System* MS Word [MG]

A catalog record for this book is available from the British Library

Library of Congress Cataloging in Publication Data
Wandel, Lee Palmer.
Voracious idols and violent hands : iconoclasm in Reformation Zurich,
Strasbourg, and Basel / Lee Palmer Wandel.
p. cm.
ISBN 0 521 47222 9
1. Iconoclasm – Switzerland – Zurich. 2. Iconoclasm – France – Strasbourg.
3. Iconoclasm – Switzerland – Basel 4. Reformation – Switzerland – Zurich.
5. Reformation – France – Strasbourg. 6. Reformation – Switzerland – Basel.
7. Zurich (Switzerland) – Church history – 16th century.
8. Strasbourg (France) – Church history – 16th century.
9. Basel (Switzerland) – Church history – 16th century. I. Title.
BR355.I35W35 1995
274.94´06 – dc20   94–13639
CIP

ISBN 0 521 47222 9 hardback
ISBN 0 521 66343 1 paperback

This book was published with the generous assistance of the
Frederick W. Hilles Publications Fund of Yale University.

Contents

Acknowledgments

Over a decade ago, over raspberries in Tübingen, Bob Scribner and I puzzled over the connection, so explicit in Zurich, between images and the poor. In 1986, he invited me to talk about the "sociology of iconoclasm" at the Wolfenbütteler Arbeitsgespräch, "Bilder und Bildersturm im Spätmittelalter und in der frühen Neuzeit," which he and Martin Warnke directed. As I listened more closely to the words, attended more carefully to the acts of Lorentz Meyger, Lorentz Hochrütiner, Claus Hottinger, Hans Ockenfuß, and other Zurich iconoclasts, I realized that these acts and words did not fit comfortably into the explanations that had been offered to date. Thus this book has it origin in two different sorts of conversations, one with a friend, in joyous moments of playful thinking, one with those long dead, who resisted conclusion, closure, and who continued to demand to be heard.

The generosity of institutions has enabled me to reconstruct the iconoclasts' speaking. Libraries and archives gave me access to those documents that are the bedrock of this study: I am grateful to the staffs of the Stadtsarchiv Zürich, in particular Thomas Schärli, and of the Staatsarchiv Basel for facilitating my research, conducted under the constraints of time American scholars know so well, curtailed by the impatience of an 18-month-old; one could not ask for greater help in the pursuit of fragments of stories, pieces of puzzles that had not yet taken shape. I join all the American scholars of Strasbourg in my special gratitude to Monsieur Fuchs of the Strasbourg Municipal Archives; I, too, benefited from his profound knowledge of the archives, his learning, and his extraordinary hospitality. The staffs of Green Library at Stanford University and of the Sterling Memorial Library at Yale University tirelessly purchased or found books for me, no matter how obscure or minimal the reference. I am grateful to the Beinecke Rare Book and Manuscript Library of Yale University, and in particular Vincent Giroud, Curator of Modern Books and Manuscripts, for the reproductions of the maps of the three cities. So, too, various institutions have provided the funding that makes such research possible. Stanford University provided some of the funding for the research on iconoclasm in Zurich. At Yale University, a Morse Faculty Fellowship provided a year for writing, and a Griswold Research Fellowship enabled a summer's research. The book was published with the assistance of the Frederick W. Hilles Publications Fund of Yale University.

The answers posed by this book have been forged in dialogues with books and with many friends, colleagues, and students. The Herzog August Bibliothek, and in particular, Dr. Sabine Solf, graciously enabled a group of us to talk about images and iconoclasm intensively for four days in the lovely setting of the library and its town. There Margaret Aston, Eamon Duffy, and Ivan Gaskell shared with me the findings of their own research, some of which each has subsequently published. In Zurich and Wolfenbüttel, Peter Jezler and Christine Göttler generously shared their research on iconoclasm in Zürich and the meaning of images to sixteenth-century laypersons.

It is a particular pleasure to acknowledge those longer-standing conversations that one has with friends. Bob Scribner was also one of the readers for Cambridge University Press; his insights, criticisms, and encouragements have strengthened this book in many ways. One hopes for such a broad vision in a reader. I am also indebted to the anonymous second reader for Cambridge, whose careful reading disclosed opacities in my argument or in my prose, places where I was needlessly confusing, or even misleading, and who led me to give the discussion of theologians' positions on images greater prominence. The discerning reader will hear echoes of conversations with Hans-Christoph Rublack, whose work on idiosyncratic Lutheran pastors and laity of various confessions offers the sort of textured understanding of "Reformation" this book seeks to craft. Though this book is not empirical enough for her, Miriam Chrisman has read drafts of each of the chapters, challenging my "too symbolist" readings, recalling me to the grittiness of the past, and sharing with characteristic generosity her own findings and thoughts, enriching my understanding of Strasbourg and sharpening my arguments. Hans Guggisberg has been a gracious host in Basel and a generous scholar of its history. Among the many improvements he brought to the chapter on Basel, certainly none is more delightful than my education in Basler Fasnacht, with its moving and breathtaking Morgestraich: His and Grety Guggisberg's was an extraordinary gift of friendship, to rise at 3 A.M. and escort an American then living in austere New England down to watch the predawn beginning of Fasnacht. On this side of the Atlantic, conversations with Virginia Reinburg have deepened my knowledge of late-medieval Christian practices and sharpened my sense of their relation to formal theology.

Most of this book has been talked and thought through within the community of friends, colleagues, and students I have found at Yale. George and Shelagh Hunter, Christine Kooi, Lawrence Manley, Gary Miller, and Claude Rawson have listened to and helped me to think about many of the issues this book addresses. While visitors here, Linda Seligman and Wayne te Brake shared with me the ways of approaching ordinary people they had developed in their own work. One venue deserves particular mention: the Colloquium on Agrarian Studies, directed by Jim Scott. There I have had the chance to read and listen to the research of scholars whose fields are removed from my own, but whose work offered ways of thinking I found enormously fruitful; and there, I had the chance to have the chapter on Basel read with a wonderful attentiveness, to talk about collective action with anthropologists, political theorists, historians, and sociologists. Bob Harms gave a sensitive and illuminating critique of it; it is clearer and more self-conscious in its analysis for his reading. I am very grateful to Jim Scott, whose generosity of mind and spirit make possible the best kind of dialogue.

Acknowledgments

Four colleagues and friends read the manuscript closely in its entirety. All have contributed to the breadth of the frame for my own work. Though Scotland does not play as prominent a role in this narrative as he hoped, Geoffrey Parker led me both to a geographic breadth in my vision of iconoclasm and a greater conviction of the importance of local context for the meaning of iconoclastic acts. Conversations with Jary Pelikan have deepened my knowledge of theology and led me to a more nuanced understanding of theologians' discussions of images. David Underdown has encouraged my attention to the local, the "ordinary"; our discussions have confirmed the importance, as well as the pleasure, of studying each community closely, attentive to details of all sorts. This book owes a special debt to Skip Stout. The Introduction is an expression of a longer dialogue with him over the relation of theology to praxis and on the importance of laypersons in the formation of every church and its doctrine; its clarity and directness, such as it has, are the effect of his close reading, his questions, his curiosity, and his encouragement to speak forthrightly.

It is, as so many know, difficult to put a name to the sort of conversation that lies behind books, those conducted in private within the rhythms of daily life over years, in which one is encouraged to think more boldly, to trust more fully one's insights, and challenged to think through more rigorously the implications of those thoughts and insights. Lord Peter Wimsey named one such conversation "the great striding fugue." I think Larry Winnie would like the metaphor of the fugue; it intimates both the melody and the counterpoints of our dialogue.

It seems only appropriate, finally, to dedicate a book on iconoclasts to Matt.

x

A note on orthography

The spelling of words in sixteenth-century Alemannisch is inconsistent, not only from one town to the next (leaving aside the great differences with modern conventions), but even within the usage practiced by each of the three towns. The texts quoted in the original, therefore, offer widely varying orthography. I have sought to provide the sixteenth-century names for various things in the texts: agencies, objects, offices, titles. In those cases where modern scholarship has already determined a conventional spelling, I have deferred to those conventions: the offices of *Ammeister* and *Stettmeister* in Strasbourg, *Oberzunftmeister* in Basel; the *grosser Rat* for the Senate in Strasbourg and *großer Rat* for the Senate in Basel. Although most modern scholars agree to various forms of anglicization, I have chosen to retain the German *Bürgermeister* to signal the particular configuration of authority, privilege, and obligation that each town attached to the office. For other words, I have chosen the spelling that predominates in the sources. In the case of the names of churches and chapels, I have given English names for almost all, which gets round, in the case of Strasbourg, the multiple names that the buildings had over the years in both Alsatian and French. Thus, for example, the Cathédral in Strasbourg and the Dom in Basel are both designated "Cathedral." On the other hand, I have retained the Alemannisch and German name Grossmünster for the main church in Zurich, rather than anglicizing it to Great Minster; it, more than either Cathedral, was a local, if also major, church. In the case of various feast days, I have anglicized those that are celebrated internationally, and retained the Alemannisch for those celebrated locally: Carnival, instead of Fasnacht/Fastnacht, but Kleine Fastnacht and Schmützigen Donnerstag.

On gendered language: I have sought throughout to use terms that reflect the inclusion or exclusion of women as appropriate. For sixteenth-century Christians, God and Christ were considered "male"; I have used, therefore, the male pronoun, capitalized, in accord with their sensibilities.

Introduction

For the past two decades, much of the discussion of the early years of the Reformation, the 1520s, has been dominated by what I would like to call a two-tiered model of culture.[1] One tier was "elite," that of the "learned elites," those who had access to a specific kind of education, who were trained in particular disciplined modes of interpretation and whose vocabulary and syntax were drawn primarily, perhaps exclusively, from texts.[2] The other tier was "popular," those cultural practices and beliefs of the great majority of Europeans, who had not had that education.[3]

[1] The now classic statement of this model is Peter Burke, *Popular Culture in Early Modern Europe* (London, 1978). See also, *Understanding Popular Culture: Europe from the Middle Ages to the Nineteenth Century*, ed. Steven L. Kaplan (Berlin & New York, 1984); *Rethinking Popular Culture: Contemporary Perspectives in Cultural Studies*, ed. Chandra Mukerji & Michael Schudson (Berkeley, 1991), esp. pt. 1; *Religion and Society in Early Modern Europe, 1500–1800*, ed. Kaspar von Greyerz (London, 1984), esp. pt. 2. For an early challenge to that model, see Natalie Davis, "From 'Popular Religion' to Religious Cultures," in *Reformation Europe: A Guide to Research*, ed. Steven Ozment (St. Louis, 1982), pp. 321–41. For more recent efforts to move round that model, see Hans-Christoph Rublack, "The Song of Contz Anahans: Communication and Revolt in Nördlingen, 1525," in *The German People and the Reformation*, ed. Ronnie Po-chia Hsia (Ithaca, 1988), pp. 102–20; and Robert Scribner, "Varieties of Reformation," which he shared with me in typescript.

[2] Many studies of individual theologians place them primarily, if not exclusively in dialogue with other theologians, both living and dead. Among the exceptions to this are Heiko A. Oberman, *Luther: Mensch zwischen Gott und Teufel* (Berlin, 1982), trans. as *Luther: Man between God and the Devil* (New Haven, 1989); and William Bouwsma, *John Calvin: A Sixteenth-Century Portrait* (Oxford, 1988).

[3] For a discussion of the problems inherent in the term "the people," see, for example, James S. Amelang, "The Artisan as Icarus: Popular Autobiography in Early Modern Europe," a paper he presented at the Wesleyan Renaissance Seminar, Nov. 1993, pp. 5–7; and Marc Venard, *Réforme protestante, réforme Catholique dans la province d'Avignon au XVIe siècle* (Paris, 1993), pp. 1045–6. For discussion of some of the recent work on the "people" and the Reformation, see Thomas A. Brady, "Peoples' Religions in Reformation Europe," and Tom Scott, "The Common People in the German Reformation," *The Historical Journal* 34 (1991): 173–82, 183–92, respectively.

Most often these two tiers are treated as severable, often in tension or even opposition.

While enormously fruitful – it has led us to attend to "the people" in ways we did not before – this model has also engendered many problems in the ways we speak about "the Reformation." "Learned elites," in particular Martin Luther, Huldrych Zwingli, and John Calvin, have been distanced from their communities, those for whose souls they were held partially, if not fully, accountable. We hear less forcefully the rich metaphors and emotionally powerful allusions that made these preachers, along with their fifteenth-century predecessors Bernardino of Siena and Geiler von Kaysersberg, so influential in their own time, as they addressed specific congregations and sought to engage their minds and souls. So, too, insofar as these men have been treated more as authors rather than preachers, their theological formulations have lost something of their resonance, their concreteness, their application. More troubling, the "people" have lost much of their agency in this model. The great majority of late-medieval and early-modern Europeans have been denied much creative role in the formation of learned culture or the "Reformation," and are, most often, relegated to the role of audience, their function to receive, to respond, frequently to misapprehend.[4] Peter Blickle's work notwithstanding, the early years of the Reformation, the 1520s – when ordinary people[5] were participating variously, sometimes collectively, sometimes individually, sometimes violently, frequently vociferously, but participating actively in "Reformation" within their communities – have lost their sense of electric tension, of potentiality, their exhilaration and the terrifying specter of anarchy as individual Christians chose to act in ways no authority, secular or ecclesiastical, had sanctioned, defined, or articulated.

Perhaps the greatest damage this two-tiered model has done, however, is to our discussion of Christianity in sixteenth-century

[4] Even Franziska Conrad's wonderful study, *Reformation in der bäuerlichen Gesellschaft: Zur Rezeption reformatorischer Theologie im Elsass* (Stuttgart, 1984), frames the peasants' relation to Reformation in terms of response and reception; see esp. chap. 2.

[5] I follow Wayne te Brake here in the use of the term "ordinary people." See, for example, "Revolt and Religious Reformation in the World of Charles V, 1516–1555," Working Paper no. 151, New School for Social Research.

Europe. Implicitly it divides two dimensions of Christianity from each other. On the one hand, it treats theology as the formal discourse on the nature of God and on the relations among the three persons of the Trinity, whose terms, vocabulary, syntax, and conceptual structures are historically determined by textual traditions. "Learned elites" discuss theology, most often in the medium of the written word. Separate, indeed often viewed as autonomous from theology, on the other hand, are the cultural practices of the "people." In distinguishing theology from the practice of Christianity, that model denies the practices and actions of ordinary Christians their theological content. In doing so, it denies Christianity its immediacy, its vitality: Christianity becomes less a lived religion than a set of doctrines and their (mis)applications. It also makes much more difficult to explain the participation of hundreds of laymen and laywomen in the enterprise of Reformation: *Why* was the mass such an abomination to so many if they were not theologically sensitive? *Why* was it so important to have evangelical preachers – to hear "the Word" preached by those who would not distort it? *Why* were so many willing to risk imprisonment, fines, even execution to destroy the images in the churches?

This book seeks to redress the distortions of the two-tiered model in two ways: first, to return to ordinary people their agency in the process of reform and, thereby, to suggest a more dynamic vision of "Reformation"; second, to recover something of their theologies,[6] their conceptions of the nature of God and of humanity's relation to Him. To do so, it takes up iconoclasm, the earliest and the most dramatic expression of reform among a broad spectrum of Europeans, lay and clerical, artisan and magistrate, rural and urban. In the sixteenth century, in dozens of towns and villages, otherwise ordinary people – parish clergy, bakers, carpenters, gardeners, most employed and most of them citizens – broke into local churches and smashed up or burned thousands of long-beloved, familiar, treasured objects: altars, altar

---

[6] As will become evident in the discussion that follows, I am broadening the use of the term "theology" to encompass those thoughts ordinary people held on the nature of God and His relation to humankind that were not articulated in the formal language of the discipline of Theology as it was taught in the schools.

retables, crucifixes, carved and painted triptychs and diptychs, panel paintings, architectural and free-standing sculptures, chalices, patens, candlesticks, and oil lamps. Many were brought to trial, the earliest to face the charge of blasphemy, a capital crime in many communities. When their judges and critics, magistrates and neighbors, asked them why they had destroyed these precious objects, many responded as Hans Zirkel of Basel did: "for the honor of God and the betterment of one's neighbor."[7] For them, iconoclasm was an act of piety. For them and for a number of the chroniclers who recorded their acts, iconoclasm was central to the reformation of Christian life: To "do away with the images" was to "reform."

Work in a number of fields enables us to dismantle the conception of "culture" the two-tiered model predicates and thereby to revise our understanding of iconoclasm in the process of Reformation. Some cultural anthropologists have developed models of culture as exchange and conflict, in which all members of a community, variously defined, participate, albeit oppositionally, in a whole that is constituted out of their confrontations and negotiations.[8] Other anthropologists have sought to cross the divide between verbal cultural forms and gestural or behavioral cultural forms, developing ways of excavating the meaning of acts within specific cultures, acts that have not been verbally explicated by their contemporaries.[9] A number of literary theorists have gone a long way in breaking apart a unified vision of readers; response theory, deconstruction, as well as semiotics argue for a much more nuanced understanding of the transmission, the reception, and the interpretation of cultural products. Following the impact of various areas of literary theory, readership and audience have become more variegated, less homogeneous. So, too, art historians have argued for a more varied viewership: Beginning with the work of Michael Baxandall and Svetlana Alpers, art historians

---

[7] *Aktensammlung zur Geschichte der Basler Reformation in den Jahren 1519 bis Anfang 1534,* ed. Paul Roth, vol. III (Basel, 1937), no. 86.

[8] See, for example, David I. Kertzer, *Ritual, Politics, and Power* (New Haven, 1988). For a recent and important discussion of the relation between "person" and "culture," see Richard A. Schweder, *Thinking Through Cultures: Expeditions in Cultural Psychology* (Cambridge, Mass., 1991).

[9] See, for example, the work of Gilbert Lewis, *Day of Shining Red* (Cambridge, 1980).

have delineated important differences among different viewer-ships, according to a range of "contexts," economic, political, social, even educational.[10] The work of microhistorians, such as Giovanni Levi, Ed Muir, and Elizabeth and Tom Cohen, has shifted the perspective from broad divisions between social and political "elites," on the one hand, and "the people," on the other, to delineating various networks of influence and patronage within communities, be they large, such as towns, or small, such as families, thereby articulating dynamics between members of different social groups, dynamics that underline negotiation, exchange, connection.[11]

Within the field of Reformation history, the work of Bob Scribner has done much to undermine that model, articulating a much more textured feel for the practices of ordinary Christians than had been previously done, and a powerfully prismatic vision of "the people."[12] So, too, the writings of William Bouwsma, Heiko Oberman, Jaroslav Pelikan, and Charles Trinkaus have underlined the human dimensions of theologians' work – their immediate audiences and influences, the human presences in every text. The work of social historians of Christianity, such as Pierre Chaunu, Eamon Duffy, A. N. Galpern, Virginia Reinburg, Jacques Toussaert, and Bernard Vogler, has provided a much richer vision of the culture of Christianity, one that incorporates the ever more refined understanding of social variation within its definition of the practices and institutions of Christian-

[10] Baxandall, *Painting and Experience in Fifteenth Century Italy* (Oxford, 1972) and *The Limewood Sculptors of Renaissance Germany* (New Haven & London, 1980); Alpers, *The Art of Describing: Dutch Art in the Seventeenth Century* (Chicago, 1983) and *Rembrandt's Enterprise: The Studio and the Market* (Chicago, 1988).

[11] Levi, "On Microhistory," in *New Perspectives in Historical Writing*, ed. Peter Burke (University Park, Pa., 1993), pp. 93–113; Muir, Introduction to *Microhistory and the Lost Peoples of Europe*, ed. Edward Muir & Guido Ruggiero, trans. Eren Branch (Baltimore & London, 1991), pp. vii–xxviii; and Elizabeth S. & Thomas V. Cohen, "Camilla the Go-between: The Politics of Gender in a Roman Household (1559)," *Continuity and Change* 4(1989): 53–77, and *Words and Deeds in Renaissance Rome: Trials before the Papal Magistrates* (Toronto, 1993).

[12] In addition to the essays collected in *Popular Culture and Popular Movements in Reformation Germany* (London & Ronceverte, 1987), see "Volkskultur und Volksreligion: zur Rezeption evangelischer Ideen," in *Zwingli und Europa*, ed. Peter Blickle, Andreas Lindt, & Alfred Schindler (Zurich, 1985), pp. 151–61; and "The Impact of the Reformation on Daily Life," in *Mensch und Objekt im Mittelalter und in der frühen Neuzeit: Leben - Alltag - Kultur* (Vienna, 1990), pp. 315–43.

ity.[13] Finally, the work of William Christian, Jr., has sought, with considerable success, to realign our perspective, moving it from the global and broadly sociopolitical to the local: that location, he argues, for Christianity as it was understood and realized by all Europeans, except, perhaps, the Pope.[14]

This book rests upon a conception of "culture" derived from reading in these areas. While that conception receives fuller explication in the following chapters, let me offer a few words here about its commitments. First, as the work of cultural anthropologists and literary theorists has argued, "culture" cannot be so easily divided into two groups: Culture as often provides a field for conflict as it does the means of cohesion; levels of "learning" differ within each group; "reading," and other forms of cultural exchange are more individuated than the two-tiered model allows. Thus, in the discussion that follows, I have sought to delineate one dynamic with many participants who adopt various cultural media, including acts, to articulate their conceptions of Christianity and of "Reformation." Second, as the work of John Boswell, Pierre Chenu, and Reinburg has argued, theology was expressed in the cultural practices of Christianity:[15] in the patterns of behavior of the clergy, in the ritual gestures of processions and the mass, in the modes and forms of liturgy, and in the ethical behavior of all.[16] As is evident in all sorts of sources, from chronicles to trial records to pamphlets, for the great major-

---

[13] See, for example, Chaunu, *Église, culture et société: essais sur Réforme et Contre-Réforme (1517–1620)* (Paris, 1981); Duffy, *The Stripping of the Altars: Traditional Religion in England 1400–1580* (London & New Haven, 1992); Galpern, *The Religion of the People in Sixteenth-Century Champagne* (Cambridge, 1976); Reinburg, *Praying the Book of Hours: Traditional Religious Practices and the Reformation in France* (Ithaca, forthcoming); Toussaert, *Le sentiment religieux en Flandre à la fin du moyen âge* (Paris, 1960); and Vogler, *Vie religieuse en pays rhénan dans le seconde moitié du XVIe siècle (1556–1619)*, 3 vols. (Lille, 1974).

[14] William Christian, Jr., *Local Religion in Sixteenth-Century Spain* (Princeton, 1981).

[15] Boswell, *Christianity, Social Tolerance and Homosexuality: Gay People in Western Europe from the Beginning of the Christian Era to the Fourteenth Century* (Chicago, 1980); Chenu, *La theologie au douzième siècle* (Paris, 1957), parts of which were translated as *Nature, Man, and Society in the Twelfth Century: Essays on New Theological Perspectives in the Latin West*, ed. and trans. Jerome Taylor and Lester K. Little (Chicago, 1968).

[16] In *Always Among Us: Images of the Poor in Zwingli's Zurich* (Cambridge, 1990), I argued for the interconnections between formal theology and the practice of communal ethics.

ity of Christians, European and then American,[17] where and how one worshiped God – both liturgy and ethics – were the expression, the outward form, of one's theology, one's understanding of God and His relation to humankind. With these commitments, let us return to iconoclasm during the early years of the Reformation.

Iconoclasm was not new to Christianity in the sixteenth century.[18] There had been violence against the images in churches throughout the history of Christianity, most dramatically in the eighth century, during the Byzantine iconoclastic controversy. At no time, however, had attacks on the images in the churches encompassed as broad a range of the people. Unlike its antecedents, Reformation iconoclasm was initially the expression not of secular or ecclesiastical authorities, emperors or bishops. It was not even the original intent of theologians, as the work of Margarethe Stirm, Hans Freiherr von Campenhausen, and Charles Garside has shown.[19] Martin Luther and Huldrych Zwingli called into question the value of the images in the churches in the ear-

---

[17] See David D. Hall, *Worlds of Wonder, Days of Judgement: Popular Religious Belief in Early New England* (Harvard, 1989), for Anglo–American Christian practices.

[18] Helmut Feld provides a history predominantly of the discussion of iconoclasm among theologians in the West, beginning with Gregory the Great (590–604), in *Der Ikonoklasmus des Westens* (Leiden, 1990). On the earliest iconoclasm, see Leslie W. Barnard, *The Graeco-Roman and Oriental Background of the Iconoclastic Controversy* (Leiden, 1974), esp. pp. 89–103, and "The Theology of Images," in *Iconoclasm*, ed. Anthony Bryer and Judith Herrin (Birmingham, England, 1977), pp. 7–13; and Paul C. Finney, "Antecedents of Byzantine Iconoclasm: Christian Evidence before Constantine," in *The Image and the Word: Confrontations in Judaism, Christianity and Islam*, ed. Joseph Gutmann (Missoula, Minn., 1977), pp. 27–47. For a narrative of iconoclastic controversies from the seventh to the ninth centuries, see Edward James Martin, *A History of the Iconoclastic Controversy* (London, 1930). On medieval iconoclasm, see Horst Bredekamp, *Kunst als Medium sozialer Konflikte: Bilderkämpfe von der Spätantike bis zur Hussitenrevolution* (Frankfurt a.M., 1975); William R. Jones, "Art and Christian Piety: Iconoclasm in Medieval Europe," in *The Image and the Word*, pp. 75–105; Anthony Ugolnik, "The Libri Carolini: Antecedents of Reformation Iconoclasm," in *Iconoclasm vs. Art and Drama*, ed. Clifford Davidson & Ann Eljenholm Nichols (Kalamazoo, 1989), pp. 1–32.

[19] Stirm, *Die Bilderfrage in der Reformation* (Gütersloh, 1977); von Campenhausen, "Die Bilderfrage in der Reformation," in *Tradition und Leben: Kräfte der Kirchengeschichte* (Tübingen, 1960), pp. 361–407, and "Zwingli und Luther zur Bilderfrage," in *Das Gottesbild im Abendland* (Witten & Berlin, 1959), pp. 139–72; Garside, *Zwingli and the Arts* (New Haven, 1966). Most recently, Sergiuz Michalski has endorsed the previous scholarship in *The Reformation and the Visual Arts: The Protestant Image Question in Western and Eastern Europe* (London & New York, 1993), esp. chaps. 1–2.

7

ly 1520s; Zwingli would move late in 1523 to call for their removal, but Luther ultimately endorsed the presence of certain kinds of images in the churches.[20]

Given the breadth of participation in the iconoclasm of the 1520s, in which literally hundreds of Christians, lay and clerical, urban and rural, participated actively in the reformation of worship, it is most puzzling that Reformation iconoclasm has been much less studied than the Byzantine iconoclasm of eight centuries earlier. Moreover, studies of Reformation iconoclasm have centered upon the theologians, Luther, Zwingli, and Calvin, who themselves did not instigate the earliest incidents but sought to mitigate, interpret, and, in some cases, stop acts of iconoclasm.[21] Much of the work on continental iconoclasm that has been done up to now has rested upon the two-tiered model of culture: Preachers motivated people to attack the images, sometimes intentionally – in the cases of Andreas Bodenstein von Karlstadt in Wittenberg,[22] Leo Jud and Zwingli in Zurich, and Martin Bucer in Strasbourg – and sometimes unintentionally. Yet Karlstadt did not publish his treatise *Concerning the Removal of Im-*

---

[20] On Luther's attitude toward images, see (in addition to von Campenhausen and Stirm) Carl Christensen, *Art and the Reformation in Germany* (Athens, Ohio, 1979), chap. 2; Michalski, *The Reformation and the Visual Arts,* chap. 1; and Martin Warnke, "Lutherische Bildtheologie," pp. 282–93.

[21] In addition to the studies of von Campenhausen, Eire, Stirm, and Michalski, Herbert Smolinsky has done a comparative study of Karlstadt and Emser's conflict over the proper attitude to images in "Reformation und Bildersturm: Hieronymous Emsers Schrift gegen Karlstadt über die Bilderverehrung," in *Reformatio Ecclesiae: Beiträge zu Kirchlichen Reformbemühungen von der Alten Kirch bis zur Neuzeit* (Festgabe für Erwin Iserloh), ed. Remigius Bäumer (Paderborn, Munich, Vienna, & Zurich, 1980), pp. 427–40. The earliest modern study of Reformation iconoclasm, Friedrich Fischer, "Die Bildersturm in der Schweiz und in Basel insbesondere," *Basler Taschenbuch* 1(1850): 1–43, provides the most details of the acts of destruction themselves, as well as an important argument about the correlation between the extent and specific victims of iconoclasm on the one hand, and the form of Protestantism instituted on the other.

[22] Carlos Eire attributes to Karlstadt a "revolutionary iconoclastic theory," which called for the violent, if necessary, removal of the images in the churches, *War Against the Idols: The Reformation of Worship from Erasmus to Calvin* (Cambridge, 1986), pp. 62–5. Both Hermann Barge, in *Andreas Bodenstein von Karlstadt* (Leipzig, 1905), vol. I, pp. 387–407, and Paul Sider, in *Andreas Bodenstein von Karlstadt: The Development of his Thought 1517–1525* (Leiden, 1974), pp. 165–73, argue the contrary, that Karlstadt did not intend to provoke either the violence or popular seizure of the initiative of the removal of the images.

ages[23] until after the iconoclasm in Wittenberg in 1522; and Ludwig Häetzer did not publish the other famous iconoclastic pamphlet, *Our God's Judgement, How One Should Conduct Oneself With All Idols and Images,*[24] until after that, in 1523. Moreover, these two treatises, which may reveal something of the content of Karlstadt and Jud's[25] iconoclastic preaching, help little to explain the precise acts of iconoclasm. The treatises consist primarily in biblical injunctions against representing God, injunctions that do not explain most of the "images" iconoclasts attacked: oil lamps, liturgical utensils, and representations of Mary and of the Deposition – not images of the Incarnation or of moments in Christ's life. If we look to the acts themselves, they reveal perceptions of the objects in the churches that differ at points from those articulated by the preachers. These pamphlets do not explain the acts of the iconoclasts – neither their focus, the specific objects they attacked, nor their timing, the specific moments the iconoclasts chose to attack objects in the churches. People did not take up, moreover, other biblical injunctions in support of redistribution of wealth, of charity toward the poor, of the reordering of social ethics, with equal passion or effect.

Till now, the acts of iconoclasts have not been the focus of study. Implicitly they have been treated, following the two-tiered model of culture, as the response of the laity to preachers, as the extension into action of the perceptions and attitudes of theologians. If we adopt a different conception of culture, however, one of dynamic and exchange, the acts of iconoclasm are no longer explained by the words of the preachers. Quite the contrary, they pose a series of questions. The question that drives this book is

---

[23] *Von abtuhung der Bylder* [Wittenberg: Nickell Schyrlentz, 1522], published as "Von Abtuung der Bilder" in *Flugschriften der frühen Reformationsbewegung (1518–1524),* ed. Adolf Laube, Annerose Schneider, with Sigrid Looß, vol. I (Berlin, 1983), pp. 105–27.

[24] *Ein vrteil gottes vnsers ee gemahels wie man sich mit allen goetzen vnd bildnussen halte sol* [Zurich: Christoph Froschauer, 23. IX. 1523], published as "Ein Urteil Gottes . . ., wie man es mit allen Götzen und Bildnussen halten soll," in *Flugschriften der frühen Reformationsbewegung,* vol. I, pp. 271–83. Cf. Charles Garside, "Ludwig Haetzer's Pamphlet Against Images: A Critical Study," *Mennonite Quarterly Review* 34 (1960): 20–36.

[25] At the time he published *Our God's Judgement,* Haetzer was still living in Zurich, active in the reform movement there, and closely linked to the evangelical leadership, among whom was Jud.

Why? Why would ordinary people choose to destroy objects that may well have been a part of their practice of Christianity, objects long familiar, objects that, as the outcry at their destruction attests, were beloved, treasured by many in their communities? To view the iconoclasts' acts as simple response obscures the question *Why*, as well as the agency of ordinary people: They *chose* to act. Why did they risk fines, imprisonment, even death to destroy objects in churches? It also denies their initiative: Not all acts of iconoclasm follow iconoclastic preaching; some *precede* it – evidence that the relationship between these acts and such preaching is a more complex dynamic among persons of differing modes of expression.

Iconoclasts risked a great deal, sometimes their lives, to communicate something to their communities. This book takes up their story, viewing the acts of the iconoclasts as themselves a form of "speaking," as a mode through which ordinary Christians entered into the dynamic of "Reformation." In so doing, it seeks to return to their actions that belief they experienced individually and privately, to explore the acts as an outward expression, sometimes individual, sometimes collective, of ordinary people's understanding of the central tenets of Christianity. This book seeks, in other words, to discern in the actions of "the people," most often understood in terms of their political and social dimensions,[26] their theological content. In treating the acts this way, this study seeks both to suggest how those acts of violence might have contributed to the preachers' and the magistrates' understanding of the place of images in traditional worship, and to explicate the relation between the images in the churches and "Reformation."

If iconoclasts have received less attention than the theologians, it is in part that the iconoclasts communicated in a form much

---

[26] Martin Warnke has argued for the social content of iconoclasm; for the Reformation period, see "Durchbrochene Geschichte? Die Bilderstürme der Widertäufer in Münster 1534/35," in *Bildersturm: Die Zerstörung des Kunstwerks*, ed. Martin Warnke (Frankfurt a.M., 1988), pp. 65–98. His argument is supported by Matthias Müller, *Von der Kunst des calvinistischen Bildersturms* (Marburg, 1993), which locates iconoclasm against objects in the Elizabeth church in Marburg in the later sixteenth century. Eire argues that iconoclasm was a "revolutionary tactic," *War Against the Idols*, pp. 151–60.

less accessible than the treatises and sermons of Luther, Karlstadt, Zwingli, and Jud. Iconoclasts "spoke" primarily in acts of violence against objects, and only secondarily in words, to their witnesses, their accusers, and finally, the magistrates who adjudicated their "crime." Iconoclasts "spoke," in other words, in that most vulnerable of modes of communication: the act.[27] Iconoclastic acts were even more transient and ephemeral, less fixed than either gestures[28] or the scripted performance of theater.[29] Iconoclasts themselves provided little verbal frame for their acts, meager explication; and that, as we shall see, was offered either to witnesses who would subsequently turn them in or to magistrates who were sitting in judgment. What iconoclasts meant to communicate has been mediated through the perceptions, sensibilities, sympathies, attitudes, and judgments of others: Iconoclasts' acts were recorded – and thereby interpreted – by others who may or may not have shared their vision of true Christianity.

In part, then, the purpose of this book is to suggest ways of excavating the meaning of the acts of those who did not have access to more protected and fixed forms of communication – the treatise, the pamphlet, the sermon, even the visual image.[30] It seeks to discern beneath or behind the commentary, the judgment of others, what iconoclasts may have sought to communicate with their acts – insofar as it is possible after so many years

[27] On individual acts as a mode of communication, see Otto Bruner, *Acts of Meaning* (Cambridge, Mass., 1990); and Lewis, *Day of Shining Red*. The notion of an act's "vulnerability" I draw from Thomas Greene, *The Vulnerable Text: Essays on Renaissance Literature* (New York, 1986), esp. pp. 101–4.

[28] Gestures, according to Moshe Barasch, have a certain conventional quality, enabling them to be a precise and relatively consistent form of communication, *Giotto and the Language of Gesture* (Cambridge, 1987).

[29] Victor Turner, *The Anthropology of Performance* (New York, 1987), esp. the chapters "Images and Reflections: Ritual, Drama, Carnival, Film, and Spectacle in Cultural Performance" and "The Anthropology of Performance"; and *From Ritual to Theater* (New York, 1982).

[30] Denis Crouzet, in *Les Guerriers de Dieu; La violence au temps des troubles de religion, vers 1525–vers 1610*, 2 vols. (Seyssel, 1990); Natalie Zemon Davis, in "The Rites of Violence," *Society and Culture in Early Modern France* (London, 1975): 152–87; and David Sabean, in *Power in the Blood* (Cambridge, 1984) suggest fertile ways of uncovering the religious resonances of acts of violence. For a comparison of E. P. Thompson and Natalie Zemon Davis on questions of popular agency and the meaning of acts by ordinary people, see Suzanne Desan, "Crowds, Community, and Ritual in the Work of E. P. Thompson and Natalie Davis," in *The New Cultural History*, ed. Lynn Hunt (Berkeley, 1989), pp. 47–71.

11

and so much distance, both cultural and temporal. Each chapter has different problems in that process. Each takes up differing kinds of evidence – predominantly trial records or chronicles – and seeks to reconstruct with as much precision as possible the acts themselves in their fullness. In most cases, that reconstruction remains static: We have no description of the movement, the moment of violence itself. However, we do have other pieces of the story: The accounts sometimes identify the actors, the iconoclasts, and sometimes the objects, the victims of iconoclastic acts; most important, those accounts almost invariably provide broader cultural frames of reference for the acts of iconoclasm – the time and the place of iconoclasm. Those temporal and spatial frames provide important clues as to the meaning the iconoclasts sought to convey.

Thus, in the chapter on Zurich, we meet a number of individual iconoclasts and learn a great deal about their acts: both the specific objects they attacked and those motives they were willing to articulate before their witnesses and judges. In the chapters on Strasbourg and Basel, we meet no individual iconoclasts, but the acts point toward broader matrices, "cultural" referents. Their very agency indicates the directions we should look to interpret the meaning of their acts – the specific locations and times of the acts. We glimpse different aspects of the acts through the differing sources, but the hermeneutic remains the same: to set the acts within broader frames of reference, within their cultural context, in order to illumine the theological content of the acting. Before we turn to the acts of iconoclasm, let me offer here some general observations about the actors, the iconoclasts, and the context of their acting that this book will highlight, lived Christianity. Chapter 1 offers a brief discussion of the objects in the churches and the theology they embodied.

The actors

The earliest iconoclasts of the Protestant Reformation did not, on the whole, act in such dramatic aggregate as later iconoclasts did in France, the Low Countries, and Scotland, where, at best, the Reformed Churches publicly sanctioned or, at worst, turned a nonjudgmental eye upon complete iconoclasm.[31] Their political contexts differed from those of French Huguenot and Dutch Calvinist iconoclasts: They were not seeking to institute minority religious communities within a hostile state of increasingly effective centralized power. Quite the contrary, the iconoclasts of this study acted within communities of much more precisely circumscribed political power: the Swiss city-republics of Zurich and Basel and the Imperial Free City of Strasbourg. The configuration of religious and political communities was essentially different: All three cities experimented for a while at least with complete identification of the religious community with the jurisdictional boundaries of the political community. The iconoclasts were "speaking" not to some distant sovereign, but face-to-face with members of some more immediate community: neighborhood, parish, urban or rural commune.

In German-speaking Europe, iconoclastic "riots" were rare. The sheer number of iconoclasts in Basel in 1529, some 200, shocked contemporaries: They had never witnessed nor heard of such numbers of people acting violently against images. Icon-

---

[31] Cf. for France, most recently, for example, Olivier Christin, *Une révolution symbolique: l'iconoclasme huguenot et la reconstruction catholique* (Paris, 1991) and Crouzet, *Les Guerriers de Dieu;* and for the Low Countries, most recently, Phyllis Mack Crew, *Calvinist Preaching and Iconoclasm in the Netherlands 1544–1569* (Cambridge, 1978); Solange Deyon & Alain Lottin, *Les casseurs de l'été 1566* (Westhoek & Lille, 1986); Henk F. K. van Nierop, *Beeldenstorm en burgerlijk verzet in Amsterdam 1566–1567* (Nijmegen, 1978); Geoffrey Parker, *The Dutch Revolt* (London, 1977), pp. 74–84; J. Scheeder, *De Beeldenstorm* (Bussum, 1974); J. G. C. Venner, *Beeldenstorm in Hasselt 1567* (Leeuwarden, 1989). Allowing for the differences in orientation between Dutch and French historiographies of their respective Reformations, all argue for the religious intent and content of iconoclasm, although individual scholars differ as to what part of religion iconoclasm attacked: Crew, for example, sees iconoclasm as a challenge to the clergy's power, whereas Christin, Deyon, and Lottin argue for its symbolic "purification" of religion. All treat iconoclasts in aggregate, though van Nierop and Venner provide prosopographies of the iconoclasts in appendices. English iconoclasm is again a different beast. See the excellent work of Margaret Aston, *England's Iconoclasts, vol. I: Laws Against Images* (Oxford, 1988); and Eamon Duffy, *The Stripping of the Altars,* pt. II; as well as Patrick Collinson, *From Iconoclasm to Iconophobia: The Cultural Impact of the Second English Reformation* (Reading, 1986); John Phillips, *The Reformation of Images: Destruction of Art in England, 1535–1660* (Berkeley, 1973); and Robert Whiting, *The Blind Devotion of the People: Popular Religion and the English Reformation* (Cambridge, 1989). On Scottish iconoclasm, see D. McRoberts, "Material destruction caused by the Scottish Reformation," in *Essays on the Scottish Reformation 1513–1625* (Glasgow, 1962), pp. 415–62; I am grateful to Geoffrey Parker for this last reference.

oclasts in the early years of the Reformation acted singly and in small groups. These early iconoclasts, moreover, are not easily categorized. The great majority remain faceless and nameless, but those individuals whom we can identify span cultural and social divisions: Categories of class, social or political status, even education or literacy are inadequate to characterize iconoclasts or to explain participation in iconoclasm. Iconoclasts were lay and clerical, rural and urban. We find prosperous and prominent artisans conversing with powerful town councilors on the virtues of iconoclasm, regional administrators turning a blind eye to the iconoclasm of their subjects – cooperation between groups often cast on opposite sides. Gradations of participation further blur social and cultural distinctions: Though no nobles or merchants seem actively to have participated in iconoclasm,[32] they present a range of degrees of involvement, from begrudging acquiescence through tacit acceptance to formal recognition and approbation. If the most prominent citizens of towns continued in their public actions to reflect their formal endorsement of standards of "order," many also removed privately, without public notice, those images in the churches their families had bestowed and over which, therefore, they had certain rights: Their iconoclasm differed in manner, in style, in conduct, but not in substance.

Most of the iconoclasts identified in the following chapters were politically enfranchised, neither powerful, authoritative within their communities, nor marginal, living outside the periphery of political decision making. They were socially stable – familiar within their communities, their towns and neighborhoods, but not prominent or possessing the influence of status. They were, to borrow a designation from English history, "of the middling sort." They were not particularly young – most had reached the age of professional majority and citizenship – nor were they poor. None that can be identified had a criminal record. They were like so many other Europeans of this time: rural or urban workers of stable employment, possessing citizenship within their towns or canton, undistinguished by political power, social status, economic prosperity, or by the complete absence

[32] In Geneva, patricians did participate in iconoclasm, Eire, *War Against the Idols*, pp. 162–3.

of any of these. Only one characteristic seems to define iconoclasts in the towns featured in this study: They were all men – although, even here, partial vignettes of women smashing objects belie any clear characterization of iconoclasts. What links iconoclasts, finally, is not some political identity – though most might be designated as "the common man," as Peter Blickle has defined him[33] – but the focus of their violence: Christian images.

The chapters on Zurich, Strasbourg, and Basel each attempt to discern as much as possible about the individual iconoclasts – what ties of kin, neighborhood, and parish they had; what other gestures or words of religious content they articulated – though the results are very uneven. As we move from Zurich to Basel, the details of identity, both individual and collective, of the iconoclasts become rarer and rarer. Throughout, however, I have sought to give social nuance to their acts, working against that aggregate, "the people," to discern iconoclasts more variously, to differentiate them, insofar as the sources allow.[34] Iconoclasts articulated a range of notions of piety and of the practice of Christianity: In Zurich and Strasbourg, iconoclasts did not present themselves as they have been treated – in the aggregate – but as individually pursuing the reform of Christian practice. Even at Basel, where it was the *Gemeinde,* as one chronicler designated the crowd, iconoclasts acting en masse, who broke into the churches and destroyed the images, their collective concern was voicing a vision of reformed Christian practice that differed not only from that of the magistrates or of the clergy, but also from a number of other ordinary citizens. I have also sought in all cases to articulate a textured experience of Christianity, as experienced

---

[33] Unlike the revolutionaries of 1525, iconoclasts did not direct their acts of violence against their lords or even their lords' abbeys, towers, castles, property, but against images, almost exclusively in churches. The revolutionaries of 1525 and Reformation iconoclasts may have shared visions of the true Christian community, and some may have even participated in both movements, but the two groups are not identical. What little evidence we have for the iconoclasts detailed in the following chapters does not place them in revolt against their lords.

[34] "In other words, although customs and the use of symbols are always polysemic, nevertheless they assume more precise connotations from the mobile and dynamic social differentiations. Individuals constantly create their own identities, and groups define themselves according to conflicts and solidarities, which however cannot be assumed priori but result from dynamics which are the objects of analysis," Levi, "On Microhistory," p. 105.

both individually and collectively, as at once a field of conflict and a location for community – as a "culture" in which various persons participated variously.

Context

The great majority of objects of known iconoclasm were located in churches, and those few that were not, were crucifixes, explicitly Christian images. These were the kind of images to which authorities attended, whose destruction they prosecuted. Images in private homes did not concern the magistrates. In the eyes of the magistrates, the objects of iconoclasm were public,[35] complexly interwoven with the public practice of Christianity. This, then, is the "context" for the images and the acts of iconoclasm that this book emphasizes: Christianity as it was enacted within specific communities. Other "contexts" – the setting of specific urban republics, with their particular forms of authority, networks of social ties, even their political myths – will be sketched at the beginning of each subsequent chapter, but the overarching frame for our discussion of iconoclasm will be Christianity as it was practiced within each these towns. This context enables us to discern the religious content of acts of iconoclasm; within it, the images acquire their greatest "power."

The following chapters take as their premise that the people in each of the towns were Christian, not necessarily as people of faith, but culturally, in the sense that Christianity shaped how they experienced their world: It gave rhythm to time, divided physical space between sacred and secular places, provided moral norms for the conduct of various kinds of human relations, and, as we shall glimpse in the next chapter, presented them with a way of conceiving of the material world.[36] For the pious, the rhythms and geography of Christianity had numinous meaning; for the less devout and for non-Christians, they

---

[35] They could, however, be privately owned.

[36] This position is in sympathy with, but not identical to that pursued by John van Engen in "The Christian Middle Ages as an Historiographical Problem," *American Historical Review* 91(1986): 519–52.

were an insistent reminder of the Christian ordering of the world.[37]

That Christian ordering of the world began with the structuring of time.[38] By the sixteenth century, most towns had at least one church endowed with bells to mark the eight "hours" of the day, which broke the day into times for prayer and for mass. Chroniclers would employ that division of the day to set events. These "hours" were set by the Church not only in number, but in length, measured in relation to sunset and sunrise, thus varying with the daylight hours of each town and structuring the time in each town according to the particular church that rang the bells. As Eamon Duffy has pointed out, there was no autonomous "secular time" in the years before the Reformation: Chroniclers, town councils, all those who marked time did so in terms of the Christian calendar.[39] Each year was calibrated according to two distinct cycles: the Temporal, which organized the year into "seasons," only one of which was fixed to specific dates; and the Sanctoral, of more than 200 fixed dates throughout the year. The Temporal structured into the year one of Christ's "pres-

---

[37] The following sketch derives from reading over a number of years for a course on Christianity. Among the works consulted, in addition to those cited elsewhere in this section: Gregory Dix, *The Shape of the Liturgy* (London, 1945); Edouard Dumoutet, *Le Christ selon la Chair et la Vie Liturgique au Moyen-Age* (Paris, 1932); Adalbert Hamman, *Vie liturgique et vie sociale* (Paris, 1968); John Harper, *The Forms and Orders of Western Liturgy from the Tenth to the Eighteenth Century* (Oxford, 1991); *Liturgies of the Western Church*, selected by Bard Thompson (Philadelphia, 1961); R.W. Scribner, *Popular Culture and Popular Movements in Reformation Germany* (London, 1987), esp. chaps. 1–5; *The Study of Liturgy*, ed. Cheslyn Jones, Geoffrey Wainwright, Edward Yarnold, SJ, and Paul Bradshaw (Oxford, 1992); and James F. White, *Introduction to Christian Worship* (Nashville, 1980).

[38] Every Christian life was also supposed to be marked by certain sacraments: baptism, that birth or initiation into the Church; First Communion, that recognition of spiritual adulthood (normally no earlier than seven years of age); and last rites, to mark the passing through death to afterlife. Some lives were marked by marriage, which the Church had come to administer by the sixteenth century, and some by ordination to the priesthood. Finally, every Christian life was to be imprinted with an annual rhythm of confession and penance, repentance and forgiveness, and taking the Eucharist, communion with the community of all Christians. It is not clear how much this structuring of human lives was effective; anecdotal evidence suggests a number of people who were nominally Christian did not marry in church, confess, or take annual communion, though they seem to have been baptised and buried as Christians.

[39] Duffy, *The Stripping of the Altars*, chap. 1. See also Arno Borst, *Computus. Zeit und Zahl in der Geschichte Europas* (Berlin, 1990).

ences," dividing it into seasons according to those key events in the mystery of Christ: Incarnation (the season of Advent and Christmas), Death and Resurrection (the season of Easter). Even Pentecost, the season of the Holy Spirit, which began with Trinity Sunday, embraced the important Corpus Christi celebrations, another kind of "presence" Christ had among living Christian communities. Within each of those Great Seasons, other events in Christ's life were marked with feast days: Epiphany, Circumcision, Presentation in the Temple, the forty days of Lent, Passion Week.

The Sanctoral Cycle was a second layer of temporal referents, marking some 200 days in the year as feast days, to celebrate those persons significant in the life of the Church: the apostles, Mary Magdalene, the Church Fathers, early martyrs, and those saints who were important locally to each town, its own patrons in the hierarchy of sanctity. Attached to this second cycle were the feast days of Mary: Birth, Presentation in the Temple, Annunciation, Purification, Death and Assumption. Each feast day was marked by special masses, and many were marked by processions of clergy and laity, both around the interiors of the churches (usually the largest church in town, either Cathedral or Münster) and in a circuit through the town, whose route would be familiar, traditional. Thus, the Christian experience of time was marked by greater cadences of the mystery of Christ and smaller festivals in celebration of human sanctity. In Chapters 2 and 3 we shall see how iconoclasts may have set their acts within specific temporal frames, with their specific references.

Christianity also structured people's experience of space. Pilgrimage had carved a particular configuration of geography: shrines and paths to those places where Christians might touch relics of extraordinary holiness, might come closer to sanctity, where the likelihood of witnessing a miracle was greater.[40] This practice had dwindled by the sixteenth century, thanks in large

---

[40] On the geography of pilgrimage, see Jean Chélini and Henri Branthomme, *Les chemins de Dieu: Histoire des pèlerinages chrétiens des origines à nos jours* (Paris, 1982); and *Tradition und Mode: Empirische Untersuchungen zur Aktualität von Volksfrömmigkeit*, ed. Martin Scharfe, Martin Schmolze, & Gertrud Schubert (Tübingen, 1985). See also Jonathan Sumption, *Pilgrimage: An Image of Medieval Religion* (London, 1975).

part to the abuses Chaucer satirized, but it had not died out: Einsiedeln, where Zwingli preached before being called to Zurich, continued to receive hundreds of pilgrims each year, pilgrims whom Zurich sought to prevent from passing through the town; and the local shrine of St. Anna in the countryside would be silenced only through the violence of iconoclasts' hands. The towns' skylines were dominated by the spires of their churches – indeed, travelers would first know of approaching a town by glimpsing those spires. Churches were frequently the largest public structure in towns, providing space not only for worship but for meetings and informal gatherings. Within the towns, processions for various feast days also carved a particular geography, linking parish churches to their constituent neighborhoods or the main church, Cathedral or Münster, to all the parishes.[41] Corpus Christi processions marked pathways for the host to travel through a town or village, departing and returning to a particular church and thereby linking that church to the parish or neighborhoods through which the host passed. Churches also contributed to the division of towns into lay and clerical spaces, as we shall see more fully in Chapter 2. Moreover, as the grievances of 1525 make clear, it mattered whether the ownership of one's land was secular or ecclesiastical: Even in economic practices, the spatial division the Church had extended, to separate secular and sacred places, had resonance.

Those grievances also pointed to another way in which the Church had come to structure human lives: the conduct of human beings toward one another. As we shall see in the discussion of images, acts and gestures in Christ's life provided models for Christians in the conduct of their own lives. Images depicted Christ's posture, the positioning of his body in relation to others, invoking individual Gospel stories with their morals, suggesting the outstretched hand of mercy, the expression of that love of neighbor Christ had preached.[42] By the sixteenth century, the

---

[41] On processions, see Young, *The Drama of the Medieval Church*. On Corpus Christi processions, see Miri Rubin, *Corpus Christi: The Eucharist in Late Medieval Culture* (Cambridge, 1991).
[42] Cf. Michel Mollat, *Les Pauvres au Moyen Age: étude sociale* (Paris, 1970); *Études sur l'histoire de la pauvreté*, ed. Michel Mollat, 2 vols. (Paris, 1974); Wandel, *Always Among Us*, esp. the Introduction and Conclusion.

Church had articulated norms of conduct of neighbor to neighbor, of man to wife, of father to child, of child to parent, of subject to ruler, and of prosperous to poor. Christ provided a model for some, though indeed few of these forms of human relations: toward neighbor, ruler, and poor. Within towns, various religious – monks, canons, friars, hermits, even some priests – invoked other forms of human conduct also attributed to Christ: celibacy, meditation, obedience, and asceticism.

These were ancient forms of Christianity's structuring of human experience. In the fourteenth and fifteenth centuries, the forms and kinds of Christ's "presence" among Christians had multiplied. Beginning in the twelfth century, the Eucharist had been the focus of a burgeoning devotion among the laity, many of whom seem to have come to the mass simply to gaze upon the host.[43] Monstrances to house the host were becoming ever more exquisitely crafted; these belonged to the increasing mobility of the host, as it was carried around the interior of churches at most masses and through the towns or villages on feast days. The celebration of Corpus Christi, whose origins can be traced to the twelfth century, crested in the fifteenth century, as the numbers of towns holding processions and plays increased, and the processions themselves became more and more elaborate.[44] The Birth, Childhood, Passion, Death, and Resurrection of Christ were performed in churches on their respective holidays in increasing detail and increasingly, with their own "images," such as the Palm Sunday ass. Even the number of holidays devoted to moments in Christ's life increased with the addition of the Presentation in the Temple and the Transfiguration.

Christianity was rooted in the rhythms, cadences, and customs of specific locales. It was practiced within specific local contexts, with their own constellations of saints, patrons, sacred presences,

---

[43] Peter Browe, *Die Verehrung der Eucharistie im Mittelalter* (Munich, 1933) and *Die eucharistischen Wunder des Mittelalters* (Breslau, 1938); Edouard Dumoutet, *Le Désir de voir l'hostie et les origines de la dévotion au Saint-Sacrament* (Paris, 1926); Charles Zika, "Hosts, Processions and Pilgrimages: Controlling the Sacred in Fifteenth-Century Germany," *Past and Present* 118 (1988): 25–64.

[44] Dumoutet, *Le Christ selon la Chair;* V. A. Kolve, *The Play Called Corpus Christi* (Stanford, Calif., 1966); and Rubin, *Corpus Christi.*

their own refinements of the greater rhythms of the Christian year, and their own particular geography of churches and religious houses. Iconoclasts were acting not only in reference to Rome, but also in dynamic with specific concerns of a more immediate community: their parish, their town or village, their "canton." Within such local contexts, images acquired additional layers of association, their meaning nuanced from the most general to the most personal and private associations.

Thus this volume is not an exhaustive study of iconoclasm throughout Reformation Europe. The iconoclasm studied herein *took place:* It had location as well as time. The places whose specific acts of iconoclasm I have chosen to study are three city-states: Zurich, Strasbourg, and Basel.[45] In its structure, in other words, this study of iconoclasm follows the juridical boundaries of three urban republics and Imperial Free Cities. These three are distinguished among the centers of Reformation for a number of reasons. In all three, iconoclasm was completed. In all, the removal of all painted and sculpted images, all crucifixes, all liturgical objects, all altarpieces, tabernacles, reliquaries, candelabra, all the objects in the churches was ultimately authorized and overseen by civil magistrates.[46] They provided important examples for later communities pursuing the reform of Christian culture; most, though not all, of the major theologians of the Reformed tradition lived in them early in their careers. These were theologians who would travel, as John Calvin did, to Geneva, or as Heinrich Bullinger did, to England, to spread in midcentury

---

[45] Although Zurich and Basel were more autonomous of the emperor than was Strasbourg, within their walls and over their *Land,* all three extended similar jurisdiction and authority. As shorthand, therefore, I shall use the terms "city-state" and "urban republic" to describe all three.

[46] Thus they differ significantly from Wittenberg, which I do not treat. The fame of the iconoclasm in Wittenberg rests not in the earliness of the iconoclasm there – at least a few acts of iconoclasm preceded iconoclasm in Wittenberg – but rather on the fact that Luther made his home there. This fame is all the more puzzling, given Luther's ambivalence toward images; Karlstadt opposed them and probably contributed at least unintentionally to iconoclasm there, but Luther's reaction has received the greater portion of attention. Most important for our purposes, iconoclasm in Wittenberg did not have the same impact as that in Zurich, Strasbourg, or Basel. For the most recent discussions of iconoclasm in Wittenberg, see Christensen, *Art and the Reformation in Germany*, pp. 35–41; Eire, *War Against the Idols*, pp. 62–5; Michalski, *The Reformation and the Visual Arts*.

a conception of the "Reformed" Church in which there were no images. Iconoclasm in these three city-states captured the imagination of contemporaries as the aborted iconoclasm in Wittenberg did not. The legalized iconoclasm in Zurich became a model for authorized iconoclasm throughout Reformed Europe. The long-term iconoclasm in Strasbourg was discussed beyond its walls over a period of years. No other iconoclasm before that of the Low Countries in 1566–7 so transfixed Europeans as did the iconoclasm of February 9–10, 1529 in Basel: It was the single greatest incident of *illegal* iconoclasm before the 1560s.[47] These three city-states also enable us to view iconoclasm more fully, enacted in places where the preachers did not shut down iconoclasm, as Luther had. They form a coherent grouping, connected not only by water, but through the bonds of friendship among the preachers Zwingli in Zurich, Bucer in Strasbourg, and Oecolampad in Basel, by diplomatic and commercial ties, and through the less visible links of artisans journeying from one of the towns to another. They may also have been linked by stories of iconoclasm in Zurich traveling to Strasbourg and Basel.

Important for iconoclasm, these three urban republics have also been important in modern scholarship. They have been studied more than some of the other locations of iconoclasm, which makes possible a richer, more textured description both of political and social arrangements within each and, in particular, of the practices of Christianity. It is possible, in other words, to delineate much more completely that "context" within which we shall seek to place the acts of iconoclasm. This is especially true in the case of Strasbourg, where the sources are more distant from the acts of iconoclasm, but our knowledge of lived Christianity among the best for sixteenth-century centers of reform.

Dividing the chapters along juridical boundaries enables us to pursue parallel concerns. On the one hand, this division emphasizes the distinctive stamp each locale gave to iconoclasm, and allows us to explore in some depth the different aspects of iconoclasm prominent in each city-state. Iconoclasm exhibited multiple dimensions in all three, but one dimension was predominant

---

[47] Bern also witnessed widespread rioting, but only after the town council had decided formally to remove all the images from the churches.

in each. Thus, in Zurich, the legal and ethical aspects of iconoclasm are most perceptible, in Strasbourg, the liturgical, and in Basel, the lay recovery of the structuring of Christianity. At the same time, this division enables us to see what defined iconoclasm across regional differences. Each iconoclastic act had many dimensions, and the prominence of these varied according to local associations, local configurations of Christian practice, local dynamics of secular and ecclesiastical authority; but in the early years of the Reformation in German-speaking Europe, each such act also shared in some way with the others.[48] Finally, I hope that this division restores to iconoclasm its immediacy, its complexity, its rich texture, and helps to make more tangible its extraordinarily important role in Reformation.

Most of the acts of iconoclasm discussed in subsequent chapters occurred within urban contexts, with their distinctive political and social arrangements. Significantly, a number of acts of iconoclasm occurred *auf dem Land,* in the rural villages and wayside shrines in the country; some of these are treated in Chapter 2. For the iconoclasts, the "context" for their acts might not coincide with the juridical boundaries of the town and its "land." For some, the parish boundaries might be the context of their acts, that "boundary" most meaningful in the practice of Christianity. For some, as we shall see in Zurich, the "context" was rural; for them, the Christian community was not urban, but began with the rural villages in which they lived. Iconoclasm was not an exclusively urban event, nor was it defined by an urban context; but its nature meant that it could be more easily discovered and prosecuted within the urban context, where the magistrates' authority was more immediate and their powers of investigation more effective.

This book is very self-consciously *not* about the theologians. It is about the theologies of ordinary people, as they were expressed not in treatises, but in acts, in the physical expressions of belief.

---

[48] Iconoclasm in Reformed Europe – Huguenot strongholds in France, as well as Reformed communities in the Low Countries, England, and Scotland – shares some of the concerns of this earlier iconoclasm, but also was driven by others, as I suggest above, deriving from hostile political environments.

In seeking to provide an interpretive model that will enable us to recover the agency and the theology of ordinary people in our understanding of "Reformation," in seeking to hear more clearly the voices and perspectives of ordinary people, this study has muted the theologians in its narrative of iconoclasm – it, too, skews our view of the past. Yet its intent is not to sever those acts from formal theology. Indeed, Chapter 1 explores theologians' discussions of images, to delineate the possible connotations images may have had for Christian men and women. It is placed before the narrative of iconoclasm in order to build in another of this study's commitments: to frame discussions of theology in dialogue with the practices of the laity. Formal theology was not autonomous of the laity, and this study posits another relation between the two – not dissemination and reception, but *resonance*. The writings of the theologians and the acts of ordinary Christians speak to one another: The meaning of each resonates in the cultural activity of the other.

Thus, this book explores another vision of "Reformation": It takes as its model not acculturation, nor imposition and reaction, but dynamic, dialogue, in which different persons "spoke" through different forms, according to their education and their social and political place within the community, each bringing to that dialogue his, or sometimes her, vision of true Christianity, and articulating that vision in that cultural form he or she found most accessible. Theologians, for example, spoke primarily in the forms of sermon, preaching, and the pamphlet, writing in the language of their intellectual discipline; magistrates, in laws, in the language of legislation, and its enforcement. The people with whom this book is concerned spoke primarily not through those forms most accessible to us – pamphlets, manuscripts, and laws – but through their actions, their "acts." This book explores those acts as one mode by which hundreds of ordinary people themselves sought to enact reforms and enter into dialogue with the theologians and secular authorities – to enter into "Reformation," which encompassed preachers, magistrates, and ordinary folk. By them, the iconoclasts helped to forge "reformed" Christian communities. Indeed, their acts became essential to the process by which various communities came to define what it meant to

24

be Christian. We seek, then, to recover something of the exhilaration and the terror of the early days of "Reformation," to discern in the acts, both individual and collective, of ordinary Christians the outlines and something of the content of *their* visions of Reformation, to contribute at least a partial answer to the question, What was at stake for them in Reformation?

The images in the churches

Iconoclasm is defined by its objects, its "victims," the focus of its violence. In this book, "iconoclasm" is defined as an attack, violence, either verbal or physical, usually physical, often combined with violent words, against Christian "images," predominantly, but not exclusively in churches.[1] Iconoclasts' attacks were directed against much more than representational art – altar retables, panel paintings, diptychs, triptychs, murals, freestanding and architectural sculpture. Reformation iconoclasts also attacked lamps, candlesticks, liturgical implements – all the material culture of Christianity. If we take their attacks as something more than "rites of destruction,"[2] then they suggest something very important about how ordinary people conceived of "images." Ordinary people, from parish priests to carpenters to magistrates, embraced many more objects under the rubric "image" than "high art," or event art with "content" as we would conceive it today.[3] The following chapters explore what iconoclasts' acts reveal of their specific understanding of the nature, meaning, and function of the images. To give those acts their

[1] For the interplay of anticlericalism and iconoclasm, see Chapter 4 on Basel. Phyllis Mack Crew has articulated a different relation of iconoclasm to the priests in the Low Countries in *Calvinist Preaching and Iconoclasm in the Netherlands 1544–1569* (Cambridge, 1978).

[2] The phrase is Sergiuz Michalski's, in his catalogue of iconoclasms in sixteenth-century Europe: "Iconoclasm: Rites of destruction," chap. 3 in *The Reformation and the Visual Arts: The Protestant Image Question in Western and Eastern Europe* (London & New York, 1993).

[3] This distinction, argued by David Freedberg in *The Power of Images: Studies in the History and Theory of Response* (Chicago, 1989), is all the more distorting for religious art, whose "content" is rarely explicit or immediate to the uneducated viewer.

full resonance, let me sketch here the debates on images, the traditions, that provided the referents, some of the terms, and signal something of the context for the iconoclasts' own contribution to the debate.

All would have agreed that images belonged to the physical world, the world of matter. All would have agreed that images were artificial – themselves created and not creators. However, the relation of the physical world to its human observers was conceived differently than it is today. Various theories of sight, most deriving from Aristotle and arriving through Arabic science, accorded the perceived world agency: Objects emanated their "rays" or "species" through distance to reach the eye.[4] In understandings of sight before Kepler, images were physically active, reaching over space to the eye. Thus, images *acted* upon the eye, and the eye was passive.[5] To put it another way, images were the agent and human eyes were the recipient.

In addition, for Christians, lay and clerical, learned and "rustic," the physical world remained a medium through which God acted, most dramatically in the form of miracles. For them, the physical world held the potential for wonder, for divine intervention and communication. Images belonged fully to that world with its potential for miracles.[6] Their execution or their beauty could be "miraculous": beyond the ability of the most skilled master without the help or intervention of God. Their placement could be "miraculous": transported to their appropriate, their right location through divine help. Most often, images participated in miracles: They served as the locus toward which the pious directed prayers and petitions. Images were that place, the physical location, where the pious might address holy per-

---

[4] David Lindberg, *Theories of Vision from Al-Kindi to Kepler* (Chicago, 1976).
[5] Thus the subjectivity of David Freedberg's formulation of "response" would be strange to sixteenth-century viewers, who conceived of the images' "power" as of an essentially different nature, and accorded the images an autonomy impossible in Freedberg's formulation.
[6] See, for example, Caesarius of Heisterbach, *Dialogus Miraculorum*, 2 vols., ed. Joseph Strange (Cologne, Bonn, & Brussels, 1851), esp. vol. 2, Distinctio 7, in which he describes some miraculous images of the Virgin. Ernst Kitzinger has traced the emergence of the Christian view of images as miraculous in "The Cult of Images in the Age Before Iconoclasm," in *The Art of Byzantium and the Medieval West: Selected Studies* (Bloomington & London, 1976), pp. 91–156.

sons long dead – the saints, the apostles, Mary, or even Christ
Himself.

For Christians, the relation of the physical world to divinity
was nuanced through a range of possible connections, articulated over the centuries in debates about images.[7] By the sixteenth
century, a number of those positions had become a part of the discourse on images. In the sixth century, Pope Gregory the Great
had written to the iconoclastic bishop Serenus that in an image
(*pictura*) even the unlearned could see what they ought to follow,
in it, even those who knew no letters (*litteras*) could read, whence
for the people (*gentibus*) the image stands for reading (*pro lectione
pictura est*);[8] it soon became the commonplace that images were
the books of the illiterate. In the ninth century, the *Libri Carolini*,
the West's own iconophobic response to the Byzantine image crisis, had nonetheless condoned images as models for the illiterate
to emulate; in the twelfth century, many theologians had referred in passing to images as the literature of the laity (*laicorum
litteratura*), and at least one had come to name stained-glass windows "*doctores.*"[9]

Gregory's pronouncement set an important tension for Christianity. In designating images the cultural medium of the unlearned, Gregory attached them to a group whose cultural place
would decline in the next six centuries: By the twelfth century, a
particular kind of textual learnedness would become highly valued, and those learned would occupy places of authority and significance. That tension may not have been intended by Gregory
or even by those theologians of the next centuries who adopted its

---

[7] Since my concern is to establish the relationship between images and Christian
theology, my discussion of medieval treatments of images follows the categories suggested by Edwyn Bevan, *Holy Images: An Inquiry into Idolatry and Image-Worship in
Ancient Paganism and in Christianity* (London, 1940), rather than Sixton Ringbom,
Icon to Narrative: The Rise of the Dramatic Close-up in Fifteenth-Century Devotional Painting
(Doornspijk, 1984). In keeping with this concern, I have chosen to use the term "divinity" throughout this discussion because it lends itself to greater precision than the
term "holy," and shifts the focus to the more clearly theological issue of the relation
between the Christian God and images.

[8] *Patrologiae Latinae*, ed. J.-P. Migne [hereafter *PL*], vol. 77, col. 1128. For a slightly
different formulation, see an earlier letter to Serenus, cols. 1027–8.

[9] Gerhard B. Ladner, "Die Bilderstreit und die Kunst-Lehren der byzantinischen und
abendländischen Theologie," in *Images and Ideas in the Middle Ages: Selected Studies in
History and Art*, vol. I (Rome, 1983), pp. 26–32.

reduced formulation: Popes, bishops, theologians, monks, and mendicants lived surrounded by images – those who were illiterate had far less access in their daily lives to images than did those who lived in monastic and ecclesiastical establishments. Also, Gregory's formulation was subtler than the commonplace it became: Images were to the illiterate what the written word was to the literate; they were a source of education for the great majority of Europeans who were illiterate, *analogous* to those written texts to which the learned had access. Gregory distinguished the quality of the two cultural media – words were the better medium – but he did not set them in opposition nor divide the two kinds of "readerships" into two distinct groups. He had, however, linked images to the illiterate. In the sixteenth century, that linkage would find new resonance, as literacy and verbal learnedness acquired ever greater value.

> We use all our senses to produce worthy images of Him, and we sanctify the noblest of the senses, which is that of sight. For just as words edify the ear, so also the image stimulates the eye. What the book is to the literate, the image is to the illiterate. Just as words speak to the ear, so the image speaks to the sight; it brings us understanding. (John of Damascus) [10]

In the early years of the Church, images came to occupy an increasingly significant role in Christianity, yet it would not be until the Byzantine image controversy of the eighth century that the nature of images was discussed in any fullness. Among those who took up the defense of images and the explication of their nature and place within Christianity, none was more influential than the Syrian saint John of Damascus.[11] Many of the positions subsequently articulated in Aquinas and others have been traced to the range of relations John put forward in his defense of

---

[10] St. John of Damascus, *On the Divine Images: Three Apologies Against Those Who Attack the Divine Images* [hereafter *ODI*], trans. David Anderson (Crestwood, N.Y., 1980), p. 25.

[11] My understanding of John of Damascus has essentially been guided by Jaroslav Pelikan, *Imago Dei: The Byzantine Apologia for Icons* (Princeton, 1990). See, in addition, Bevan, *Holy Images,* pp. 127–46.

the images in the eighth century.[12] John gathered a number of earlier orthodox writers' opinions on images, often written for other purposes, such as the cult of the emperor, and drew from them a subtle, multifaceted, and deeply resonant formulation of images, their relation to divinity, and the proper attitude of devout Christians toward them.[13] His *On the Divine Images: Three Apologies Against Those Who Attack the Divine Images*, with the *Ancient Documentation and Testimony of The Holy Fathers Concerning Images* and its commentary that accompanied each apology,[14] articulate a conception of the nature of images and an explication of the relation between images and divinity crucial to understanding their "power" in the sixteenth century.

For John, images could not be divided simply between divine and human. Quite the contrary, he anchored his definition of an image in his Christology:[15]

> An image is of like character with its prototype, but with a certain difference. It is not like its archetype in every way. The Son is the living, essential, and precisely similar Image of the invisible God, bearing the entire Father within Himself, equal to Him in all things, except that He is begotten by Him, the Begetter. It is the nature of the Father to cause; the Son is the effect.[16]

That most difficult, most discussed, explored, and controversy engendering of relations, between God the Father and Christ the Son, was the first model John posited for the relation between im-

---

[12] On the western medieval connections to the eastern image controversy, see Johannes Kollwitz, "Bild und Bildertheologie im Mittelalter," in *Das Gottesbild im Abendland* (Witten & Berlin, 1959), pp. 109–38. For official exchanges between eastern and western ecclesiastical authorities during the Byzantine image crisis, see Gert Haendler, "Kirchpolitische Rückwirkungen des byzantinischen Bilderstreits auf das Papsttum bis zur Frankfurter Synode 794," in *Der byzantinische Bilderstreit: Sozialökonomische Voraussetzungen – ideologische Grundlagen – geschichtliche Wirkungen*, ed. Johannes Irmscher (Leipzig, 1980), pp. 130–48, and more fully, *Epochen karolingischer Theologie. Eine Untersuchung über die karolingishe Gutachten zum byzantinischen Bilderstreit* (Berlin, 1958).

[13] Among the authors upon which he drew were Dionysius the Aeropagite, St. Basil, Gregory of Nyssa, John Chrysostom, Ambrose, Anastasius, Eusebius, and Gregory Nazianzus.

[14] Anderson's translations of John's titles.

[15] In the following pages, John's Christology is illumined only insofar as it pertains to the discussion of images that would continue in the West.

[16] *ODI*, p. 19.

ages and divinity.[17] In invoking it, John connected any discussion of images to the great tradition of Christological debates in the Church.[18] He also indicated how very complex he understood images' relation to divinity to be, the multiplicity of interconnections they had with their "prototypes." In invoking Christ's relation to God the Father, John set from the start the parameters of an image's relation to its prototype: An image was neither identical to, nor divisible from its original; their interconnections were manifold, on a range of levels.

Images, John next asserted, could also be within God: "There are also in God images and models of His acts yet to come: Those things which are His will for all eternity, which is always changeless."[19] The relation of images to divinity began with those images, invisible to human eyes, within God, eternal, capturing that which was to come. These were images not of God or Christ, but of the future. They served as plans. John thus introduced another key characteristic of images: They bridge time. Images within God delineate what is to come; images within human experience were less explicit:

> Again, an image foreshadows something that is yet to happen, something hidden in riddles and shadows. For instance, the ark of the covenant is an image of the Holy Virgin and Theotokos. . . . The brazen serpent typifies the cross and Him who healed the evil bite of the serpent by hanging on it.

Images within human experience provided more cryptic signs of the future. They also served as bridges of a particular kind to the past:

> Again, things which have already taken place are remembered by means of images, whether for the purpose of inspiring won-

---

[17] On the inter-Nicene discussions of Christ's nature as it pertained to images, see Christoph von Schönborn, *L'Icone du Christ: Fondements Théologiques* (Fribourg, 1976).
[18] "The iconoclastic controversy begun in the eighth century by the Byzantine emperor Leo III (717–41) and continued by his successor Constantine V (741–75) cannot be considered in isolation from the Christological controversies of the preceding centuries," Anderson's Introduction to *ODI*, p. 7. See also Pelikan, *Imago Dei*. Peter Brown argued the contrary: "the Christological background of Iconoclasm is far from certain," "A Dark-Age crisis: Aspects of the Iconoclastic controversy," *English Historical Review* 88(1973): 3.
[19] *ODI*, p. 19.

der, or honor, or shame, or to encourage those who look upon them to practice good and avoid evil.[20]

The distinction is subtle but important: Images do not represent the past, but are the *means* by which the past is remembered. As with many points in his argument, John draws out the subtler resonances of earlier formulations. Like Gregory, John of Damascus articulates a delicate and precise relation between images and the past. Images enable human remembrance of the past, and human response to past events. Images themselves did not record the past: "when we record events and good deeds of the past, we *use* images."[21] They functioned mnemonically: They spoke to human memory, evocatively, facilitating its recovery of knowledge and experience.

Images that function in this way, John continues, are of two kinds: "words written in books, as when God had the law engraved on tablets and desired the lives of holy men to be recorded, or else they are material images, such as the jar of manna, or Aaron's staff."[22] Words could be "images" as well, according to the Damascene, an argument Luther himself would make seven centuries later.[23] Thus, images were not restricted to those forms of art known as "representative." They were not descriptive, but evocative.

Finally, those images "made by words or artistic representation" were preceded by "the natural image": "First we have a human being; only then can we have words or pictures."[24] Images thus ranged from those that God had made, Christ and man, down to those art forms human beings made. For John, creation itself formed a hierarchy of imagery, from that which God had made directly, more and less perfectly in His own image, to those images humans made in words or pictures.

In all of the Damascene's definitions, images were neither stat-

---

[20] Ibid., pp. 20–1.
[21] Ibid. italics mine.
[22] Ibid.
[23] Hans Freiherr von Campenhausen, "Luther und Zwingli zur Bilderfrage," in *Das Gottesbild im Abendland*, pp. 160–1.
[24] *ODI*, pp. 74–8.

ic nor still: They prefigured; they signaled; they evoked past experience; in some significant way, they bridged time, either past to present, or present to future. Images were a source of mimesis. They were that place where actions to be emulated, "mirrored," were expressed: the movements, gestures, and acts of Christ, the apostles, Mary, and all the saints. "Of like character," but not identical to their prototypes, images were not purely descriptive or directly and immediately representative. They did not "carry" meaning; they were a *mode* of divine foreknowledge; they *enabled* human memory to engender meaning. They were evocative. It was not in the representing, but in the interplay between mind and image that an image acted.

John's *On the Divine Images* is important to us for two reasons. It was incorporated into the western Christian tradition's own defense of images, as we shall see.[25] More important, however, is that he signals an understanding of the relation between image and divinity that circumnavigates "representation." That understanding enabled John of Damascus to meet successfully the criticism iconoclastic theologians leveled against images: Any representation of God was idolatrous.[26] In suggesting, as he had in each of his kinds of image, that the image was similar to, but different from, its prototype, John had undercut the iconoclast position: Images did not "represent" in the simple manner iconoclasts implied, but functioned more obliquely, evoking memory, mood, experience, or, as in the case of the ark of the covenant, some larger frame of reference.

John had also articulated the foundation for the place of images in Christian churches. From the start, he provided the most powerful justification: God Himself had created one "image" of Himself, man, and begotten one "image" of Himself, Christ. Through the second image, God had reconciled Himself and man – the reconciliation was, in the words of Leslie W. Barnard,

---

[25] Damascus was translated into Latin in the twelfth century, Kollwitz, "Bild und Bildertheologie im Mittelalter," p. 110, n. 7 (p. 132).

[26] This position can only be deduced from iconophilic polemic; iconoclastic writings did not survive the reinstitution of icons in the East, Bevan, *Holy Images*, p. 128; Pelikan, *Imago Dei*, pp. 47–9. On the various reasons Byzantine emperors might have had for seeking to eliminate the images, see Pelikan, *Imago Dei*, chap. 1.

"mediated through matter."[27] That second "image" justified images in Christian churches:

> If we attempted to make an image of the invisible God, this would be sinful indeed. It is impossible to portray one who is without body: invisible, uncircumscribed, and without form. Again, if we made images of men and believed them to be gods, and adored them as if they were so, we would be truly impious. We do neither of these things. But we are not mistaken if we make an image of God incarnate, who was seen on earth in the flesh, associated with men, and in His unspeakable goodness assumed the nature, feeling, form and color of our flesh. For we yearn to see how He looked, as the apostle says, "Now we see through a glass darkly." Now the icon is also a dark glass, fashioned according to the limitations of our physical nature. Though the mind wear itself out with effort, it can never cast away its bodily nature.[28]

Christianity had its origin in that moment when God took on human form: "So the Word became flesh; he came to dwell among us, and we saw his glory, such glory as befits the Father's only Son."[29] God the Father, was, in the words of early theologians, "uncircumscribable": invisible, infinite, eternal, without limit or demarcation. He had, however, "taken on flesh," become incarnate. Christological debates would contribute essentially to the increasing distance between East and West, but John's central assertion, that God had "assumed the nature, feeling, form and color of our flesh," held. God Himself had produced the first images, the one flawed, man, the other, much more closely similar to the prototype, yet still distinct, sharing but not identical in nature – Christ. The nature of the "incarnation," Christ's physicality, would be debated, both among theologians and in visual images, for the next millenium,[30] but the fact of Christ's physicality and its inseverability from His divinity would not. Important for our purposes here is the establishment

[27] Barnard, *The Graeco-Roman and Oriental Background of the Iconoclastic Controversy* (Leiden, 1974), p. 103.

[28] *ODI*, pp. 52–3.

[29] John 1:14, *The New Oxford Annotated Bible*, Rev. Std. Version (New York, 1977).

[30] Cf. Caroline Walker Bynum, "The Body of Christ in the Later Middle Ages: A Reply to Leo Steinberg," *Fragmentation and Redemption: Essays on Gender and the Human Body in Medieval Religion* (New York, 1991), pp. 79–117.

of the theological basis for images: Insofar as the Christian God had become incarnate – "becomes visible to flesh," "empties Himself and takes the form of a servant in substance and in stature and is found in a body of flesh" – one could "depict," "draw," and "show" Him, "use every kind of drawing, word, or color."[31]

The Damascene's argument extended beyond the assertion of God's taking on human form. The Incarnation had altered the relation between God and matter on the one hand, and the meaning of matter for man on the other: "I worship the Creator of matter who became matter for my sake, who willed to take His abode in matter; who worked out my salvation through matter."[32] Matter served human salvation, insofar as God was working through it.[33] Just as it was heretical to sever Christ's divine and human natures, to sever Christ's spirit from his flesh, so, too, were iconoclasts heretical to deny matter its role in human salvation. The Incarnation was not merely the moment of divine embodiment. It marked an essential change in the relation between divinity and the material world: No longer could the two be separated, for the one who had taken "His abode in matter" worked through matter to touch human souls, to save them. God spoke through matter to man.[34]

The Seventh Ecumenical Council (Nicea, 787) asserted the orthodoxy of this formulation.[35] The Council reaffirmed that Christ's two natures were inseparable, and declared heretical any effort to separate the two. Like John of Damascus, the Council asserted that Christ's "flesh" could be depicted; to deny that was heretical. At the Council, the orthodox position on images for the Church, both western and eastern, was established: Christ Himself could be depicted, and images of Christ, along with those of saints, apostles, Mary, and other holy persons, belonged fully to

[31] *ODI,* pp. 18–19.

[32] Ibid., p. 23.

[33] Anderson's Introduction, pp. 8–10.

[34] Thus, John of Damascus' position differs significantly from that Peter Brown attributes to Byzantine iconodules, that icons were "holy" in essentially the same way as God was "holy," Brown, "A Dark-Age crisis," pp. 5–12.

[35] See esp. the Third Volume, trans. and pub. Daniel J. Sahas in *Icon and Logos: Sources in Eighth-Century Iconoclasm* (Toronto, 1986), pp. 80–96. Peter Brown asserts, "There is little evidence that the Byzantine clergy knew of [John of Damascus' *On the Divine Images*] at the Council of Nicea in 787," Brown, "A Dark-Age crisis," p. 3.

the practice of Christianity. Images served to induce and preserve conversion, to educate, as a source of mimesis, to shape patterns of behavior into orthodox practices, and to evoke piety itself:

> Thus the holy catholic Church of God, using many different means, attracts those who are born within her to repentance and to the knowledge of how to keep the commandments of God. . . . When these [icons] are before our eyes, the hearts of those who fear the Lord rejoice; faces bloom; the disheartened soul turns cheerful, singing along with David, the forefather of Him Who is God: *I remembered God and rejoiced.* Therefore through the icons we are continually reminded of God. (Sixth Session of the Seventh Ecumenical Council)[36]

John of Damascus also articulated a psychological reason for images: "for we yearn to see how He looked." Not only did God work through the material world, but human beings, by their nature, sought to see God in the physical. This insight would also survive in the West. It was essential to their nature for human beings to wish to see God: "Though the mind wear itself out with effort, it can never cast away its bodily nature." Human nature made images a necessary element in spiritual knowledge: "Anyone would say that our inability immediately to direct our thoughts to contemplation of higher things makes it necessary that familiar everyday media be utilized to give suitable form to what is formless, and make visible what cannot be depicted, so that we are able to construct understandable analogies."[37]

What distinguished Christians was not the desire to see the invisible and infinite in material form, but discernment:

> But to us it is given, on the other hand, as Gregory the Theologian says, to avoid superstitious error and to come to know God in the fullness of truth; to adore God alone, to enjoy the fullness of divine knowledge. . . . We are no longer under custodians, but we have received from God the ability to discern what may be represented and what is uncircumscript.[38]

The iconoclastic controversy of the eighth century led John of Damascus and other apologists for images to formulate what we

---

[36] Sahas, *Icon and Logos*, pp. 171–2 (see also p. 175).
[37] *ODI*, p. 20.
[38] Ibid., p. 18.

might call a Christian epistemology. That epistemology posited two interdependent claims. First, the physical world was a medium through which God acted; it was "an abode" for God. The Incarnation, as they articulated it and as it was affirmed as orthodoxy, represented that moment when God altered the relation between the spiritual and physical worlds. The latter became a locus for meaning: God worked through the physical world; and God Incarnate was present not merely as speaking, but as acting, as gestures, acts that could be imitated. Second, human beings, *by their nature*, depend upon the physical world – they "construct understandable analogies" from the visible and physical world – to understand the spiritual. The physical world provides the metaphors by which human beings may grasp an "uncircumscribable" God, a God whose eternity, omnipotence, and infinity were opposite human mortality, frailty, and finitude.[39]

Such an epistemology privileged sight as a central vehicle of cognition. If the physical world was a locus for divine communication with humanity, the eye was the sole sense that could gaze upon matter and discern meaning. In this epistemology, images became a medium of religious knowledge. Through them, Christians could contemplate the Incarnation – that mystical interplay between finite physicality and infinite divinity. God Himself remained invisible, infinite, formless; but His "presence"[40] in the physical world in all its multiplicity – through Christ, saints, miracles – could be intimated, suggested, "evoked" in images.[41]

---

[39] Cf. George Lakoff & Mark Johnson, *Metaphors We Live By* (Chicago, 1980) and Mark Johnson, *The Body in the Mind: The Bodily Basis of Meaning, Imagination, and Reason* (Chicago, 1987).

[40] This term has been taken up in recent discussions of image theory. See, for example, Jean-François Lyotard, "Presence," pp. 11–34, and Salim Kemal & Ivan Gaskell, "Art History and Language: Some Issues," esp. pp. 2–3, both in *The Language of Art History*, ed. Salim Kemal & Ivan Gaskell (Cambridge, 1991). By this term, however, I wish to invoke obliquely debates on the nature of "presence" in the Eucharist, a topic I shall take up more directly in the future.

[41] This view of images and their relation to divinity explains, I think, those examples Bevan (*Holy Images*, pp. 145–6), and Freedberg (*The Power of Images*, chaps. 6– 7, e.g., pp. 124, 149) cite as evidence of the identification of specific images and divinity. Huldrych Zwingli would challenge this place of images in Christian epistemology. See my "The Reform of the Images: New Visualizations of the Christian Community at Zürich," *Archive for Reformation History* 80(1989): 115–20.

This epistemology did not go undisputed. In the ninth century, Agobard, Bishop of Lyon, would challenge any effort to represent sanctity and reject images of saints as a mode of understanding the qualities inherent in divinity.[42] The monastic tradition, with its asceticism, directly questioned the value such an epistemology placed upon material objects. The most famous among the monastic critics of images, Bernard of Clairvaux, criticized images in terms that would be echoed from the eleventh century to the sixteenth. Images for Bernard belonged to the world of matter valued purely for itself. They distracted the pious from meditation upon more spiritual things. Far more important, however, was their larger role within the economy of Christianity: Images took sustenance from the needy, as the pious gave money for the maintenance of images instead of the human poor.[43] Yet even Bernard, who would be cited (and miscited) so often, did not call for the elimination of images. He sought instead their devaluation, to turn the attention of the pious from these images to the enactment of his particular conception of charity, the realization of divine love among human beings. Bernard's criticism of images resonated over centuries, as other proponents of a more "spiritual" or "ascetic" Christianity – John Wyclif, the Lollards,[44] some of the more austere Hussites, Bernardino of Siena, John of Capistrano, Konrad Summenhart, Savonarola[45] and Erasmus – challenged images' central place in Christianity. However, even Bernard's own order continued to grace its monasteries, its chapels, its refectories with an artistic style known not only for its simplicity, but for its beauty, its sensitivity to visual values. Even St. Francis himself, Bernardino of Siena and John of Capistrano's

---

[42] "Liber contra eorum superstitionem qui picturis et imaginibus sanctorum adorationis obsequium deferendum," *PL* 104, esp. cols. 209–11.

[43] *PL* 182, cols. 895–918. Although references to Bernard's letter to William, Abbot of St. Thierry, refer only to that one section concerning images and the poor, the entire letter is concerned with the question of charity as it pertains to the practice of Christianity, and explains the basis for Bernard's asceticism in terms of the practice of love.

[44] On Wyclif's and Lollard critiques of images, see Margaret Aston, *Lollards and Reformers: Images and Literacy in Late Medieval Religion* (London, 1984), esp. chap. 5, "Lollards and Images."

[45] Helmut Feld, *Der Ikonoklasmus des Westens* (Leiden, 1990), chaps. V–VI.

spiritual model, would bring added attention to the crucifix as a focus of devout meditation.

For the great majority of Christians in the West images were a medium of religious knowledge. For John Beleth, Sicardus of Cremona, and Durandus, images depicted more than examples of the Fathers or the saints, evoked more than acts the virtuous could imitate.[46] Thomas Aquinas would echo John of Damascus in attributing to images an evocative power. Images, according to Aquinas, served three purposes in Christianity: first, for the instruction of the crowd (*rudium*), they educate as if they were books for them; second, that the mystery of the Incarnation and the example of the saints might be greater in memory, as they are daily represented (*repraesentantur*) to the eyes; third, for exciting the mood (*affectum*) of devotion, which is more efficaciously aroused through sight than through hearing.[47] So, too, the Franciscan Bonaventure's justification for the use of images in Christianity asserted their evocative power, again on three counts: "because of the simplicity of the crowd [*ruditatem*], because of the slowness of piety [*affectatem*], and because of the slipperiness of memory."[48] For the great Dominican and Franciscan theologians, as for John, images evoked, recalled to memory the lives and acts of Christ, Mary, and the saints, and interacted with the memory and experience of their viewer to engender a mood, an emotion, a disposition to piety.[49]

Indeed, some would echo those larger claims John had made for images, of their necessary place in a hierarchy of revelation. In his treatise, *The Journey of the Mind into God* (*Itinerarium mentis in deum*), Bonaventure suggested a similar gradation of cognition, in which images might lead the mind to contemplation of God,

---

[46] Kollwitz, "Bild und Bildertheologie im Mittelalter," pp. 121–5.

[47] Latin text, Commentary on the *Sententiae* of Peter Lombard, Lib. 3, dist. 9, qu. 1, art. 2 (ed. Rome, 1570; vol. 7, pp. 35H–J), cited in Ladner, "Die Bilderstreit und die Kunst-Lehren," p. 29; my translation. This position was echoed by the fourteenth-century *Praeceptorium*, attributed to Nicolas of Lyra, cited in Michael Baxandall, *The Limewood Sculptors of Renaissance Germany* (New Haven & London, 1980), pp. 51–2.

[48] Bonaventure, *Sent*, lib. 3, dist. 9, qu. 2, cited in Kollwitz, "Bild und Bildertheologie im Mittelalter," p. 137, n. 115, my translation.

[49] On other twelfth- and thirteenth-century theologians' statements on images, which follow the lines articulated here, see Kollwitz, "Bild und Bildertheologie im Mittelalter," pp. 121–31.

"and through sensible things [*sensibilia*], which they see, they are borne [*transferantur*] to intelligible things [*intelligibilia*], which they do not see."[50] The visions of mystics such as Hadewijch and Henry Suso further blurred the distinction between "seeing" and spiritual "illumination" or knowledge.[51] In the fifteenth century, Nicolaus of Cusa would employ the metaphor of an icon, the eyes of which always appear to look into the eyes of its beholder, to explicate his understanding of the "gaze of God" and speak of the metaphoric mode of human cognition.[52]

John's formulation reminds us that modern understandings of the relation between divinity and images are much less nuanced than medieval conceptions, linked as they were to highly sophisticated Christologies. Images occupied a place of particular complexity in medieval theology. Like Christ himself, images' relation to divinity was not simple identity. Images were not God or gods, nor even saints or Mary. They did not "represent" in the sense that has come to dominate since the Renaissance. They provided the means for Christians to *imagine* a God who was unknowable; they were metaphors for a God who acted through the physical world, but was not Himself physical. Medieval religious images participated in collective meditations on the nature of God's presence in the world. No one mistook images for God – even the most hostile of critics of images did not assert that. Nor, on the other hand, did Christian theologians seek to sever images from the divinity they "represented" in the medieval sense[53] – that would be to commit the greatest of heresies, to suggest that the physical nature of Christ was somehow severable from the divine. Images were neither themselves divine nor exclusively material, physical. They enabled the pious to conceive of divinity and of the quality of holiness in terms that were themselves comprehensible – in terms that functioned as metaphors,

---

[50] Bonaventure, *Itinerarium mentis in deum*, ed. Werner Höver (Munich, 1970), bk. II, art. 11.

[51] On the interplay of mystics' visionary experiences and images, see Alfred Peltzer, *Deutsche Mystik und deutsche Kunst* (Strasbourg, 1899); and Ringbom, *Icon to Narrative*, pp. 15–22.

[52] Pauline Moffitt Watts, *Nicolaus Cusanus: A Fifteenth-Century Vision of Man* (Leiden, 1982), esp. chap. V.

[53] Margaret Miles, *Image as Insight* (Boston, 1985).

providing analogies, associations, evocations, themselves elusive, transient, and powerful. Like the mystery of Christ Himself, images' relation to divinity escaped precise definition – no matter what the words used, conceptualization remained personal, private, in the heart of each pious Christian.

Such an epistemology helps to explain more fully – and sympathetically – a range of other practices. In enshrining relics in images of a range of kinds – crucifixes, busts, arms, shrines, full sculptured forms – Christians were linking two different modes of physical presence, bones and man-made images. These images, too, served mnemonically, to evoke knowledge of the particular saint, his or her acts and gestures, the forms and expression of his or her piety. In praying to those images that enshrined relics, tens of thousands in number by the sixteenth century, Christians were addressing that physical location where the saint might be present – not *in* the image, but "present" as God was present, acting *through* the image.[54] They were looking to the image as the medium through which they might speak to someone long dead, whose relation to the physical world had been altered, but not severed. The "truth" of the image lay not in the accuracy of its representation, but in the evidence of the saint's "presence": answers to prayers, intercessions, and miracles.

The second great tradition of debate, interconnected with the first on the nature of images, centered upon the relation of the viewer to religious images: What was to be the attitude of the pious Christian toward images? What was to be the place of images in worship? As early as the sixth century, Gregory had sought to define that relationship: In the same letter to the bishop, Gregory wrote, "For it is one thing to worship [*adorare*] an image, it is another to discern [*addiscere*] through pictures [*per picturae*] the story of that which is to be worshiped [*adorandum*]."[55] Again,

---

[54] The particular linking of holiness and physicality saints embodied is a separate and more complicated question. An excellent consideration of this is Caroline Walker Bynum, *Holy Feast and Holy Fast: The Religious Significance of Food to Medieval Women* (Berkeley, 1987), as well as, more recently, "In Praise of Fragments: History in a Comic Mode," in her *Fragmentation and Redemption*, pp. 11–26.

[55] *PL* 77, col. 1128.

John of Damascus provided the fullest explication of the relation of viewer to Christian images.

John had distinguished two ontologically[56] different kinds of worship: absolute, "adoration" or *latreia,* and relative, "veneration" or *proskinesis.* He established two spheres of worship, the one directed toward the creator and the other directed toward the created world. The first sphere encompassed five different attitudes of the pious directly toward God:

1. "adoration, which we give to God alone";
2. "the awe and yearning we have for God because of the glory which is His by nature";
3. "thanksgiving for all the good things He has created for us";
4. that worship "inspired by our needs and hopes for His blessing"; and
5. "repentance and confession."[57]

The second sphere distinguished different relations between the pious and various aspects of creation. There were, according to John, seven different ways one venerated creation:

1. toward those "created things," the saints, who were "truly gods, not by nature, but because they partake of the divine nature . . . obedient servants and favored friends, but they are not the King Himself";
2. toward "those places and things by which God has accomplished our salvation," such as "Mount Sinai, and Nazareth, the cave and manger of Bethlehem, the holy mountain of Golgotha, the wood of the cross, the nails, the sponge, the reed, the holy and saving lance, the robe, the seamless tunic, the winding-sheet, the swaddling-clothes, the holy tomb which is the fountain of our resurrection, the stone which sealed the sepulchre, holy Mount Zion and the holy Mount of Olives, the pool of Bethsaida, the blessed garden of Gethsemane" – "all matter which partakes of divine power . . . all God's holy temples, and everything where God's name is found," including angels and men;

---

[56] The term is Anderson's. See his Introduction, pp. 8–11.
[57] *ODI*, pp. 82–3.

3. toward "objects dedicated to God, such as the holy Gospel and other books," as well as "patens, chalices, censers, candlesticks, and altars";
4. toward "those images which were seen by the prophets . . . such as Aaron's rod . . . or the jar of manna," and other images that assure past events will be remembered: ". . . the honorable figure of the cross, or the likeness of the physical features of God, or of her who gave birth to Him in the flesh, and everyone who is part of Him";
5. toward "each other, since we are God's inheritance";
6. toward "those who have been given the authority to rule over us"; and, finally,
7. that veneration servants offer to their masters.[58]

The second sphere linked those images he had already designated – prophetic images, the cross, likenesses of Christ, Mary, and the saints – in an ontological hierarchy to saints, those places and objects connected immediately with the person of Christ, the Gospel, liturgical objects, and all humanity, as well as to various figures of authority and "masters." Images belonged within a network of connections of "veneration," of a certain kind of honor. In that hierarchy of relations between divinity and creation, images were inferior to "those places where God, who alone is holy, has rested," Mary and the saints, who "bear in themselves Him who is by nature worshipful." They were superior, however, to persons of authority and masters, whose veneration derived solely from the most general divine ordering of human relations.

John of Damascus' essential distinction between *latreia* (*latria* in Latin), the adoration due God alone, and *proskinesis* (or *dulia*, as it would be known in the West), the reverence one paid the created world as it reflected divinity, rested upon his subtle understanding of representation. John organized his hierarchy of veneration in terms not of animate–inanimate creation, but of the immediacy of that creature's relation to holiness. Thus, for John, worship mirrored the hierarchy of revelation. Images were to be venerated not for their matter, their participation in the physical-

---

[58] Ibid., pp. 84–8.

ity of creation. The veneration directed toward images was offered "to those who are portrayed through matter in images. Any honor given to an image is transferred to its prototype, as St. Basil says."[59] Subsequent theologians, among them Aquinas, would take up this understanding of worship, but they would articulate it in an environment dramatically different from that of John of Damascus, or even of Gregory the Great.

Beginning in the mid-tenth century, the place of images within the churches began to change.[60] Images began to play an increasing role, and occupy increasing space, within the practice of Christianity. They grew in both number and kind. In the central portions of the Carolingian empire a new genre of image emerged, the freestanding sculpture. This new genre was employed to render a number of Madonnas with the Christ child and patron saints, many of which became the focus of pilgrimages, such as the Golden Madonna of the Essen Cathedral treasury and Saint-Foy at Conques. These freestanding statues became quickly intertwined with the burgeoning cult of relics: The development of bust reliquaries occurred simultaneously. By the sixteenth century, the largest churches possessed hundreds of images in dozens of chapels and on thirty to forty altars. The sheer density of images – as Kollwitz, following Keller, intimated – altered their relation to the practice of Christianity: They *were* the environment in which Christians worshiped. They became ever more elaborate, demonstrating greater and greater skill on the part of their designers and the wood- or stonecutters, woodcarvers or sculptors, painters, and gilders who made them. By the sixteenth century, even modest churches housed elaborately carved and delicately painted altar retables of multiple wings, freestanding sculptures, as well as panel paintings, crucifixes, and carved altars. Everywhere one looked within any church, one encountered "images."

By the twelfth century, as Kollwitz has suggested, general discussions of the liturgy frequently took into account images. Different kinds of images had come to be placed on altars: Freestanding reliquaries and, after the twelfth century, altar retables

[59] Ibid., p. 89.
[60] Kollwitz, "Bild und Bildertheologie im Mittelalter," pp. 112–17.

were placed alongside or in front of crucifixes, between candlesticks, behind patens and chalices. Thus Honorius Augustodunensis, John Beleth, Sicardus of Cremona, and Durandus would each treat of the specific relation of images to worship in works on the liturgy.[61] Durandus, Sicardus, and Beleth all affirmed Gregory's distinction: One honored not the image itself, which would be wrong, but what the image represented. Images were nonetheless an important medium of communication in the liturgy. As Durandus said and the others echoed, images were more powerful than books, for they "moved the spirit more forcefully."[62] For Durandus, images not only made visible moments in Christ's life, reminding the pious of their meaning; they could make immediate the majesty and power of Christ and "arouse" the devout's joyous expectation of Paradise. They were not merely sources of mimesis, but a medium of wonder and hope.[63]

For Sicardus, Bishop of Cremona, images contributed to the liturgy's message of mystery and redemption, and for him, many objects served as images. Although he divided the ornamentation of churches, specifically their sculptural and pictoral programs, from the "utensils of the church [*utensilibus ecclesiae*]," in separate chapters in his *Mitral*, a summa of ecclesiastical offices, all these material presences participated in the visual rendering of Christianity's central truths. For Sicardus, the crucifix belonged not to the ornamentation of the church, but to "utensils"; this object that had acquired so much evocative power, "placed in the middle of the church, that we might see the sign of victory in public, that we might love the means of our redemption in our hearts," belonged to the implements of the liturgy. So, too, did candelabra: "[H]ere is Christ, who illumines all who come [to Him] in this world."[64] Images and liturgy were linked in an interplay of meaning, each conveying epigrammatically central truths of Christianity. Images were becoming the visual "book" for those biblical stories invoked in the liturgy, for those patristic

[61] Ibid., pp. 121–5.
[62] Durandus, quoted in ibid., p. 121, my translation.
[63] Ibid., pp. 123–4.
[64] Sicardus of Cremona, "Mitrale seu de Officiis Ecclesiasticis Summa," *PL* 213, cols. 49–56.

and saintly examples that gave the liturgy historical depth and gestural resonances;[65] and all the objects in proximity to the performance of the mass, all the candlesticks, the crucifixes, the patens, chalices, even the cloths upon the altars, were "images," conveying, evoking Christianity's mystery and its meaning for humanity.[66]

In the thirteenth century, Thomas Aquinas linked images much more closely to that which they represented in his understanding of their relation to Christian worship:[67]

> Honour or reverence, as has already been pointed out, is due to rational beings only. If it is to be paid to inanimate creatures this is only by reference to a rational nature. Two cases may be envisaged: the inanimate thing may either symbolize the rational nature or else be in some other fashion connected with it. . . .
>
> Both reasons combine to provide the motive for our veneration of the true cross on which Christ was crucified. For it is, in the first place, a symbol of Christ's body stretched out on it, and, in addition, it came into contact with the limbs of Christ and was bathed in his blood. For these two reasons, it receives the same form of veneration as does Christ himself, that is to say, divine worship [*latria*]. This explains why we address the true cross and pray to it as we would to Christ himself. (*Summa theologia*, pt. III, Question 25, On Reverence Due to Christ)[68]

---

[65] On gestural resonances – the specific movements of the priest and their associations – see Mosche Barasch, *Giotto and the Language of Gesture* (Cambridge, 1987), pp. 7–10; O. B. Hardison, "The Mass as a Sacred Drama," in *Christian Rite and Christian Drama in the Middle Ages* (Baltimore, 1965), pp. 35–79; Hélène Lubienska de Lenval, *La Liturgie du Geste* (Casterman, Belgium, 1956); Virginia Reinburg, "Liturgy and the Laity in Late Medieval and Reformation France," *Sixteenth Century Journal* 23 (1992): 526–46; and Karl Young, *The Drama of the Medieval Church*, 2 vols. (Oxford, 1933), vol. I, chap. 1.

[66] As Carlos Eire emphasized, images were essentially linked to worship in the sixteenth-century debates among theologians as well, *The War Against the Idols: The Reformation of Worship from Erasmus to Calvin* (Cambridge, 1986). Luther and Zwingli each spoke of images in relation to worship, von Campenhausen, "Luther und Zwingli zur Bilderfrage." Zwingli took up images in his efforts to reform the mass, linking the two again and again.

[67] On Aquinas, see Bevan, *Holy Images*, pp. 150–1; Feld, *Der Ikonoklasmus des Westens*, pp. 63–5; Kollwitz, "Bild und Bildertheologie im Mittelalter," pp. 125–6.

[68] St. Thomas Aquinas, *Summa Theologiae, vol. 50, The One Mediator* (3a. 16–26), ed. Colman E. O'Neill (Blackfriar's ed., London, 1965), art. 4, pp. 196–9. This statement occurs in the midst of Thomas's discussion of the worship due Christ, divided into six inquiries: 1. Are Christ's divinity and his humanity to be paid one and the same

Thomas was in accord with Damascus, whom he cited often, on the nature of images.[69] His concern in discussing worship was not the images themselves, but what they "represented." In his understanding of representation, Thomas drew upon Aristotle's theory of perception: As he asserted in the same Question, "the movement of the mind to an image is identical with movement to the object represented."[70] Thus, "the adoration of an image is forbidden in the measure that adoration of the object which it represents is forbidden." Any adoration was directed toward that which an image "represented." Idolatry, which Thomas had treated much earlier in Part II, was therefore not the worship of images per se, but "a profession of unbelief by outward forms of worship."[71] What the image "represented," however, as he makes explicit in the above passage, depended upon prior knowledge that enabled the viewer to "read" the image, to understand its signaling. Thomas did not allow images as active a role in human cognition as had John;[72] but he nonetheless held representation to be a complex interplay between each image and its viewer, the image evoking on the one hand, and the viewer recognizing on the other. Moreover, even for Thomas – whose position on the relation between an image and its "prototype" would not receive wide acceptance – images were an integral part of worship.

The cross and images of Christ were to receive *latria*, because they were reverenced for what they represented and were therefore inseparable from the worship due Christ Himself. The person of Mary, however, posed a different problem:

since the Blessed Virgin is no more than a creature and is ratio-
nal, she must not be paid divine worship, but simply the venera-

reverence? 2. Is his flesh to be paid divine worship? 3. Is divine worship to be paid the image of Christ? 4. Is such worship to be paid the cross of Christ? 5. Is it to be paid his mother? 6. What honor is to be paid the relics of the saints?

[69] Kollwitz, "Bild und Bildertheologie im Mittelalter," p. 126.

[70] "[I]dem est motus in imaginem et in rem, eo modo prohibetur adoratio imaginis, quo prohibetur adoratio rei cuius imago est," *Summa Theologiae*, pt. III, Qu. 25, art. 3 (vol. 50, pp. 194–5). Cf. Damascus quoting St. Basil, above and *ODI*, p. 91.

[71] *Summe Theologiae, vol. 40, Superstition and Irreverence,* ed. Thomas Franklin O'Meara and Michael John Duffy (2a2ae. 92–100) (London, 1968), Qu. 94, Idolatry, art. 1.

[72] Cf. *Summa Theologiae*, pt. I, Qu.12, art. 2.

tion known as dulia; however, since she is Mother of God, this should be of a higher form than that given other creatures. For this reason the veneration paid her is termed hyperdulia, to indicate it is more than ordinary dulia.[73]

Thomas further refined the discussion of worship and images: *Hyperdulia* would be separated from *dulia*, the former now reserved for the Mother of God, the latter for images of the saints, one degree further removed from God Himself. This tripartite division would be shifted: *Hyperdulia* would come to be that reverence directed toward images of Christ, themselves more closely connected to divinity than images of saints, the object of *dulia*.[74]

Thomas's division of grades of worship also enables us to understand better the interconnections of saints and images with Christian worship. For him, saints were to be worshiped insofar as they were servants of God – as God acted through them.[75] Although more distant from God than Christ or Mary, the saints were nonetheless connected to God more closely than were ordinary humans, in a hierarchy of the presence of holiness in the world. Furthermore, following Aristotle's theory of perception, images of the saints were worshiped because of the saints they represented – they received the same *dulia* as the saints' persons, because the sole justification for their place in worship was the person or persons they depicted. Thus, saints and their images both occupied a place more removed from God than Christ or His Mother, but closer to God than those human beings who prayed to their images. Saints' images were not the saints themselves, but a place where the pious might direct devotion ultimately, but not immediately, addressed to God. Following Thomas's understanding of Aristotle's theory of perception, one could speak to an image as though the saint were there, because in one's mind one was speaking to the saint him- or herself. The image was the

---

[73] *Summa Theologiae*, pt. III, Qu. 25, art. 5 (vol. 50, pp. 200–1).

[74] Michael Camille finds in Thomas's discussion of this Question evidence for attributing to Aquinas the tripartite division of worship into *latria*, due the cross, *hyperdulia*, due representations of Jesus as human on earth, and *dulia*, due images of saints, *The Gothic Idol: Ideology and Image-Making in Medieval Art* (Cambridge, 1989), p. 207. For fifteenth-century treatises echoing these discussions, see Baxandall, *The Limewood Sculptors*, pp. 53–4.

[75] *Summa Theologiae*, pt. III, Qu. 25, art. 6 (vol. 50, pp. 202–5).

medium for the devout to address persons of greater holiness along a precisely graded spectrum of God's presence in the world.

For John, and for the tradition that would echo his understanding, images were not an *object* of devotion – not the thing itself – but a *medium*, interconnected with divinity in the functioning of each pious person's mind, in the process of cognition. In all the discussions, images, saints, Mary, and Christ were all positioned along a spectrum of revelation, each a medium through which God was "present," and that place where the devout might address Him or His agents.[76] Images received devotion insofar as one could discern Christ or Mary or a saint's "presence" through them. As Sixton Ringbom has argued so eloquently, images served as a focus of pious devotion, themselves not the object of that devotion, but the medium.[77] Images linked divinity and humanity, but, unlike Christ Himself, belonged to neither.

These discussions provide an important framework for the practices of medieval Christians toward images. Christians knelt before, addressed their prayers to, placed gifts before, and endowed the production and maintenance of images; they seem to have knelt most often before images of Mary and the saints, who would intercede on their behalf before a judging God (although in those places where Franciscans held sway, crucifixes received much more devotion); they addressed their prayers to Mary, the saints, and Christ. As the wealth of all sorts of images evidences, they gave, according to their means – through confraternities or guilds, or privately, through families – for the production and maintenance of altars, altarpieces, liturgical implements, panels, sculptures, stained-glass windows, crucifixes, crosses, and even some of the clothing of the clergy. Within the framework of the Damascene's apology, with its echoes in later western theologians' writings, these practices become evidence of belief in a God who revealed Himself in and through the physical world, the persons of saints, and the material of their representations.

[76] Cf. for the modern period Régis Debray, *Vie et mort de l'image: Une histoire du regard en Occident* (Paris, 1992).
[77] Esp. chap. 1.

Images participated in this larger enterprise of Christianity. They helped to make Christ "present" in the lives of urban and rural populations. Images of Christ helped to give specificity to the life of Christ, detail to the narrative of those moments in His life of extraordinary meaning. They helped to make the mystery of Incarnation "real": depicting an infant, a 12-year-old boy, a young man, the physical pain, suffering, and death of a man of 33. Images of saints enabled Christians to understand better God's agency through humanity. Images themselves were reminders of the mystery of God's "presence" in the world, experienced both with the eyes and with the knowing soul.

Images inhabited a delicate position between divinity and pure physicality, vulnerable to the dual imbalances of immanence and materialism. In the fifteenth century, Lollards and radical mendicants would reject the place of images in worship, invoking a more "austere" Christianity. Yet images were integral to the epistemology Christians had formed over the centuries, integral to a religion whose God revealed Himself in and through the physical world; and by the fifteenth century, they had become integral to the worship of that God. Altarpieces sought to represent central concepts of Christian theology: Incarnation, Resurrection, and transubstantiation, the miracle of the Eucharist.[78] Altar retables would be opened and closed, panel paintings would be uncovered and covered according to the rhythms of the Christian year. Some images, such as the Palm Sunday ass, would be developed strictly for the purpose of the celebration of a particular holy day – in this case, the procession imitating Christ's entry into Jerusalem on an ass. Other images, such as the crucifix, would travel with steady regularity around the church whenever the priest prepared to come to mass.[79] Great crosses, such as the one in Strasbourg, would stand above and behind the main altar, presenting the congregation with a magnificent im-

---

[78] The theological content of altarpieces has been surprisingly little studied. See, for example, Barbara Lane, *The Altar and the Altarpiece: Sacramental Themes in Early Netherlandish Painting* (New York, 1984); and Maurice Vloberg, *L'Eucharistie dans l'Art*, 2 vols. (Grenoble, 1946).

[79] Karl Young, *The Drama of the Medieval Church*, vol. I, chap. 1.

age of God's suffering and sacrifice, signaling human redemption.

The discussions of John of Damascus, Pope Gregory I, Thomas Aquinas, and others enable us to discern the rigidity of the term "cult of the image," used by some modern scholars to refer to the relation between an image and its viewer.[80] These modern studies accept those medieval critics' description of the place of images in worship and, following their medieval predecessors, attach a particular psychology to a pattern of behavior. Yet I have found no evidence – nor do they cite any – demonstrating ordinary people's perceptions of images or their understanding of images' relation to divinity. We have, in other words, descriptions of practices – kneeling before, addressing prayers to, endowing – but we know very little of the conceptions of images and their relation to divinity held by the majority of European Christians before the Reformation.

The discussions of medieval theologians suggest the range of conceptions of the place people *might* have accorded images in the practice of Christianity. The following chapters seek to elucidate some of the perceptions and evaluations of images in the churches ordinary people had in the 1520s. As (I hope) they make evident, the words and acts of iconoclasts *resonate* with the discussions of medieval theologians, and central among those resonances is the notion of "presence." For the iconoclasts, as for the medieval theologians, the images represented more than social or political arrangements. They were one of those places where the laity looked to envision God's presence in the world.

---

[80] See, for example, Hans Belting, *The Image and Its Public in the Middle Ages: Form and Function of Early Paintings of the Passion*, trans. Mark Bartusis & Raymond Meyer (New Rochelle, N.Y., 1990); and *Bild und Kult: Eine Geschichte des Bildes vor dem Zeitalter der Kunst* (Munich, 1990).

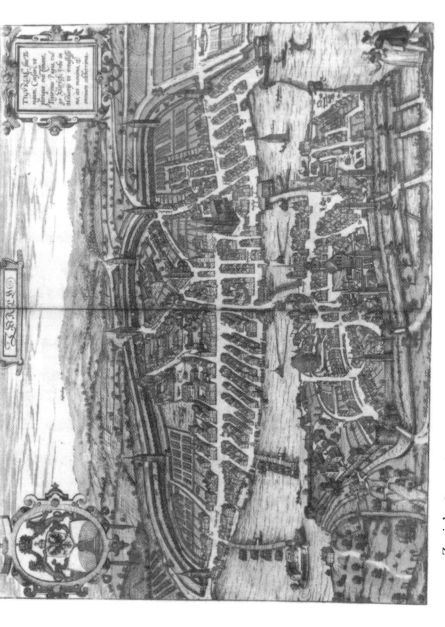

Zurich. *Source:* Georg Braun & Frans Hogenberg, *Civitates orbis terrarum*, vol. III (1581). Beinecke Rare Book and Manuscript Library, Yale University.

2

Zurich

In the summer of 1520, Uly Anders of Kennelbach, in the *Grafschaft* (county) of Toggenburg, was beheaded by the Zurich town council for blasphemy. Uly Anders had a history of "blaspheming": At another time, he had ridiculed the servant of a cardinal, for "if you serve him, so have you served an ass clearly"; attacked the cardinal himself, threatening to hack him up "like a butcher chops up meat"; and sworn, in front of witnesses, both that God in heaven should be more dear to them than God's flesh, and that God's five wounds did nothing for him.[1] The "blasphemy" for which Uly Anders paid his life, however, was of a different sort: In an inn in Utznach, he had beaten, torn apart, and thrown out a window a painted and sculpted image of Christ on the cross, with Mary and John at either side. As he did so, he claimed, "the idols bring nothing and they will help nothing."[2]

In 1520, verbal and physical attacks on the material culture of Christianity were still considered blasphemy by the town council – an attack against God's power, His suffering, His five wounds, or His flesh. They constituted a crime as serious and as dangerous as theft or murder: These three crimes alone were punished consistently with death in early sixteenth-century Zurich. Moreover, in 1520, acts of blasphemy were linked in their punishment and in the way they were perceived to crimes that

[1] Stadtsarchiv Zürich [hereafter StAZ], B VI 248, *Liber Baptistalis 1520*, f. 31.
[2] "[D]ie götzen nützent nüdt da vnnd sy möchtind nüdt gehelffen." StAZ, B VI 248, *Liber Baptistalis 1520*, f. 31. In order to retain the distinction between *götzen* and *abgötterei* found in the original testimonies, which I believe is an important one, I have translated *götzen* as idols and kept *abgötterei*, for which there is no exact English equivalent, alongside the translation, "idolatry."

53

threatened the community. Blasphemy was prosecuted as an affront to God, an assault against God, and it was punished as the expression of those who did not share in the community's values, its attachments, who sought in some way to endanger it. Uly Anders, whose words now foreshadow so directly the sentiments of Reformation iconoclasts, was prosecuted not as a pious Christian but as a traitor to the common good, and was executed as such. In 1520, his reasons for destroying the image, articulated to witnesses, had no broader resonances for his judges, the Zurich town council: They conceived and judged his act as the capital crime of blasphemy. Iconoclasm was not new to the sixteenth century; it had a history as individual, isolated acts that were defined as a particular crime, with a prescribed punishment. Uly Anders's case reminds us that something extraordinary happened in sixteenth-century Europe, the 1520s in the Holy Roman Empire: Acts that had been construed as a grave crime against God and against the community became one of the expressions of "Reformation."

Uly Anders provides us with a glimpse of sentiments, opinions, and values that would receive definition and approbation in the process of Reformation. In 1520, Zurich was still undistinguished in the eyes of its contemporaries for any religious or intellectual activity. Huldrych Zwingli, the powerful and charismatic preacher, had been preaching the pure Word of God for but one year, since New Year's Day 1519. In 1520, however, small changes intimated the more dramatic changes to come. Zwingli resigned his papal pension that year – a clear signal of his increasing distance from the traditional church. The Word of God, as he preached it, offered a very different vision of Christian life from the one people were living. Within two years after his arrival in Zurich, Zwingli was preaching against many of the ancient practices: the penitential system with its false indulgences, pilgrimages, the cult of Mary and of all the saints, processions, the vows of the clergy (in particular, celibacy), and the "artifices" of Rome. Furthermore, in 1523, Zwingli brought Leo Jud, his friend and fellow evangelist, to Zurich, to be the preacher at the oldest parish church in Zurich, and possibly in all of Switzerland: St. Peter's (see map, at center, below river).

In January 1523, the increasing tension in the town – between those who opposed Zwingli and his vision of Christian life, and Zwingli along with his supporters – led the town council of Zurich to call the First Disputation, held on January 29. The town council invited the Bishop of Constance, and all the priests, parish and lay, chancel and monastic, who held benefices in the canton, to attend. The Disputation diverged from its medieval predecessors on two counts: All discussion was to be anchored in the "true divine Scripture," and it was to be held in German.[3] At the Disputation, Zwingli presented Sixty-seven Articles, drawn from his understanding of Scripture. Those Articles were not successfully repudiated by Johannes Faber, the bishop's representative, and at the conclusion of the Disputation, the town council confirmed Zwingli's insistence upon the sole authority of Scripture to determine not only the substance of theology and Christology, but the practice of Christianity.

Reformation in Zurich was dramatic, rapid, and among the most complete. It took place not in a university center or a major commercial center, but in a middling-sized town of guilds and ancient religious foundations. Zurich's population was smaller than the other two cities we shall consider, its intramural population roughly 5,700.[4] It was a town through which people passed: merchants on their way from Italy to the great cities on the Rhine; pilgrims on their way across Lake Zurich to the famous holy shrine at Einsiedeln; clergy on their way between the episcopal sees of Basel and Strasbourg to the west and the see of Constance to the east.

The religious – monks, nuns, canons, priests, mendicants, tertiaries – were the earliest settlers on the site of a Roman customs station at the mouth of Lake Zurich. Like so many other towns north of the Alps, Zurich had its origins in the expansion of the Church and its settlement of sites of isolated sacred lives. According to legend, the Grossmünster and the Fraumünster had been

---

[3] Emil Egli, *Aktensammlung zur Geschichte der Zürcher Reformation in den Jahren 1519–1533* (Zurich, 1879; reprint Aalen, 1973), hereafter EAk, no. 318. All references to EAk are to document numbers.

[4] Walter Claassen, "Schweizer Bauernpolitik im Zeitalter Ulrich Zwinglis," *Sozialgeschichtliche Forschungen*, vol. 4 (Berlin, 1899), p. 30.

founded in the eighth century by Charlemagne and his nephew Ludwig the German, respectively, to house the relics of the early Christians, Felix and Regula, who had been martyred by the Romans.[5] The two churches stood opposite each other to the north and south of the Limmat, their towers and mass providing dual anchors for the urban life that developed around them. In 1520, the religious still dominated Zurich, not so much politically or socially, where their influence was all but gone, but physically. The two Münster were the largest buildings in Zurich; their towers, along with those of St. Peter's, the Dominican and Franciscan churches, the Water Church, and the Augustinian canons' church, still defined the horizon of Zurich; and the town's physical geography was structured by the three parishes.

If the religious houses dominated the physical landscape, guilds dominated the political and social one. In 1336, artisans allied with patricians had overthrown the political authority of the merchants and restructured the government of the town to give themselves an equal voice in decision making: twenty-six seats for guild members and twenty-six for the Constaffler, which comprised the former regime of rentier, nobles, mine owners, knights – those who would become the town's patriciate – and merchants, goldsmiths, and moneychangers. Reforms of the government in 1489 and 1498 gave the craft guilds the majority in the town council. It was possible in Zurich for artisans to acquire political influence, wealth, even social prominence, though some crafts, such as fishing and weaving, and some professions, such as domestic servants, remained poorly paid and socially marginalized.

Guilds provided the structure for the town council, the governing body of the town and canton. Guild membership was necessary for election to it. The town council comprised two chambers or "Councils" (*Räte*) set by the Charters of 1489 and 1498: the Great and the Small. In the Great Council sat 162 men: Each of the twelve guilds sent twelve representatives, and the Constaffler sent eighteen. In the Small Council, whose authority was increasing in this period, sat fifty men: twenty-four guildmasters,

---

[5] Rudolf Pfister, *Kirchengeschichte der Schweiz*, vol. I (Zurich, 1964), pp. 24–5, 150–1, 92.

two from each guild; four of the Constaffler; twelve guildsmen, each elected for life from the Great Council; two Constaffler, also elected for life from the Great Council; six councillors elected freely, also for life, from the Great Council; and the two *Bürgermeister,* whose authority alternated every six months. According to those same charters, anyone who was a guildsman – and therefore also a citizen of Zurich – could be elected to the town council.[6] In the 1520s, there were roughly a thousand citizens within the town's population, a little less than one-fifth the total.[7] The great Council continued to reflect something of that ideal in the 1520s: Most of its members still lived from their craft.[8] The Small Council was becoming ever more elite: The *Bürgermeister* and key officers within it belonged to one of only a dozen families, and their worth was typically at least 500 Gulden.[9] Yet, as we are reminded by the career of Bürgermeister Hans Rudolf Lavater (d. 1557) – who rose from a lesser profession, glazier, and a less powerful guild, the Gerwe, to become the single most influential man in Zurich[10] – the artisans in Zurich retained access to decision making in Zurich through channels increasingly regulated, but not yet closed.

The town council ruled not only over the residents of the town, but also held dominion of various kinds over the large *Landschaft,* or "land," as I shall inadequately translate it here, over the canton of the same name.[11] In 1520, that canton had a popu-

---

[6] My description of the town council derives primarily from Walter Jacob, *Politische Führungsschicht und Reformation* [Zürcher Beiträge zur Reformationsgeschichte, vol. I] (Zurich, 1970).

[7] Paul Guyer, "Die soziale Schichtung der Bürgerschaft Zürichs vom Ausgang des Mittelalters bis 1798," *Schweizerische Zeitschrift für Geschichte* 2(1952), 576.

[8] Hans Morf, *Zunftverfassung und Obrigkeit in Zürich von Waldmann bis Zwingli* [Mitteilungen der Antiquärischen Gesellschaft in Zürich, vol. 45.1] (Zurich, 1969), p. 60.

[9] Ibid., p. 3; Jacob, *Politische Führungsschicht,* pp. 4–5.

[10] Heinzpeter Stucki, *Bürgermeister Hans Rudolf Lavater 1492–1557* [Zürcher Beiträge zur Reformationsgeschichte, vol. III] (Zurich, 1973).

[11] "Countryside" suggests something rather more bucolic, and certainly less settled, than the land in the canton was in the sixteenth century. "Land" is the choice of most scholars to capture both the agricultural use and the pattern of rural settlement that existed in most of the canton. In order to distinguish forms of collective life, I have used "urban" to refer to life within the town walls of Zurich (and it would apply to Winterthur as well), and "rural" to refer to all other forms, from those of isolated farms or tiny villages to those of villages of substantial size whose economy, however, remains predominantly if not exclusively agricultural.

lation of roughly 48,100–58,790, ten times that of the town.[12] There were 193 *Landesgemeinden*, rural communes or villages, ranging in size from a dozen residents to about three hundred.[13] More than 85 percent of the rural population, the great majority, was agricultural; no more than 5 percent was engaged in a trade, such as milling, or crafts, such as weaving. Those who did have a craft frequently practiced it in addition to their agricultural work. Most peasants in the canton of Zurich owned some land, in a ratio of 8.5 to each day laborer. Beginning in the 1520s and reaching crisis after 1550, the rural population grew out of proportion to wages, land fertility, and productivity; at midcentury, the peasants would increasingly become divided between wage laborers and those who continued to own their own land.[14] During the iconoclasm of the 1520s, however, the peasants of Zurich were not divided among themselves by marked disparities of wealth, property, or labor. We shall glimpse something of that moment of general community among the rural residents, for the town council adjudicated all iconoclasm within the canton, whether the acts occurred intra- or extramurally, whether the accused were residents or citizens of the town or resided anywhere else within the canton. Indeed, it would be rural acts of iconoclasm, iconoclasm in the churches in villages and not within the town of Zurich itself, that would immediately precede the town council's decision to "do away with the images or idols [*götzen*], everywhere where they are honored."[15]

January 1523 marked one turning point in Zurich's movement toward reform. It was not conclusive, setting a path down which the people of Zurich would move flawlessly, smoothly, directly; but it set a principle – the authority of Scripture – that the people of Zurich would apply in the next two years in their discussions of

---

[12] Werner Schnyder, *Die Bevölkerung der Stadt und Landschaft Zürich vom 14. bis 17. Jahrhundert* (Zurich, 1925), p. 108.

[13] For the following discussion, I have relied upon Claassen, "Schweizer Bauernpolitik im Zeitalter Ulrich Zwinglis."

[14] Otto Sigg, "Bevölkerungs-, Agrar- und Sozialgeschichtliche Probleme des 16. Jahrhunderts am Beispiel der Zürcher Landschaft," *Schweizerische Zeitschrift für Geschichte* 24(1974), 1–25.

[15] EAk 546.

the nature and forms of Christian life. They would apply that principle variously. As the stories of the iconoclasts detailed below make manifest, the process by which "Reformation" was realized in Zurich comprised a multivocal dynamic. Some of the voices are already well known. The reformer Zwingli, whose theology offered a vision of Christians living in community, preached the return to the simplicity of the apostolic church. His closest ally, Jud, who had followed Zwingli first to Einsiedeln and then to Zurich, preached a more urgent Reformation. Other evangelical preachers, among them Simon Stumpf, Ludwig Häetzer, and Conrad Schmid, were preaching reform in the land; some, such as Stumpf, a more active reform than others.

The town council comprised another range of voices, some, such as Ulrich Trinkler, actively supportive of reforming religious life, and others, such as Bürgermeister Marx Roist, equally forcefully resisting dramatic changes and seeking to maintain order and equipoise. The town council would ultimately legislate Reformation, from the reform of the images and the mass to evangelical social ethics. It was the people of Zurich, however, mostly lay, but some clerical – people whose profiles are less prominent in the story of Reformation, whose voices are not well known, indeed, are not always audible – who gave "Reformation" in Zurich its specificity and definition through their acts in the years 1522–6: the widespread iconoclasm, the clergy's abdication of their clerical state and their transferral of their property to the town council, the attacks on the mass. In dynamic with Zwingli and Jud's preaching and with the town council's decisions and indecisions, the people's actions made concrete, locally meaningful, "Reformation." They gave it physical expression, cultural form; and the drama of their acts brought the town of Zurich prominence.

Of all the cities in which iconoclasm took place, Zurich was arguably the most influential. Wittenberg witnessed an earlier iconoclasm in February 1522, urged by Andreas Bodenstein von Karlstadt, but those acts found no completion, having been aborted through the combined opposition of Martin Luther and the Wittenberg authorities. Iconoclasm in Zurich came only a little later and intensely: Most of the acts took place between September and November 1523. In Zurich, the town council, the ruling secular authority, came to participate in iconoclasm, to recognize the validity of iconoclasts' acts, and, ultimately, to oversee the removal of the images from all the churches – to direct, in other words, the completion of iconoclasm. In Zurich, iconoclasm came to be legislated. For the first time in the West, the very activity of iconoclasm acquired a legitimacy it had not held before. This provided a potent paradigm for reform.[16]

In Zurich the records for iconoclasm are predominantly of trials of iconoclasts; they present the discussion of iconoclasm as it took place before that secular authority, the town council, that adjudicated crimes against the common good.[17] The trial is thus the immediate frame for discussions of iconoclasm in this chapter.[18] The records in Zurich consist in testimonies of accusers, then of the accused, made before the council. As such, they provide details other accounts cannot: of the iconoclasts themselves, as their accusers identify them; of their perceptions of the objects they attacked; of their explanations for their acts, in which they present motives; and of their definitions of what constituted "idols" and "idolatry."

These records allow us to hear more approximately the iconoclasts' own voices, which are mediated only through the notary's or scribe's hand: first, as he sought to record what the accused and their accusers said in the various dialects of the canton; and second, as he may have abstracted from a more rambling testimony the "essentials," those pieces that gave coherence to a nar-

---

[16] Among the towns that looked to Zurich for guidance in formalizing iconoclasm were the two studied in this volume, Strasbourg and Basel, as well as Bern, Constance, Schaffhausen, Ulm, Augsburg, and possibly Geneva.

[17] In *Zwingli and the Arts* (New Haven, 1966), esp. chaps. 4–7, Charles Garside offered the first narrative of iconoclasm in Zurich in English. My narrative of events differs from Garside's at a number of points, in part because I was able to draw upon archival sources, many of which provided details, even entire accounts not available in Egli.

[18] Much more work has been done on the dynamics of English trials. See Thomas A. Green, *Verdict According to Conscience* (Chicago, 1985); John H. Langbein, *Prosecuting Crime in the Renaissance: England, Germany, France* (Cambridge, Mass., 1974); Cynthia Herrup, *The Common Peace: Participation and the Criminal Law in Seventeenth-Century England* (Cambridge, 1987).

rative.[19] It is also possible to delineate some of the iconoclasts' identities with some depth: Their accusers and the notaries who recorded the trials provide rare details of profession, kin, home, place of origin. It is possible in Zurich, as it is not for Strasbourg or Basel, to locate individual iconoclasts within the human map of Zurich, within a number of matrices: social, political, religious.

We do not hear the iconoclasts speaking freely, however; we hear them before the town council. That context may have led them to describe their acts in terms of particular resonance to their judges, to frame those acts in terms of values that were publicly held in Zurich, values that the iconoclasts – and increasingly the town council – believed gave those acts legitimacy. We cannot know the degree to which the civil context shaped their testimonies, though there are suggestions of negotiation, of conversation between the iconoclasts and those who would judge them. We do know that they achieved an extraordinary success: Certain attacks were not punished as blasphemy, as *Gotteslästerung*, as a treachery against the community. In that exchange of testimony and judgment we can trace the increasingly clear differentiation of certain acts of iconoclasm from the genre of blasphemy that the town council continued to prosecute fully throughout this period. In at least three cases within the town, and many more in the land for which we have accounts, the defendants were not punished with death. How did these iconoclasts differentiate their acts from Uly Anders's?

The reformers' preaching may well have contributed to the town council's ultimate acceptance of specific acts, but it cannot explain, cannot provide the "cause" for, iconoclasm. It may be, as the chronicler Bernhard Wyss has it, that Zwingli spoke against the images in the First Disputation in Zurich in January 1523.[20] Leo Jud did in fact preach against them in St. Peter's church the week before the first attacks on the objects in the churches.[21]

---

[19] This second mediation is more difficult to discern, especially since some testimonies are indeed more rambling than others, and no one notarial or scribal hand presents terser narratives than another. In the construction of the testimonies, however, there are sufficient caesura to suggest some editing on the notary/scribe's part.

[20] *Die Chronik des Bernhard Wyss 1519–1530* [hereafter Wyss], ed. G. Finsler [Quellen zur schweizerischen Reformationsgeschichte, vol. I] (Basel, 1901), p. 12.

[21] See Lorentz Meyger's testimony, StAZ A27, 4, Kundschaften und Nachgänge.

Simon Stumpf preached their removal, encouraging specific acts of destruction of the objects in the churches, in Höngg, which during his tenure there became a center of iconoclasm; indeed, he would be banished from the canton for his incendiary preaching.[22] Zwingli, Jud, Ludwig Häetzer, Stumpf, Conrad Schmid, and other preachers were all calling for the restoration of the simplicity of the apostolic church, and by the end of 1523 all were also not merely preaching against images, but calling explicitly for their removal from the churches.

Yet, as I hope becomes evident in the stories that follow, the iconoclasts' acts, the objects they attacked, the times and the locations of iconoclasm, are more precise, more specifying, than the preachers' citation of the biblical injunctions against all images in the churches. To accord to preaching the motive, the catalyst, is to obscure or to ignore the choice each individual iconoclast made: to act. It is to ignore their responsibility, their rationality, their enfranchisement in the enterprise of reform. It is also to miss the communication of their acts. The preaching of the reformers inspired no other actions in Zurich as immediate, as violent, and as widespread as the attacks on the idols. Moreover, for each of the iconoclasts in Zurich, iconoclasm was still a capital crime: Here was no empty gesture, but an act of significance and great risk. The preaching made "sense," in the way that Clifford Geertz has argued – "what the mind filled with presuppositions . . . concludes"[23] – but we cannot assume it therefore provided a motive. At least one iconoclastic act preceded reform preaching. Each iconoclast chose to act, chose the object of that attack, with its specific location, and probably even the time. Those acts of successful iconoclasm were directed against specific images of specific meaning within collective life in Zurich.

If we place the objects within the material culture of Zurich, they become more than the "idols" of iconoclastic theory; they become objects of local significance, specific identifications and connotations. Let us then turn to, and listen to, the iconoclasts themselves as they explain why they had destroyed sacred ob-

---

[22] See esp. the testimony of Jacob Nötzli, StAZ E I 30.59, Pfrundakten Höngg.
[23] Geertz, "Common Sense as a Cultural System," in *Local Knowledge: Further Essays in Interpretive Anthropology* (New York, 1983), p. 84.

jects, as they distinguish their attacks from blasphemous ones. In this way, and by exploring the iconoclasts' links of kinship, guild, friendship, and enmity within the community, we can discern the meaning iconoclasts accorded the objects of Christian material culture within collective life in sixteenth-century Zurich.

On September 19, 1523, Lorentz Meyger, assistant at St. Peter's church, Zurich, stood before the Zurich town council.[24] An altar retable and various ornaments and church documents in St. Peter's had been destroyed sometime in the night of September 6–7, the Sunday night one week after Jud had preached against the images in the church. At the time, only Meyger had been found in the church, though not near the image. Four witnesses provided details suggestive of Meyger's culpability, but none had seen him do it or heard him admit to it.

The first witness before the town council, Hans Kolb, stated that he had entered the church about three in the morning on the night of Our Lady, early Monday, to discover a "wild mess [*wilds gerumppel*]" – specifically, a shattered retable and scattered objects and documents. He had seen no one but Meyger, whom he had found in the choir. They had decried the affair and then gone back to view it more fully. The following morning, Kolb had been sitting peacefully before Hermann Mertzhuser's house, discussing the previous night's events, when Meyger had passed by. Hearing the nature of their discussion, Meyger had stopped and inquired what they were talking about. Upon perceiving their puzzlement as to who might have done this, he had replied that whoever had done such a thing would come forward and announce it. Two other witnesses, Hermann Mertzhuser and Felix Steinbruchel, confirmed Kolb's account of the morning conversation, though both were careful to state they knew nothing of "it," as they had not been inside (the church, it seems). Steinbruchel added that whoever had done this was a church thief,

---

[24] The chronology for Zurich, with specific reference to acts of iconoclasm, has been prepared by Christine Göttler & Peter Jezler in *Bilderstreit; Kulturwandel in Zwinglis Reformation* [hereafter *Bilderstreit*], ed. Hans-Dietrich Altendorf & Peter Jezler (Zürich, 1984), pp. 149–59.

and not as good as he.[25] The last witness, Chaplain Jörg of St. Peter's, testified that he was the one who adorned the altars for marriages, feasts, and other days, for which he received an annual income. On St. Mary Magdalena's or St. Jacob's evening, as he was adorning the altar, Meyger had said to him, "nothing would please him more than that he find the idols [*götzen*] gone from over the altar."[26]

Meyger was not an artisan, but a member of the staff of one of the town's churches and one of the centers of evangelical preaching. Meyger was only about 26 years old at the time, but he had already been a canon at Heiligenberg before coming to St. Peter's. He was a native not of Zurich but of Winterthur, to which he returned as deacon at the end of 1523.[27] In December of that year he married.[28] In 1524, he moved to Stammheim as their preacher; there, in that same year, two retables in the St. Anna chapel, a famous pilgrimage shrine, were burnt.[29] Meyger was not a marginal member of St. Peter's church's staff: He became a preacher within a year after the attack in St. Peter's; that is, he became one of those who sought actively to bring the Gospel into collective life.

In his testimony, Meyger provided the narrative linking himself to the destruction of the retable and offered the fullest description of the object: "an old retable, on which was painted Our Lord God's descent from the cross, as our Lady holds him on her lap."[30] The retable, according to Meyger, had been not an image of particular saints or donors, but Christ, with Mary, in a scene from the Passion – similar to the image Uly Anders had destroyed. The retable stood on the oldest altar, the great or high altar, which had been founded in the twelfth century.[31]

---

[25] StAZ, E I 1a, Religionssachen, no. 1.64.

[26] "In gelüste nüdt bas dann dass er einfart die götzen vber den altar abhin gehygte." Ibid. Meyger's own testimony confirms this conversation, StAZ, A27, 4: Nachgänge 1510–23.

[27] Wyss, p. 29, n. 3.

[28] Ibid., p. 29.

[29] Ibid., p. 43.

[30] "[S]tunde daruff ein ["bild" crossed out] Alts täffeln daran gemalet werent vnsers her gots ablößung vom krüz wie Im vnser frow uff der schoß hett." StAZ, A27, 4.

[31] Arnold Nüscheler, *Die Gotteshäuser der Schweiz*, vol. III, pt. 2: *Zürich* (Zürich, 1873), pp. 377–9.

In his reconstruction of the link between himself and the destroyed objects, Meyger suggested another way of conceiving of church art. The first characteristic he attributed to the retable was age. In explaining how the retable came to be broken, he again centered upon physical aspects of the retable: first its location and then its age. As he told the town council, he "discovered" the retable upon the altar, turned to his fellow assistant, Hans Pfifer, and asked, "What is that picture doing there and who brought it there?" The question itself is ambivalent, suggesting surprise at the image's presence on the altar, as though it had not been there before. As he continued, he then sought to move the retable to one side, but the frame, being "very old, broke apart."[32] Thus, his testimony underlined two aspects of the retable: It did not "belong" on the altar – someone had put it there without authority – and it was fragile – it had a kind of mortality. At no point in his narrative did Meyger acknowledge that the retable was an object distinct from other objects made of wood: It was old, it fell apart.

In the second part of his statement, Meyger turned to his conversation with the chaplain of St. Peter's, giving that testimony a fuller physical context and altering the substance of their talk. He had watched the chaplain prepare the altar for a wedding by adorning it with gold and silver and other expensive things. Meyger confirmed that he had said the idols did not please him; he noted, however, that he had further said

> nothing would please him more than to knock the idols right off the altar with the candlesticks, for there were so many poor human beings who sat before the church and elsewhere, and who had nothing, but must suffer great hunger and drudgery [*arbentzäligkeit*] – those same might be helped with such expensive orna-

---

[32] "Da syg nit an, er Rette zu sinem vorberurte mit gesellen was da das bild thäte, vnnd weres da har gettrage? Uff das hett er selb gesprochenn Ich wills nebentsich thun Vnnd gebe Im daruff ein truck, das die ramen, so dann vast alt were, zerbroche." StAZ, A27, 4. I have chosen to translate both *bild* and *biltnuss* as "image" in the text, because the object referred to was often three dimensional, being both painted and carved. On the multiple definitions of *bild*, see Christine Göttler's article, "Die Disziplinierung des Heiligenbildes durch altgläubige Theologen nach der Reformation, ein Beitrag zur theorie des Sakralbildes im Übergang vom Mittelalter zur Frühen Neuzeit," in *Bilder und Bildersturm im Spätmittelalter und in der frühen Neuzeit*, ed. Bob Scribner & Martin Warnke [Wolfenbütteler Forschungen, vol. 46] (Wiesbaden, 1990), pp. 263–97.

ments. For as one finds in Ambrose, such ornaments are the food of the poor.[33]

Why did Meyger turn specifically to Ambrose in his defense? Perhaps Jud had quoted Ambrose in his sermon on the idols; perhaps Meyger himself had read Ambrose or Karlstadt's use of him in his pamphlet against the images.[34] Ambrose was one of the patristic references most frequently cited by popular pamphleteers and the iconoclasts themselves in their verbal attacks on church art.[35] Meyger's use of Ambrose also brought the terms of the argument of the third-century iconoclastic controversy into public discourse in Zurich. In quoting this particular passage from Ambrose, Meyger invoked a specific connection – between ornaments and food for the poor – that was more immediate and concrete for the people of Zurich. Since the fourteenth century, the canons of St. Peter's had been the caretakers of the hospital for the poor.[36] St. Peter's had received a larger proportion of endowments for the poor than for decorations.[37] The people of Zurich recognized and reinforced with their gifts its public role as caretaker of the needy. Thus, in calling forth Ambrose's argument for the redirection of the wealth of Christian piety to the care of the poor, Meyger was not only drawing upon a long tradition of iconoclastic criticism. He was also placing an act that, when viewed in isolation, was purely destructive, within a matrix of connotations significant to Zurich: The retable and the ornaments embodied the currency of Christian piety, which should have been directed to the poor in the Spital.[38]

At no time, though, did Meyger claim to have destroyed the

---

[33] "[D]ann es wer so meings arms mensche das vor den kilchenn vnnd sunste allenthalb sässe vnnd wedr vmb noch an hette sondre grossen hunger vnnd arbentzäligkeit lid müßte mit wellichem kostlichen zierden den selben wol geholfen möcht. were dann man heiter finde in Ambrosio das solich gezierden ßyg ein spys der armen." StAZ, A27, 4.

[34] Andreas Bodenstein von Karlstadt, *Von abtuhung der Bilder* (Wittenberg, 1522).

[35] See, for example. Otto Brunfels, *Von den Pfaffen Zehenden* (n.p., n.d.), who also cites Augustine, Chrysostom, and Jerome in his critique of church wealth.

[36] K. Furrer, *Geschichte der Kirche und Gemeinde St. Peter Zürich* (Zürich, 1906), p. 19.

[37] See, for example, StAZ, C II 18, Spital, nos. 1074 and 1075, for the period 1520–3.

[38] The Zürcher pamphleteer Utz Eckstein attacked the endowment of church decorations, among them wooden objects: "Du hast nun leym vnd holtz bekleyt / ich hatt dir von den armen gseyt." *Concilium* [Zürich: Christoph Froschauer, ca. 1525], p. A5r.

retable for the sake of the poor: It had broken apart because of its age and construction. Nor did he ever address who had strewn the other ornaments and documents about in the church. Moreover, when the destroyed retable was discussed at Mertzhuser's house, Meyger had stated that he had not done it himself, nor did he know who had, but that he believed whoever had done it "would be seen by God Almighty as such a valiant [*dappfer*] Christian spirit and heart, that he would make himself known."[39] The town council released Meyger from jail because they could uncover nothing more.

The second incident was tried the same day. Different in tone and style, it took place on Sunday, September 13, two days after the Feast of Felix and Regula, at about five in the evening, during suppertime. Uli Richiner of Sulz testified that he had been standing in the plaza before the Fraumünster when Lorentz Hochrütiner, Wolfgang Ininger, and a third person whom he did not know had crossed the bridge. As he was going into the church, the three had run past him, into the St. Nicholas chapel. Following them there, he had seen them take down the lamps that hung before the pulpit and throw them under it, behind an old retable, so that "the oil splattered and the lamps were crumpled."[40] As he approached them, the three had then sprinkled one another with holy water, saying they wanted to swear an oath together (*beschweren*) and offering the same to Richiner. Richiner had declined because, as he said, he could well take an oath (*beschweren*) himself.[41] Richiner had then followed the three out of the church and onto the bridge. Hochrütiner had

---

[39] "[A]ls dz hort er das Ir Red von den zerrißinen taffellen were, hab er gesprochenn er bedörfftind nit also thun dann er stunde wol daruff, der solichs gehan hett vnnd sich selbs veoffnen vnnd es sagenn unnd söll niemas dafür achte noch hätte das er schuldig syge, odr sunst wüsse wer gethan, sonders habe er noch huttbitag dafur vnnd syg der meynung der so es gethan were von gott dem almechtige ein solich dappfer christenlich gemütt vnnd herz werlichem das err selbs eroffnem werde." StAZ, A27, 4.

[40] "[D]as das öll verschütt, Vnd die ampellen zer kleckt wurde." StAZ, E I 1a, Religionssachen, no. 1.63.

[41] "Vnd in disen dinge als er diser Zug Zu inen gange hettind sii einandernn mit dem wiewasser gesprengt Vnd gesprochen si weltind einandern beschweren Si seitind ouch Zu im, er söle zu inen kan, so weltind sii inn ouch beschwerenn. Vff das Rette er gütlich, er bedörffte irs beschwerens nudt, er könte sich selbs wol beschweren." StAZ, E I 1a, 1.63.

turned to him, saying that were Richiner to do anything about it, they were not afraid, for it had occurred publicly (*offentlich*), not clandestinely (*heimlich*); they would and should bear such idolatry (*abgötteri*) no more.[42] Richiner, however, had chastised the three, saying that the lamps were eternal lights and should have been left alone for other people's sake. Hochrütiner's reply gives us a glimpse of the dynamics between the iconoclasts and their witnesses, those who would later expose their acts to the authorities: "[Richiner] had been in school so long he didn't know anymore what it was, for it was nothing other than an idolatry [*abgötteri*]."[43] Two more lamps in the St. Nicholas chapel were destroyed that evening, but the witness could not say that the three accused had done this as well, since he had not seen it.

The rest of Richiner's testimony suggests the tensions between iconoclasts and those who would not join them. The following day, Richiner continued, he had run into Hochrütiner, who pointed Richiner out to another, Andresen, standing with him, as the one who had accused them and publicized the affair (*die sachen ußkunt hatt*). Richiner again asked Hochrütiner why they had not been peaceful, and said further that it was nothing to him that they wished to hold as merely idolatry (*abgötterei*) what to him were eternal lights; but he had had to allow it, since they had been three and he only one. At this, Andresen had said that "they need fear nothing, for they had done it publicly."[44]

Hochrütiner was a weaver, originally from St. Gall. In the early 1520s, like Zwingli, he preached against mercenaries – who, according to the Gospel, "were no better than those who murder and steal because of poverty" – in the presence of two town councilors, Ulrich Trinkler and Hans Schärer.[45] He was also

---

[42] "Vnd in solichem giengint Si zur kilchen ußhin uf die bruggen, Vnd seite namlich hochrütiner: wenn schon er diser Zug, das von inen seite so fruchtind si inen doch nit darumb dann es were offenlich und nit heimlich beschechenn Si weltind und möchtind solich abgötterei nit mer erliden." StAZ, E I 1a, 1.63.

[43] "[E]r diser Zug, wer so lang zuschul gange vnd wüßte nit was es were, dann es wer nudt anders dann ein abgötteri." StAZ, E I 1a, 1.63.

[44] "Si bedörffteind Inen darumb nit zuo furchte dann si hettinds offenlich getan." StAZ, E I 1a, no. 1.63.

[45] "[I]m krieg zuhe gellt vnd besoldung empfache um damit biderblütt zutod schlache denen das ir näme die Im nye leids gethan habint der selb kriegsman syg vor gott dem almechtige auch nach innhalt der Evangelischenn leer ein mörder vnnd nit

among those present on the evening of the first Lenten Sunday in 1522 when the printer, Christoph Froschauer, broke the fast by eating wurst.[46] Hochrütiner appears at moments central to the reform in Zurich, in the presence of those more powerful lay members of the community who supported Zwingli, both actively and passively challenging certain practices associated with the Roman Church.

Hochrütiner's named companion, Ininger, was a *Tischmacher*, a carpenter. The third may well have been Bartlime Pur, a baker, who appears with both Hochrütiner and Ininger elsewhere in the records. Pur was also accused, along with another iconoclast, Claus Hottinger, and two others, of harassing a Franciscan preacher.[47] Thus two of Richiner's three, we know at least, were artisans; the leader of the trio was a weaver, and he, and possibly the third member, were evangelical activists.

Why did Hochrütiner choose so deliberately – crossing the bridge and entering the church, heading straight to the St. Nicholas chapel – to destroy the lamps in Fraumünster? What was it about the place or the objects that made the lamps idolatry for him? The place, the chapel, lay near the high altar of Saints Felix and Regula, the town's patron saints. It was dedicated not only to St. Nicolas, but also, since the beginning of the fourteenth century, to Saints Laurentius, Georgius, Cornelius, Antonius, Fridolin, and Beatus.[48] Three of these saints – Laurentius, Fridolin, and Beatus – were especially known in northern Switzerland for helping the needy.[49] Why were the lamps especially offensive in this context? Hochrütiner used the term *abgötterei* to refer to the lamps, but lamps were never the focus of worship or adoration.

---

besser dann der so armutt halb murde oder stäle." StAZ, B VI 289, Kundschaften und Nachgänge, ff. 29v–30r. Trinckler was one of Zwingli's leading supporters. See Jacob, *Politische Führungsschicht*, pp. 273–6.

[46] *Ratsbuch 1524,* quoted in Thomas Schärli, "Die bewegten letzten zwei Jahre im Leben des Niklaus Hottinger, Schumacher, von Zollikon, enthauptet zu Luzern 1524," *Zolliker Jahrheft* 7(1984), p. 29. On Froschauer's *Wurstessen*, see EAk 233–4.

[47] Wyss, pp. 13–15.

[48] Nüscheler, *Die Gotteshäuser der Schweiz*, vol. III, pt. 2, p. 368.

[49] See, for example, the wall painting, now in the Schweizerisches Landesmuseum (LM20991), which stood originally in the "Haus zum Königstühl," Zürich. The upper panel presents the visit of the three kings and St. Beatus; the lower panel presents, among twelve saints, Saints Felix, Regula, Exuperantius, and Fridolin.

Hochrütiner's profession, as a weaver, offers us certain clues as to his choice of place and subject. The Fraumünster was the church to which both the linen and the wool weavers' guilds were dedicated.[50] Since the late fifteenth century, the craft guilds had been centrally concerned with the endowment of candles for their respective churches and for processions.[51] Wax was expensive, and the guilds were carefully regulated as to how many candles they could endow for processions: In the fifteenth century, the linen weavers were allotted three, the wool weavers two.[52] Lamp oil, however, was not endowed by the guilds. It may have been supported in part through private gifts, but the major source for financing the oil was the income of the churches, primarily tithes and rents.[53]

The "idol" Hochrütiner and his companions attacked was not an image of Christ or of saints, but lamps. These were objects not funded through guild endowments, not supported with collective gifts. On the contrary, they were financed primarily through exactly that form of ecclesiastical income the laity found most onerous: tithes and rents. It was, moreover, this form of ecclesiastical income that reformers, such as Caspar Hedio, and pamphleteers, such as Johannes Landsberger and Sebastian Meyer, found most opposed to popular notions of Christian brotherly love.[54] The lamps were objects that, as "eternal lights," literally burnt up pious bequests and church monies unceasingly.[55] They were distinguished by pamphleteers, such as Balthasar Stanberger, as *ölgötzen* – the idols that eat oil.[56] At least one other resident of

---

[50] Ottmar Fecht, *Die Gewerbe der Stadt Zürich im Mittelalter* (Lahr, 1909), p. 84.

[51] StAZ, A73, 1–2, Zunftwesen; A77, Verschiedene Handwerke.

[52] Fecht, *Die Gewerbe der Stadt Zürich,* p. 84.

[53] StAZ, C II 1 (probstei); C II 10 (Fraumünster), and C II 10 (Obmannamt). On the expense of candles for processions and feast days, see Peter Jezler, Elke Jezler, & Christine Göttler, "Warum ein Bilderstreit? Der Kampf gegen die 'Götzen' in Zürich als Beispiel," in *Bilderstreit*, pp. 89–90.

[54] Caspar Hedio, *Von dem Zehenden* ([Augsburg: Philipp Ulhart d. A.], 1525); Johannes Landsberger, *Ain nutzlicher Sermon* ([Augsburg: Philipp Ulhart d. A.], 1524); Sebastian Meyer, *Des Bapsts vnd seiner Gaistlichen Jarmarckt* (1535). The theme that tithes are opposed to Christian brotherly love appears in dozens of pamphlets.

[55] See Eckstein, *Concilium,* pp. A5v ff.

[56] Stanberger, *Ein Dialogus oder Gesprech zwische einem Prior Leyenbruder un Bettler* (Erfurt, 1521); Clement Ziegler, *Ain kurtz Register . . . was Abgotterey sey* ([Augsburg], 1524), p. A2r.

Zurich, Hans Pfleghar, attacked verbally, but not physically, the "filth [*dreck*] that was in the lamps that hung before the pulpit in the Fraumünster."[57] It was not that the lamps were worshiped that brought them the name of *götzen,* idols, but that they consumed.

The second incident of iconoclasm was conducted entirely in a style distinct from that of Meyger's. Meyger's narrative is flat, presenting a strictly physical and profane relationship between the object and himself. Richiner's account of the three men's handling of the holy water, however, suggests most clearly a quality that suffuses the whole incident: a humorous familiarity with sacred objects. Their treatment of the holy water reflects certain gestures and patterns of behavior associated with Carnival.[58] There is a playfulness to their gestures, an irreverence, particularly striking in reference to sacred objects; there is inversion of patterns of deference, but no malice. The three took over – appropriated – sacred objects, without expressing malicious intent. When the three were sentenced, each to three nights in the tower, it was not for the destruction of property, but for *frävel* (or *fraüel*), riotousness.

Among the forms of crime distinguished by the Zurich town council, *frävel* was significantly less serious than theft, murder, or blasphemy. Most often it designated behavior that was not malicious, but disorderly, sometimes excessively exuberant. Three nights in the tower, moreover, was a relatively lenient punishment in sixteenth-century Zurich. Fining was the most lenient, and often the town council would not fine a miscreant if he were too poor, but sentence him to a few nights in the tower. Though they had destroyed church property and played irreverently with holy water, Hochrütiner and his companions were not designated as members who were endangering the well-being of the community, and they were not severely punished.

A number of elements came to play in their case that distinguished it from that of Uly Anders. That Hochrütiner called the

[57] EAk 435.
[58] On the social meaning of Carnival, see Robert Scribner, "Reformation, Carnival and the World Turned Upside-Down," *Popular Culture and Popular Movements in Reformation Germany* (London & Ronceverte, 1987), pp. 71–101.

lamps *abgötterei* does not, in fact, clearly differentiate his attack from that of Anders, who included the image among the *götzen*, the idols. The differences lie in the relationship of the three men's attack to patterns of collective life in Zurich. First, we have seen Hochrütiner keeping company with some of the more powerful members of Zurich who were supportive of reform. Second, Hochrütiner and his companions' behavior toward the holy water recalled a traditionally recognized, if not welcomed, pattern of collective behavior, the irreverence and inversion of Carnival.[59] Third, the characteristic most important to Hochrütiner was that the act occurred publicly (*offenlich*), not clandestinely (*heimlich*).

What is the significance of this distinction? It does not seem to be so much concerned with the nature of the act itself, whether it was open or covert, because the act took place at five in the evening on Sunday – apparently not during compline, when nuns, priests, chaplains, and a few laity would be in church, but, according to the notary, "at suppertime," when most would be home. Richiner, moreover, seems to have been the only witness in the church. This distinction seems to be concerned more with the location in which the act occurred: a distinction between public and private arenas for the attack. The attack took place in the public space of the popular and guild-affiliated Fraumünster, in contrast to Uly Anders's attack, which took place in an inn, a privately owned public house.

Within two weeks after his first trial for iconoclasm, despite his imprisonment, Hochrütiner participated in another attack on a religious object, this time at the behest of Zurich's best-known iconoclast, Claus Hottinger.[60] With the help of Hochrütiner and another, Hans Ockenfuß, Hottinger uprooted and brought down a large wooden crucifix that stood in a crossroads in Stadelhofen, just outside the town gate (see right side of map). We know a

---

[59] Though Hochrütiner and his companions were only three in number, and Carnival engaged a large proportion if not all of the community, discussions elsewhere (in Höngg testimonies, E I 30.59, for example), present three actors as constituting a *gemeinde*, a community.

[60] Thomas Schärli's account of the last two years of Hottinger's life covers the incident in Stadelhofen. Peter Jezler has also explored Hottinger's destruction of the crucifix in "Tempelreinigung oder Barberei? Eine Geschichte vom Bild des Bilderstürmers," in *Bilderstreit*, pp. 75–82.

great deal about the incident because Hottinger discussed it with a number of people who later testified at his trial. The narrative not only represents the fullest statement by an iconoclast of his motives, but also gives us an insight into the variety of positions people in Zurich took toward religious objects.[61]

The first witness Hottinger approached was Heini Hirt, the miller in Stadelhofen. Hirt's testimony is the second in the records, but it precedes the others in sequence of events. I therefore begin with it, and shall call attention to those points when Hottinger's later testimony diverged from Hirt's narrative of events; otherwise, Hirt's fuller testimony provides the story of this exchange. Hottinger had run after Hirt, who was on his way to a drink with his "brothers" from the lower grain house (*Kornhuß*), and spoke to him, demanding to know when he was going to do away with his *abgötzen*. Hirt, not unlike Richiner, had responded that they did not disturb him, though he knew he must not pray to them. He wished to leave the matter to the town council because, as he had said, he was unlearned in Scripture and had no understanding of the thing. Hottinger, however, had not let him go, but had pressed him, telling him that if he were a good Christian man, he would do away with the idols because the holy word did inform him (Hirt) that the idols should not exist. At this point, Hirt had acquiesced partly, telling Hottinger that insofar as he, Hirt, had the power and the right to do away with such idols, he would give them to Hottinger as a gift, along with whatever jurisdiction (*gerechtigkeit*) he held over them. (Hirt's and Hottinger's testimonies conflict at this point: Hirt claimed to have given Hottinger the crucifix only insofar as he had the right and power to do away with it,[62] while Hottinger claimed the gift had been "für fryg eige vbergebe," his to give over freely,[63] to which Hirt finally agreed at the trial.) Hottinger had still not been satisfied and had asked Hirt to help him take down the crucifix, but at this Hirt would have nothing more to do with him. Hottinger had departed, remarking he would find others willing to help

---

[61] For the following narrative, StAZ, B VI 249, *Ratsbüch Baptistalis 1523*, f.70r; E I 1a, 1.43, 1.45, 1.46.

[62] E I 1a, 1.43.

[63] Ibid., 1.45.

him. Hirt concluded by saying that he had not realized how hot-headed Hottinger had been.

The first scene we have in the attack on the crucifix is an ex-change between Hottinger and the miller Hirt as to whether the images should be removed or retained. The miller did not feel strongly about images in the churches. His position was defined not in relation to the objects, but according to the official stance of the town council. His ignorance of the iconoclastic debate was his excuse for his obedience to the civic authorities. To this, Hot-tinger countered the "information" offered by the higher author-ity of Scripture. The exchange of the crucifix between the two men was also carefully formulated: Hirt allowed for some ambi-guity about his ownership of the crucifix and his right to destroy the object, while Hottinger received the crucifix as a gift, free and clear, to do with as he chose. Hottinger then reinforced this par-ticular relationship to the object in the next scene.

Hirt testified that, concerned about Hottinger's anger, he had followed him. Hottinger had next approached Ulrich Trinkler, then Claus Setzstab, Thoma Sprüngli, and Heinrich Trueben, all four guildmasters and town councilors.[64] (At this point, Hottin-ger's testimony is much fuller, since Hirt did not hear the entire-ty of his conversations with these men, and so, we switch to it.) From Trinkler he had sought first confirmation that the crucifix was indeed a gift, free and clear, to him from Hirt. He had then sought from Trinkler and the other three a kind of official rec-ognition of his intended destruction of the crucifix. He had not asked them for help or even for permission, but had sought "council [*Rat*]," stating his intention to each. According to Hot-tinger, all four had agreed it would be a "good work."[65] More-over, Trinkler had showed him images he had stored in his house, and confided how it had cost him a great deal to take all

[64] On the specific political and religious connections of these four men, see Jacob, *Politische Führungsschicht.*

[65] "[D]ie habint im das nit gewert sonders gesprochen das si es Irs verstands für ein gutt werck hieltind und achtotind, das sollich biltnussen hinweg komint. ... Vnd damit man nit meyne, das er erst nach der that Rat gehept hab, So syg er glich der stund als hirt im das crucifix schankte, zu M. Vlrich Trinckler gange, vnd hab er nit anders verstand dan dass er seite, er hielte es für ein gutt werch." StAZ, E I 1a, 1.45. The designation of iconoclastic acts as "good works" is a suggestive inversion of the evangelical argument on endowments for church art.

of them out of the churches in order to prevent others from worshiping them.[66]

In the second scene, we see Hottinger seeking to confirm his relationship to the object – his rights over it, and specifically, his right to destroy it. We see him seeking to engage powerful members of the community who were also associated with the reform movement in Zurich. In his testimony, Hottinger sought to link them tenuously through these discussions to his intended attack. These men were in a position to ratify his attack on the crucifix, to make it legitimate and legal in the eyes of the community, though, as Hottinger admitted, he expected to spend some time in the tower. They were also in a position to authorize the removal of all images from all churches, which they were not to do until June 1524.[67] Hottinger, then, may have also been impatient, seeking to provoke them to a more active reform, a physical as well as verbal participation in the program of reform.[68]

This case also makes most explicit a characteristic shared by almost all incidents of iconoclasm in Zurich: the degree to which they were discussed, in inns, in *Stuben,* in guildhalls, in homes, among friends, by opponents and actors. The attacks on the religious culture of Zurich were carved in the language of the town, shaped and formulated, drawing upon certain associations and connotations. So, too, as the incidents entered into the public discourse of the town, members of the community not originally present were, in an oblique manner, engaged.

In the third scene, Hottinger had persuaded first Ockenfuß and then Hochrütiner to participate in taking down the crucifix. We glimpse here something of that moment of persuasion, when Hottinger moved these two men to join him in an act neither formally sanctioned nor explicitly condemned by the authorities in Zurich. Ockenfuß, the first witness at the trial, testified that

---

[66] "Vermelter M. Vlrich zougte im ouch ettliche bilder, so in sinem huß under den stägen stündint, vnd seite er hett vil costens damit gehept vnd doch die uß der kilchen getrage damit niemas die anbättoti." StAZ, E I 1a, 1.45.

[67] EAk 546.

[68] Schärli suggests that Hottinger was impatient with the progress of the town council in adopting a program of reform, not only with regard to images, but also with regard to the mass; "Die bewegten letzten zwei Jahre," pp. 29–38.

Hottinger had approached him to help remove the crucifix, "for the miller himself had given it over freely as a gift to him as his own. Moreover, one heard daily, that such a crucifix and all other images are forbidden by God our Savior."[69] Hochrütiner, the third witness at the trial, testified that, having so recently been in prison for the incident of the lamps, he had been entirely of the opinion that my Lords would wish him to take no part of it. In fact, he had faced severe penalties for any renewal of iconoclastic activities. Hottinger had reassured Hochrütiner that both the miller and even Ulrich Trinkler had given him the crucifix for his own. Hochrütiner himself had reasoned further that, since other people were carrying images of the saints and crucifixes out of the churches, and no one minded, he did not think it wrong; so he had agreed to Hottinger's wish, and uprooted it.[70] Thus we glimpse something else: the agreement of these two to follow Hottinger in his vision of reform, their participation in his repudiation of this particular "idol."

Hottinger's own testimony is the longest of all. He detailed his talks with Hirt, Trinkler, Setzstab, Sprüngli, Trüeben, Ockenfuß, and Hochrütiner. His conversations with the miller and town councilors gave precision to the nature of the exchange of the crucifix. The councilors had validated his intended iconoclasm: They had not obstructed his plans, but had spoken to them, saying that, according to their understanding, they held and acknowledged his intended removal to be a good work. It had been the intention of the three, according to Hottinger, to sell the wood and give the money to the poor – a theme Meyger had invoked, and to which we shall return. Toward the end of his testimony, Hottinger acknowledged that his sister and his wife had both warned him that he would be put in the tower for this, and another, Ulrich Schwaben, had told him he had heard that the magistrates wished to arrest him and the others; thus Hottinger had turned himself in.

This case differs from the others in a number of ways. First, of course, no other iconoclast had approached members of the rul-

---

[69] StAZ, E I 1a, 1.43.
[70] Ibid.

ing elite before acting. This gave the incident a much more explicit public form than previous incidents had had. Second, Hottinger was one of Zwingli's most active and visible supporters. He
had not only been present at the publisher Christoph Froschauer's the night the Lenten fast was broken in 1522;[71] he had
also verbally attacked the traditional form of the mass so aggressively that the town council had forced him to retract.[72] Perhaps
most significant, he had sought to organize at least one gathering
of "good Christians" in a village near Zurich, in which the evangelical word might affect those not already moved by the Gospel.[73] Though he was a citizen of Zurich, he seems to have taken
up citizenship only later, when he married the widow of a
shoemaker and became himself a shoemaker.[74] Hottinger was
originally from Zollikon, in the 1520s one of the rural centers of
iconoclasm, as we shall see later in this chapter, and of resistance
to tithes, and home to the first Swiss conventicle of Anabaptism,
and he kept strong ties of kinship there. Thomas Schärli has suggested, rightly I think, that Hottinger would have himself become an Anabaptist with his brothers had he not been executed
for heresy in Lucerne in 1524.[75] Ockenfuß was a tailor who appears, unlike Hottinger, only one other time in the records, when
he came before the town council for accusing Zwingli of lying
in his pamphlet on baptism – for taking, in other words, a position articulated by Anabaptists.[76]

---

[71] Schärli, "Die bewegten letzten zwei Jahre," p. 40.

[72] EAk 369. Though many people in Zürich in 1523–5 protested the mass, few were
actually prosecuted by the town council. That the council would demand a retrac-
tion from Hottinger suggests not so much their position on the mass as their relationship with so independent and active a member of the community.

[73] Hottinger planned a *Schencki* for Ulrich Trinkler, who was returning from Baden,
which Schärli suggests was an implied criticism of Trinkler's "taking the cure" in
Baden; "Die bewegten letzten zwei Jahre," pp. 31–3. In his testimony, however,
Hottinger revealed that this gathering would be considerably larger than a traditional *Schencki*, but "die Evanglisch ler vnnd das wort gots, werde für und für wurken
vnnd vnder den christen zunammen Vnnd die so jetzt villicht dem Evangelio nit al-
lencklich anfangint bekert werdent." StAZ, E I 1a, 1.42.

[74] Schärli, "Die bewegten letzten zwei Jahre," p. 28.

[75] Ibid., p. 40.

[76] StAZ, B VI 249, f. 155v. Ockenfuß was apparently not among those executed for his
Anabaptist beliefs, nor was he heavily punished in this incident.

Why would a shoemaker, with the help of a weaver and a tailor, attack a wooden crucifix?[77] It was during these years of reform that the difference between crucifixes and crosses became critical. The one, the crucifix with the suffering Christ upon it, was the focus of evangelical attacks; the other, the simple and unadorned cross, was adopted as one of the evangelical movement's central symbols[78] – a reminder of man's brotherhood with the human Christ, but also, more centrally, a symbol of Christ's sacrifice for human sinfulness.[79] The timing of the destruction of the Stadelhofen crucifix may be connected to the Feast of the Elevation of the Cross, September 14. More than any other iconoclast, Hottinger seems to have determined the object and place of his act in advance. What was significant about this particular crucifix?

The Stadelhofen crucifix stood not in a church, where candles or offerings might be placed before it, but in an open square. According to Peter Jezler, it was a *Wegkreuz,* a marker, indicating both the physical, earthly path, and the spiritual.[80] It was not church art. Nor was it made or adorned with precious metals, as was the great cross in Strasbourg. It was, however, a central symbol of Christian piety, the image most representative of the old liturgy and its invocation of the Passion as well as sacrifice.

It seems clear that Hottinger wished to make his attack as public a gesture as possible. He discussed it in advance with men

---

[77] A later illustration presents it as a simple cross, *Illustrierte Reformationschronik Bullingers* (Zürich, 1605/6), f. 99r. This depiction puzzles, since the language of the trial explicitly designates the object of attack as a "crucifix."

[78] There are a number of popular pamphlets from the 1520s on the theme of taking up the cross of evangelical Christianity. See, for example, *Creütz Biechlin* ([Strassburg], 1525); Johannes Brenz, *Wie das holtz des Creutzs behawen* ([Augsburg: Philipp Ulhart d. A., ca. 1528]); Andreas Bodenstein von Karlstadt, *Auslegung unnd leuterung etzlicher heyligenn geschriften* ([Leipzig: Melchior Lotter, 1519]). The Zürcher pamphleteer Eckstein expressed the evangelical view of the cross in his dialogue between Christ and Adam: Christ tells Adam: "Das crütz muß werden ufgnon / von dem der da wil zu mir kon," *Dialogus* ([Zürich: Froschauer, 1525]), p. B4v. This new cross, as Eckstein's language suggests, was a burden to be carried, a view visualized in 1525 in a woodcut published by Hans Hager first on the title page of Zwingli's treatise, *Ein Antwurt . . . Valentino Compar* (27 IV 1525).

[79] See Eamon Duffy's article, "Devotion to the Crucifix and Related Images in England on the Eve of the Reformation," in Scribner & Warnke, *Bilder und Bildersturm*, pp. 21–36.

[80] Jezler, "Tempelreinigung," p. 78.

who adjudicated public life in Zurich. He approached the miller, one of the pivotal members of a community,[81] not of Zurich, but of a village just outside the town walls. In part, his choice of place may reflect his position in relation to the town and the land: a citizen of the town who had strong ties of kinship and friendship to the land, though not specifically to Stadelhofen.[82] The crucifix was different from the other objects attacked: It was not enclosed in a building, but stood in the open. It was in a crossroads; many passing in and out of the gate, who were not residents of the town, would see it.

The crucifix was also, like the retable, made of wood. Unpainted, its material was much more immediate to the viewer's eye than the retable's: It was explicitly wooden, and wood was a particularly important and controversial material on the land.[83] As the primary substance for both heating and building, it was vital to each household. Collecting and selling kindling was also a livelihood for some poor people. Most wood, however, did not stand on free land.[84] In the 1520s alone there were dozens of cases of theft of wood from both private and common lands.

Hottinger's comment, that he wanted to sell the wood and give the released (*erlöst*) money to the poor, suggests that he was well aware of the connection between rural poverty and wood. The crucifix imprisoned wood that could heat and shelter, that could feed the poor. However, it was not its substance alone that provoked: The crucifix also symbolized most directly and explicitly the conflicting notions of the Christian community, between the old Church of Rome and the new church of Zurich. It may have also, within Zurich, invoked conflicting visions of the new Christian community. In his preaching, Zwingli had attached to the cross the message to take up the burdens of the obedient Christian, and this message may well have been unacceptable to one whose own piety was active and assertive.

Hottinger's attack was the most public and the most publicized

---

[81] Carlo Ginzburg, *The Cheese and the Worms*, trans. John & Ann Tedeschi (London & Chicago, 1980).
[82] Hottinger's cousins and brothers remained in Zollikon.
[83] Sigg, "Bevölkerungs-, Agrar-, und Sozialgeschichtliche Probleme," pp. 6ff.
[84] Ibid., pp. 20–4.

of all iconoclastic acts in Zurich. It was also the most severely punished by the town council. On November 4, the Wednesday following All Saints', the Zurich town council passed its sentence: Hottinger was banned for two years from Zurich; Hochrütiner was also banned; and Ockenfuß, who was released after paying his court and imprisonment costs, was placed under the supervision of his guild. The town council punished the three for "great riotousness and wantonness, which Claus Hottinger had done in opposition to my Lords, who had authority over him" – they were not punished for blasphemy.[85] Here, as perhaps with earlier acts, we can discern the preachers' influence: Citing scriptural injunctions against the images and precedents of iconoclasm, they argued that the crime was not capital, but civil, a question of rebellion.[86]

On September 29, St. Michael's Day, the town council designated the town councilors Jakob Grebel, Setzstab, Binder, Berger, Wegmann, along with Konrad Escher, Hans Usteri, Heinrich Werdmüller, and the three people's priests, Zwingli, Jud, and Heinrich Engelhard, to prepare advice "concerning the images and other things."[87] On October 15, the three lay priests recommended that the town council call a Second Disputation, in order to "discuss and help find a decision out of the Holy Scripture of the Old and New Testaments concerning images and the mass: what might be done that would be most pleasing to God the Almighty, most saving to believing Christian persons, and by which might be lived the will of God and His Holy Scripture, both Testaments, in which so much error has occurred until now. And until then the prisoners should remain in prison."[88]

The Second Disputation was held October 26–28.[89] The subject of the Disputation was "Images and the Mass." As with the First

---

[85] "[G]roßen fräfel und muotwillens, so claus hottinger wider min herren sin oberheit gethan," StAZ, B VI 249: *Ratsbuch Baptistalis 1523*, f. 70r.

[86] *Huldreich Zwinglis Sämtliche Werke* [hereafter *Z*], vol. II, ed. Emil Egli et al. [Corpus Reformatorum, vol. 89] (Leipzig, 1908), p. 665.

[87] EAk 424.

[88] EAk 430.

[89] For a concise account of the major issues of the Second Disputation, as well as relevant references, see Gottfried Locher, *Zwingli und die schweizerische Reformation*, vol. 3, pt. J1 of *Die Kirche in ihrer Geschichte*, ed. Bernd Moeller (Göttingen, 1982),

Disputation, the Bishops of Constance and the other cantons were invited, as were parish and lay priests, chaplains, canons, monks, and mendicants, preachers, other prelates, provosts, and the *Vogten* from the canton of Zurich;[90] in addition, certain other laity and theologians, the Bishop of Chur, as well as the bishop and faculty from the University of Basel were invited. Some nine hundred attended, including a number of scholars, but few of those who opposed reform: No one came from Constance; of the Confederation, only Schaffhausen and St. Gall; and none of the bishops. One day was allotted for discussion of the problem of the images to be led by Leo Jud, and two for the discussion on the mass to be led by Zwingli. Even though Conrad Hoffman, canon of the Grossmünster and ardent opponent of Zwingli, spoke at some length, the discussion occurred primarily among those who considered themselves "evangelical," bound by the Word of God: Jud arguing most forcefully for the complete elimination of the images, Schmid arguing for patience and education of people's spirits before removing them, and Heinrich Lüty, preacher in Winterthur, arguing for their continuance in the churches.[91] Zwingli held closer to Jud than any of the other evangelical positions: He agreed with Schmid that preaching ought go forward first, but asserted "thus the images are not to be endured, for all that God has forbidden, there can be no compromise," and God had forbidden the images.[92] The Zurich town council, however, did not agree to this. Perhaps because the evangelicals themselves were divided; perhaps because, as Bürgermeister Roist said the following morning, all had handled themselves so unseemly that the town council was pleased with no one; perhaps because that position articulated at the end of the day did not resolve the objections of the earlier debates – the town council temporized. On October 27 it declared:

> . . . until further announcement, which will be given shortly, if God wills it, out of the Word of God, neither clerical nor lay per-

---

J 26–8. Garside also provides a narrative of the Second Disputation, structured to underline Zwingli's influence, in chap. 6 of *Zwingli and the Arts*.

[90] EAk 430.

[91] Ludwig Häetzer published an account of the Second Disputation with Christoph Froschauer on December 8 of that year, Z II, pp. 664–803.

[92] Ibid., p. 708.

son may remove or alter any image in the churches, except those who had their own images in the churches, who were given permission to remove them peacefully, but images that had been commissioned by an entire congregation or paid for through parish wealth were not to be removed or altered, without the entire congregation's knowledge and will.[93]

The lay preachers had advised the Zurich town council to call the Second Disputation. Their position, closer to the town council than to the iconoclasts, was made explicit in their "Advice Concerning the Mass and Images" of December 10–19, 1523:

First, it is our opinion that the retables should be immediately closed and not opened again until further notice. They are closed anyway during times of fasting, and the other images are covered. The silver, gold, or otherwise bejeweled images should no longer be brought out, either for weddings or for other days, but instead the highest treasures [*schatz*] of the Word of God should be carried in the hearts of human beings, not the idols before their faces.

2. Next we hold to the most recently issued order, namely that no one is to take any image whatsoever either into or out of the temples, unless he had put them therein before or the majority of an entire congregation decided itself to remove them, and that all removals should be without disgrace, sport, or wickedness, or any wanton manner that might anger anyone.

3. Last: Since it has now been discovered through the Word of God that the mass is not a sacrifice, and also that one should not have images, and since certain pastors in our city moreover agitate constantly against them, with rebellious, irritating, and unfounded words, it is our opinion, to speak to them in that or this form, [to use] fines or the stripping of their benefices, that they do not bring God's Word to nothing.[94]

Even though the preachers were speaking against the images from their pulpits, calling for their removal, even though some were prepared to speak in defense of iconoclasts once they appeared before the town council, most were not endorsing these unofficial, individual acts of iconoclasm. The three people's

[93] EAk 436.
[94] ZII, 814–15.

priests, even Jud who most forcefully opposed the images in the churches, endorsed instead the town council's efforts to maintain public order. Thus it may be that the iconoclasts themselves, both within the town's walls and beyond in villages in the canton, had given the Second Disputation's terms a concrete and specific context, its decisions particular application. Moreover, the rural iconoclasts may have been the most important component in the town council's decision to hold a formal discussion of the question. They presented the town council with a different challenge: On the land, the town council encountered *gesellen*, companions, and other, smaller, forms of community, acting collectively. In Höngg, Eglisau, Altstetten, and Zollikon, the town council found the same sorts of discussion as Claus Hottinger had conducted within Zurich, but these conversations occurred among members of the rural communes, who sought to protect what autonomy they had, and who proved in the next few years to be fervently and actively evangelical, often in direct conflict with the town council's pacing and conception of reform. Rural iconoclasts presented the town council with a more marked tension: As its sources of information became more· distant both physically and in terms of ties of loyalty, as its authority extended beyond the town walls, that authority became more attenuated, less immediate and efficacious. The cases of iconoclasm in the land of the canton are grouped according to the village in which they occurred, underlining thereby the jurisdictional divisions within the canton and also, I hope, the networks of local loyalties and hostilities that would become visible in the trials.

The first of the rural centers of iconoclasm was the village of Höngg.[95] The narrative begins with the disappearance of an image of Christ on the Mount of Olives, sometime in September 1523.[96] On Sunday, September 27, the evangelical mendicant, Simon Stumpf, preached in support of the image's removal.[97] This opened a discussion, primarily among members of two

---

[95] Though Egli has condensed many of these acts into one narrative (EAk 422–3), the testimonies of the various witnesses and actors were not only given over a period of five months, but also distinguish the dates of the different acts, placing them primarily throughout the months of October 1523 and January 1524.

[96] EAk 422, I.

[97] For the following narrative, StAZ, A27,4.

Höngg families, the Grosmans and the Nötzlis, that images should be removed from the churches. One, Heini Nötzli, claimed that he had already removed one image from the church, after which he told Stumpf that he should now be silent, because all the images would come out (of the churches) in eight days. Another, Thoma Grosman, said that he had seen the (missing) image of Christ in a square in Zurich, eating with the beggars. It made him ill (*gieng im gras*), he said, to see the image devour the grapes. On the evening of the 27th, according to the sacristan, sometime between vespers and bedtime, someone entered the church without a key and without breaking in, removed some of the images, and broke a window. A while afterward, the sacristan and his brother entered the church and stored whatever they found broken in the treasure room. Around the time of this attack, Kaspar Liechti removed two angels his family had donated from the church.[98] In the following weeks, Thoma Grosman and Hans Appenzeller threw an old shrine over the church wall and smashed it up, so that no one knew of which saint it had been an image. Another time, according to Grosman, he and a journeyman from Obermeilan, Hans Heini Schwenden of Affhofen, took three planks from a retable in the church and threw them away.[99] Grosman also met Thoma Scherer of Wipkingen, Lienhart Boumgarter, and Großhans Rütsch at a wedding, where all agreed that the idols must come out of the churches in Wipkingen. That evening they carried out the "idols [*götzen*]," chopped them up, and threw them in the lake. As the witness, Scherer, was careful to point out, they had neither sworn nor behaved unpeacefully – had not blasphemed – but had done it from the best intentions.[100] The town council requested their local official, the *Vogt,* to investigate on behalf of the three whether a consensus had occurred beforehand, because then the images might have been removed anyway.[101]

On February 27, 1524, the *Vogt* in Höngg received testimony

---

[98] Ibid.

[99] StAZ, A27, 1.

[100] "[D]arby aber nützyt kein schwür noch onfrydlichs gehandelt, vnnd sollichs nieman zu Iratz oder verachtung sonder als sy verhoffent besser meinung gethan." StAZ, B VI 289, f. 82v.

[101] EAk 423.

from two professed iconoclasts.[102] Rudolf Mumprat from Ravensburg related that he had:

taken one crucifix from a garland before a retable and placed it in the choir stalls;
taken another crucifix that stood on a board, thrown it out into the vineyard, and placed the board on the priest's station;
placed an image of St. Anthony and two other images under the choirstalls;
thrown down a retable of "Our Lady"; and, finally,
stabbed a vesper image with a wall sconce, so that the picture had fallen.

He had not taken anything with him, but left everything lying where it had fallen. Jacob Nötzli then related that, for a time after his sermon on images, Simon Stumpf and his assistant had visited him at home repeatedly and prodded him to remove the idols. Finally, he had made several trips to the church and removed a retable, two (altarpiece) wings, five images that stood on the retable, and an image of Christ on the Mount of Olives, all of which he had then burned. He had also stripped two altars of all their decorations, taken a banner, and thrown all these things in the lake.

The acts in Höngg are all similar: collective iconoclasm, in which members of the community, who were often linked by kinship or profession, participated. The objects were all removed from the church, and the actors did not notice many details about the objects they destroyed. The individual objects were significant only insofar as they were idols, and all the material culture of Christianity – altars, retables, banners, shrines, lamps, images of Christ and of the saints – were idols.

In Höngg the motives of the iconoclasts are less explicit, but it is possible, I think, to bring them into relief. In the 1520s Höngg, as well as Zollikon, was notable for attacks on two faces of Christian practice: images and tithes. A member of the Nötzli family, quite possibly one of the iconoclasts, was fined in 1523 for refus-

---

[102] I am very grateful to Peter Kamber for showing me the following testimonies from the Höngg Pfrundakten, StAZ, E I 30.59.

ing to pay the tithe.[103] The village collectively resisted paying tithes to any ecclesiastical institution, including the Grossmünster in Zurich, other than their own parish church.[104] These two forms of Christian practice – images and tithes – were linked on the land as the objects of both verbal and physical attacks. They were also the forms that embodied, and had come to consume, the currency and the gifts of pious laity. All the material forms of Christian culture were idols, which consumed and did not produce, which received gifts, but did not manifest Christian brotherly love.

Presenting the iconoclastic acts in Höngg not individually but collectively gives us another impression, another view of iconoclasm. In part, this choice is mandated by our knowing so little about the individual actors,[105] and even less about the objects they destroyed; but, in part, it affords us the opportunity to see iconoclasm as a series of individual acts carried out over time by one or more individuals who were in communication with one another. In Höngg Simon Stumpf preached against the images in the churches and even actively pressured one of the villagers to destroy them. In Höngg, acts of destruction, carried out at some distance from the regulatory eye of the Zurich town council, occurred within a community unwilling itself to apply those means of punishment at its disposal. In the case of Höngg, our view more closely approximates that of the Zurich town council: distant, strangers, outside the village's own circle of discussion and decision making.

On January 27, 1524, the Zurich town council received testimony from Ulrich Haffner of Eglisau and Marti Kopp concern-

---

[103] StAZ, B VI 249, f. 51r.
[104] Again, I am grateful to Peter Kamber, who pointed out testimonies from Höngg on the tithe and its proper use (E I 30.60).
[105] The Grosmans and the Nötzlis appear sporadically in the records for small complaints and claims of debt (StAZ, A26,1: 107–8; A27,6), at times even as joint claimants (StAZ, A26, 1:106), but with the exception of two incidents, we learn very little about them. The first incident involved Thoma Grosman and his father-in-law, Erhart Grosman, who attacked Thoma because he did not want his daughter married to a "thief" (B VI 249, *Ratsbuch Baptistalis 1526*, f. 280r). The second incident is more significant: In 1523, one "nötzli von höngg" was fined for refusing to pay the tithe (B VI 249, *Ratsbuch Baptistalis 1523*, f. 51r).

ing iconoclasm in Eglisau in mid-October 1523.[106] Haffner spoke first; his testimony is recorded in full. Fourteen days before the Feast of Simon and Jude, before the Second Disputation, and, as he carefully noted, before the town council's prohibition, he and other "good fellows [*guotgsellen*]" had been sitting together and talking generally, especially about how they in Eglisau had accepted the Word of God, almost from the first, and how elsewhere the images were removed fine and quietly, and whether they might not also initiate something in secret (*in heimlikeit*), that no one might be harmed (*verboßeren*). Then the gathering had broken up. As he and Marti Kopp were leaving together, they had said to each other, Shall we head to the city gate and take something inside with us? They then had come to a great cross in a small chapel, which the parishioners (*Harderin*) had made, where two small retables stood. They had wished to remove these. "They [the images? retables?] greeted them so badly that they dared not do it, and . . . they went home." Later, during the night, both had been badly disturbed, and in the morning Kopp had gone out and wished to put it (the great cross?) back in the chapel. They (retables?) had been broken apart. Haffner did not know what more Kopp had done with it (?). They (the images) had been in the church on St. Conrad's day, when mass had been held. On the same day, Haffner had been at Thomas Meyer's, where he had drunk and talked until midnight; thereafter he had gone home, and did not know who had removed it (the cross?). Moreover, the church had been locked so tightly that no one could have easily gotten it, nor could anyone see evidence that someone had broken in. In the morning, the images were gone, removed. The removal must have happened on the night of St. Conrad's day; and it was talked about among all the residents of Eglisau that they (the images) had still been there on St. Conrad's day, and that the following morning, Thomas Meyer had broken an image (*ein bild*) that had already been taken out. Marti Kopp confirmed Haffner's testimony and added that he had buried it (the cross?) in his vineyard, in order to prevent evil (*bößers*), and wished to say further that he had been a dozen

---

[106] StAZ, E I 1, 1a, 1.78, p. 1r [EAk 491].

times in the city where images had been thrown in the Rhine (that is, Basel).

There is much obscured in Haffner's long and rambling testimony. While he had been arrested and brought before the town council, he did not give a direct accounting of his actions. Unspecified antecedents, unspecified pronouns make opaque not only the agents, the actors, in the iconoclasm, but also the objects. Most significant and unlike other narratives, Haffner's quickly moves to speak of the images in third-person pronouns, creating distance, anonymity. Midway through his narrative, it is no longer clear to whom "they [*sy*]" refers. Indeed, his narrative at points blurs whether the images themselves are acting or being acted upon. His testimony confuses – agents and victims, antecedent and later events, locations of persons – and disorients. The town council may have shared our frustration with the obfuscation of events, chronology, causality, and culpability: They placed the two on probation, released on fifty Pfunden each bail, requiring that the parson split the cost of his bail with Kopp, and designating two from Eglisau as guarantors.

On February 10, 1524, Ash Wednesday, the town council recorded the following narrative.[107] A number of *Gesellen,* possibly journeymen or guild associates, having left a *Schencki* in Üetikon, had come upon a wayside shrine (*Heiligenhauschen*) near Obermeilen. One of their number, Heini Iringer, in his drunkenness had sung in the shrine, thrown the images here and there, and shown one of his companions an image, so that his companion laughed. A woman had come and thrown the miscreants out of the shrine by the hair. Another one of the companions, Heini Baumgarter, had put one of the images outside the shrine in order to cut off its head; but because its neck was made of iron, had instead cut off its sword. The town council fined them for the cost of the damage plus one Mark penance, along with forbidding drunkenness.

What do we learn from this fragment? It suggests yet another treatment of the images. A group of drunken *Gesellen,* companions, journeymen, throw images about and seek to decapitate

---

[107] EAk 497.

one of them. The first violence, throwing the images about, has no specific focus among the images, nor does the violence take precise form. The second violence, of Baumgarter, is resonant of English iconoclasts, performing against those images the punishment for blasphemy. In the second incident, there is ready violence and no words to explicate. Equally significant, it is more evidence of the variety of conversations on the use and place of the images that were taking place in villages: People spoke to one another about the images, seeking confirmation of choices or a consensus as to a course of action.

The next case of rural iconoclasm demonstrates most fully how much testifiers might obscure: We know neither the objects destroyed nor the agents who attacked them. In November 1523, the *Untervogt,* priest, and two parishioners of Altstetten appeared before the Zurich town council.[108] The priest testified that he had proclaimed to the congregation many times, on the basis of the Holy Word, that the idols should be removed (*dannen thun*); nonetheless, he did not know, and could not designate therefore, who had taken the idols away. The *Untervogt* reminded the town council of the ordinance (of October 27) that permitted each congregation to decide for itself, according to the majority, what it would do about the idols. Altstetten had met collectively on the issue, but had not been able to reach a decision to remove the images, so they had agreed to leave the idols until such time the town council might call upon them to remove them, or they themselves came to it. Because no one had spoken to him directly about removing the idols, he did not really know who had done it.[109] The first parishioner confirmed that the priest had said to remove the idols and that it had been discussed all around, and

---

[108] StAZ, B VI 289, ff. 90v–91 r.
[109] "[H]an schmid vndervogt zu altstette. dt. anfang habent vnser herrn inen gschriben, der götzen halb vnder andern, Ob ein gmeind der mererteil einß wurden, die götzen hinweg ze thun, daß sy danethun, die selben söllent vnd mögen uß der kilchen thun, vff daß habent sy ein gmeind gehept, Vnd als sy tzwyschen roß vnd wand sitzent Vnd besorgt übel so inen hieruß erwachsen möcht Syent sy einhellig einß worden, die götzen stan zelassen, biß vnser herrn sy wyter hiessint die dannen ze thun, oder sy selbs käment vnd die hinweg thätent. Er sye ach sydhar unendert angstrengt vm die gmeind ze halte, wol hab er gehört daß ettlich darvon geret, aber im sye nit zu komen. Wisse och gantz nit wer die götzen hinweg gthan hab." StAZ, B VI 289, f. 90v.

added that the *Undervogt* had not opposed his efforts to persuade the congregation to remove the images collectively, but that they had not reached consensus on the issue; he could no longer fully recall who had removed the idols, because the community had unanimously agreed not to remove them. The second parishioner also did not know who had removed the idols.

The case of Altstetten suggests another way in which iconoclastic acts reflected collective goals: The congregation may not have acted collectively in removing the idols, but it did so in protecting those who had. The four witnesses' testimonies each invoked the accepted practice of local and communal decisions before refusing to identify the agents, before drawing a veil over the acts of local individuals. The case of Altstetten also reminds us how many iconoclastic acts may have gone unreported – and that what we know is based upon the betrayal of neighbors, kin, and companions.

The final rural location for iconoclasm was the village of Zollikon, which lay on the north shore of Lake Zurich, had produced the iconoclast Claus Hottinger, and would later be the site of both resistance to tithes and the first Swiss Anabaptist conventicle.[110] Like Höngg and Eglisau, the parish of Zollikon was immediately contiguous to the town of Zurich. On December 23, 1523, the Zurich town council released Conrad Buman, Hans Dachßman, Claus Unholz, Rudolf Ruotschman, Hans Hottinger, Rudolf Hottinger,[111] and Hans Wüst, all residents of Zollikon, from prison. Each was accused of participation in an elaborate act of iconoclasm: dragging a wooden donkey, with the image of Our Lord God on it,[112] from the church and throwing it into Lake Zurich. Both Buman and the town council were careful to identify the donkey as the one with the image of Our Lord God on it. This was no mere farm animal for a manger scene at Christmastime, but an image from the Passion, used in Palm Sunday processions, to open the special theater of events of Holy Week and

---

[110] Fritz Blanke, *Brüder in Christo: Die Geschichte der ältesten Täufergemeinde (Zollikon 1525)* (Zurich, 1955).

[111] Hans and Rudolf seem to have belonged to the same Hottinger family as Claus, although the relationship among the three is not stipulated.

[112] "[D]en esell mitsambt der biltnuß unsers Hergotte daruff," StAZ, E I 1a, 1.70.

Easter. It was an image of particular resonance, used for a procession of particular popularity, during the time when Christians meditated most upon the physical suffering of Christ.

Each of the accused testified individually as to the extent of his participation. Buman, according to his testimony, had taken the key to the church from the sacristan, who had helped to unlock the church, and helped Buman pull the donkey and throw it into the lake. Dachßman acknowledged that he had helped drag the donkey out of the church and to throw it into the lake. Unholz had only helped to pull the donkey out of the church and no further. Ruotschman had come into the churchyard and, "as he was standing somewhat in the way," hacked at the donkey or the image of Our Lord God; thereafter he had gone to Dachßman's house, where they had drunk "a measure of wine,"[113] and decided to return, help throw the donkey in the lake, and sink it with stones. Hans Hottinger acknowledged having helped pull the donkey out of the church and, following the plea and demand of Ruotschman, to drag it up to the lake; but he had remained on the beach and not helped while the others had pulled it into the lake. Rudolf Hottinger confessed that he had been shocked at first by the affair with the donkey and would have nothing of it, and thought it dangerous or wicked; but then he had decided, as though it had fallen onto him from above, and had hit the donkey twice. Wüst, the *Vogt*'s son, had helped search for the key and, since the key had not fit the usual lock, had gone to the sacristan's house and seen Buman take the key; he had not accompanied them back to the church, and so had not helped drag the donkey out of the church or throw it into the lake. Each was fined a greater or lesser amount, according to the extent of his participation. Those who had helped throw the donkey into the lake were fined the most heavily, one Mark; others were fined one Pfund, five Schilling; Ruotschman and Hans Hottinger were fined half a Mark – neither as culpable as Buman and Dachßman, nor as innocent as Unholz, Rudolf Hottinger, and Wüst.

---

[113] "[D]ie mas wins getrunken," StAZ, E I 1a, 1.70.

We can discern in their testimonies the dynamic of this collective act of iconoclasm. Buman was the leader, the one who got the key, found the donkey, pulled it out, and ensured that it ended up in the lake. Wüst seems to have had the idea of unlocking the church, though the donkey seems not to have been his object. Ruotschman, while not the initiator of this particular episode, clearly actively encouraged others to participate and took up his own particular form of iconoclasm: hacking at the donkey. Unholz and the two Hottingers expressed degrees of resistance as well as participation: Unholz would only help take the donkey *out* of the church, not destroy it; at Ruotschman's instigation, Hans Hottinger had helped to the very edge of the lake, but would go no farther; and Rudolf Hottinger seems to have experienced something akin to conversion to the act of iconoclasm – changing his mind and attacking the donkey twice – "zwen wurff zum esel gethan."[114] There is, in the actions of each, both a readiness to participate and a clear sense of the limits to participation. In their individual choices we can trace differing degrees of opposition to the Palm Sunday donkey: One seems not to have been concerned with it at all; two were willing to remove it from the church; one struck it, but would not move it; another was willing both to strike it and to drag it into the lake; and two were willing to drag it from the church and throw it into the lake.

On May 14, 1524, the evening before Pentecost, the Zurich town council issued a mandate in an effort to still the increasing movement to reform. Paragraph 7 addressed directly the question of images:

> . . . and we bid yet again, that no one, either woman or man, young or old, religious or lay, should either take on or concern oneself with these two things, that is the images and the mass, but wait for the opinion of my Lords, who will deal with it as they think necessary and good. And if anyone ignores this [order] and does not adhere to it, [the councilors] will punish him according to their office and judgement.[115]

---

[114] StAZ, E I 1a, 1.70.
[115] EAk 530 §7.

The following day, Pentecost, anonymous iconoclasts attacked more objects in the churches in Zollikon.[116] This time they destroyed more than just an image used in a specific procession at a specific time on the liturgical calendar. We do not know which images were destroyed, but the iconoclasts in Zollikon attacked another "image" of particular importance: the altar. They destroyed those physical presences with which traditional Christianity had been practiced, especially the altar. As the Zollikon iconoclasts made clear, it would not suffice for the town council to demand peace and the restoration of order. Those who were willing to risk their lives would not be dissuaded by such a mandate. On May 21, the Saturday following Pentecost, the town council stated

> The investigation concerning the uproar in Zollikon, which began on Pentecost in the church, in which they destroyed the images and altar, is suspended, until such time that the town council arrives at a decision concerning the images and the mass. (*Ratsbuch Natalis 1524*)[117]

The extent of the violence, its embrace of more than a few objects, and perhaps its location in the increasingly rebellious land, led the town council to take up the issue of images again. The Monday after Pentecost 1524, the town council set up a commission to explore the problem of the images and the mass, comprising those same men it had designated in October 1523, prior to the Second Disputation: the councilors Jacob Grebel, Binder, Berger, Setzstab (whom Hottinger had consulted), and Wegmann; Konrad Escher, Hans Usteri, and Heinrich Werdmüller; the three people's priests in Zurich. To this group, the town council now added the Abbot of Cappel, the Comthur at Kusnach, and the Provost of Embrach.[118] Thus, in delegating the commission, the town council had added members of the "old faith," who had

---

[116] StAZ, B VI 249, *Ratsbuch Natalis 1524*, f. 108r.

[117] "Vmb die unfuuog so die von Zollikon vff den pfingst tag in der kilchen begongen vnd die bilder vnd altar zerschlagen habent ist ein frag gehalten Vnd erkent, dz sölich sach styll stan söll bis dz die ratschlag für bracht werdint der bilder vnd maß halb," StAZ, B VI 249, *Ratsbuch Natalis 1524*, f. 108r.

[118] EAk 532.

publicly continued loyal to Rome and its culture,[119] to those of the "new." Its choice of advisors suggests that it was not entirely ready, even yet, to move on the question of images; but the preachers and the iconoclasts would no longer let the issue rest. At the end of the month, the commission published its "Advice on the Images and the Mass," recommending the elimination of all images from the churches and the institution of a reformed Communion.[120] On June 3, Zwingli would write Martin Bucer in Strasbourg specifically articulating his opposition to images.

On June 8,[121] the town council issued a statement on the images and the mass. "Because," the council noted, "it is not necessary to dispute very much on [the images'] behalf, since there are a number of passages in the Old and New Testaments, and [because] we also know that these images are offered more honor than should be," it is indeed good to advise that they should be removed. However, they were to be removed "with love, without anger or divisiveness, since such images originated among Christians many hundred years ago and not long after the holy apostles and the son Christ." The council advised a five-part position on the images:

1. Those people who had made or commissioned images to be put in the churches were to remove those same images from the churches in eight days.

2. No persons, either few or many in number, either privately or publicly, were to remove images that had been made or commissioned from the church's or the congregation's common funds. Only the entire congregation or a unified majority were to decide if they wished to leave the images or not, and if the congregation or a majority agreed that the images should remain in the church, so they should, as long as it pleased them.

---

[119] See, for example, the complaint filed by the commune of Embrach with the town council because the provost and chapter at Embrach would not offer them the Word of God, but continued to demand tithes and rents from the laity, EAk 490.

[120] *Z* III, 114–31; on images, pp. 129–31.

[121] The date is that of Göttler & Jezler in *Bilderstreit*, p. 156.

3. If a congregation were to agree to leave the images, no clergy or other person was to urge others to pull, pollute, or disturb them, with either word or act, in any way, but he was to remain peaceful. Whoever failed to do this would be heavily punished. Moreover, no one was to commission any more images for the churches, nor should sculptors (*bildhower*) make them, under threat of severe punishment.

4. If a congregation agreed to leave their images and retables in the church, they were not to burn candles before them, nor place censors before them, nor cense them, nor show them any other honor, but instead turn all of these to the honor of God and Jesus Christ alone.

5. Since the crucifix "of Our Lord" does not signify divinity, but alone the humanity and the suffering of Christ, and is a sign of Christian people and the entire Christendom, such crucifixes everywhere, in the churches and on the streets, in a wayside shrine (*bildstocken*) and wherever one might find them, should remain; and no one is riotously to break them, tear them, or bring any wantonness against them, under threat of severe punishment.[122]

When, in early June, the Zurich town council began to move to remove images from the churches, its motive was not evangelical iconophobia but the maintenance of public order: the protection of the property and rights of its subjects. Its first concern was one of property: Those individuals who owned images could remove them. The town council distinguished forms of ownership among the images in the churches: images owned by individuals or individual families versus images collectively owned by congregations. Its second concern was one of consensus: Entire congregations or majorities within those congregations were to make the decision to remove or retain images collectively owned. Decisions, the town council was legislating, were to be representative of the entirety, and the remainder of its statement on images presumed that the majorities of congregations would wish to preserve the images. Its third concern was to control individuals acting autonomously: No more were preachers or other

[122] EAk 543.

clergy to call for verbal or physical attacks, no more were they to encourage acts of defacement, no more were fervent individuals to destroy images the entire congregation "possessed." Only at the end of its third statement and in its fourth did the town council turn to the issue of false worship: No more images were to be commissioned, and no one was to honor images in the many ways people had in the past. The fifth concern is perhaps the most surprising: The town council, quite possibly with Claus Hottinger in mind, singled out crucifixes for particular protection from acts of iconoclasm.

A week later, on June 15, the town council turned again to images: "that one should do away quickly with the idols [*götzen*] and images, so that the Word of God might be given in their stead." So began a discussion that concluded on that same day with the Zurich town council's mandate, "How One Should Deal with the Church Idols." On June 15, the town council moved from images (*bilder*) to idols and church idols (*götzen* and *kilchgötzen*). What had made that possible? In part, the town council's leadership had changed dramatically between June 8 and June 15: On June 13 and 15, 1524, respectively, the *Bürgermeister* Felix Schmied and Marx Roist had died. Even as one, Roist, lay dying on June 15, the council passed its mandate on images. However, their deaths simply removed resistance to a position both preachers and iconoclasts had been pressing for some time: At the beginning of the discussion on June 15, the town council charged the three lay priests and one man each from every guild to "protect that the idols would not go wantonly."[123]

On that same day, the town council legislated iconoclasm.

Since, our gracious Lords Bürgermeister, Council, and Great Council, were informed through the Holy Word and in the past discussions among their own and other learned men, and since nothing else has been discovered, than that the Almighty God has forbidden the images or idols [*götzen*] to be made, and recognizes no worship to be done them – on that our aforesaid Lords, after taking counsel, God be praised and worshiped, and so that in human hearts the same alone is worshiped and prayed to, ac-

---

[123] EAk 544.

knowledge and conclude: to do away with the images or idols in all places where they are worshiped, so that many turn them-selves from the idols entirely to the living true God, and each seeks all help and trust in the one God through Our Lord Jesus Christ, call upon and recognize in worship him alone. And the goods and expenses that have been laid upon these images should be turned to the poor needy human beings, who are a true image of God.[124]

The town council then detailed by whom and how the images might be removed. Anyone who had commissioned an image privately was to remove it to his home, without any interference. Congregations were together to remove the images and retables that the entire congregation or a majority had commissioned. Preachers were to ensure that the removal was done "modestly, orderly, and without uproar." Each and every lay priest and preacher was "to proclaim truly and earnestly the true Word of God in this and in all Christian issues, and to allow the same to work, so that all is of the divine word and not of human law."

On July 2,[125] the town council officially commissioned a com-mittee to remove the "idols" [*Götzen*]. Among the seventeen men were representatives of each guild, a stonemason, a carpenter, the three lay priests, and Ulrich Trinkler. For the next ten days, they moved from church to church in Zurich. Behind closed doors in each church, they took down the sculptures and smashed them up, turning them into cobblestones; they took down the wooden panel paintings and the altarpieces, smashed them and burned them before the churches; they carried out all the objects made of precious metals and stones, broke them up, melted down the metals, and turned them all into money for civic uses, particularly the poor; and distributed to the poor the vestments and various garments of the religious. All the "im-ages," the "idols," carved, painted, sculpted, gilded, cast, all the objects human skill had made beautiful, were returned to the substances from which they had been made – stone, wood, mar-

---

[124] EAk 546.
[125] Göttler and Jezler place the date of the commission on June 20 (*Bilderstreit*, p. 156), following Wyss. I see no reason, however, to override Egli's date for the actual appointment of the committee for iconoclasm, EAk 552, from *Ratsbuch 1524*, "Samstag nach Petri und Pauli," f. 118.

ble, gemstone, metal – and then were put to use as building material, heating material, and currency for the poor. When the committee members were finally done, they washed the walls white, so that none of the paintings of the medieval church would be visible.

Sometime during this same period the relics of Felix and Regula, the two saints around whose remains the town of Zurich had been founded and who were its patron saints, were removed from the two Münster and secretly either buried in the graveyard or thrown into the charnel house.[126] The town council forbade the organ to be played anymore in the churches, forbade the priests to bless palms, salt, water, or candles, and insisted that everyone "abstain entirely and fully from all like superstitions."[127] The organs were silenced in 1524; the one in the Grossmünster would itself fall to iconoclasm on December 9, 1527.

Nor was the official cleansing of the churches sufficient for all in Zurich. After the churches were reopened, iconoclasts "ran into [the Grossmünster] and broke in every way imaginable the stools in the church and then carried them home. And one tore this one, another tore that stool, in a half day, there were no more stools in the church."[128] On November 18, 1524, the town council advised those who wished to remove their gravestones from the churchyards and anywhere else in the town; all other gravestones were to be removed and put to the town's common use and need.[129] Finally, two years later, on July 8, 1526, altars and sacrament shrines (*Sakramentshäuschen*) were broken up and turned into building stones for the new chancel screen in the Grossmünster. In Zurich, altars and images had been separable; as we shall see in the next chapter, they were not so in Strasbourg.

Let me close the story of iconoclasm in Zurich with one last vignette of an encounter that took place sometime after the town

[126] Gerold Edlibach, "Aufzeichnungen über die Zürcher Reformation 1520–1526," ed. Peter Jezler, in *Bilderstreit*, p. 59.
[127] Bullinger, *Reformationsgeschichte*, ed. J. J. Hottinger & H. H. Vögeli (Frauenfeld, 1838), vol. I, pp. 161, 162.
[128] Edlibach, "Aufzeichnungen," p. 57; Wyss, p. 43.
[129] EAk 865.

council's mandate on images.[130] Acknowledging that the council had recently issued a mandate on images on the land (*vff das land*), Steffan Buoman of Ottikon testified that Thias Liechty had come to him and said that since the church ornaments were no longer valued, and since he was poor and had many small children, he wished to take the chalice out of the church. Liechty had asked Buoman what he thought of that. Buoman had queried, "Do you think you do nothing wrong?" Upon this, Liechty had turned, left him, and taken the chalice. Buoman did not know when or where he had taken it. Sometime after, Liechty seems to have sold the chalice and sent six *batzen* (pennies) from Winterthur to Buoman at the home of his brother Jacob. With this, Buoman bought a half-pound of salt and left for Württemberg. During this time, he did not see Liechty again, nor did he know what he had done further with the chalice. No other information, as to either Liechty or the town council's judgment, follows.

Even as the town council sought to bring the question of the images to a conclusion in Zurich, conversations about the images were taking place individually, between residents of outlying villages, and between strangers and local residents. This conversation, this vignette, like ones before it, centered upon the material wealth embodied in the chalice: A poor man expressly takes a single object for its monetary value, and, turning it into currency, not only feeds his children, but enables his witness to buy a pound of salt with his portion. The "image" became food, for poor children and for the man who would tell the town council, which had so recently legitimated iconoclasm, of the encounter. With his portion the witness would buy salt, that most common and familiar of substances, essential to any meal.

Blasphemers continued to be executed throughout the 1520s.[131] What distinguished the attacks of Lorentz Meyger, Lorentz Hochrütiner, Claus Hottinger, and the residents of Höngg, Eglisau, and Zollikon from that of Uly Anders?

[130] StAZ, A27, 4.
[131] StAZ, A27, 6; B VI 248, *Liber Baptistalis 1520*, ff.30r-v.

First, as Thoma Scherer pointed out, none swore against God or His omnipotence.[132] No one "blasphemed" in this new, more narrow definition of the crime: No one spoke against God Himself, His person. None acted "unpeacefully" (*unfridlich*), with malicious intent, against the community's well-being. Second, none attacked objects in private homes. Although the objects may have been the property of a donor's family, they were located in public spaces. These were, moreover, spaces designated for communal and lay piety: The cloisters were not attacked in Zurich.[133] Third, the earliest actors, Meyger, Hochrütiner, and Hottinger, did not have a history of disorderly and destructive behavior. On the contrary, they were familiar to the town council as active supporters of the reform of collective religious life. Their actions might have been perceived as the expression of a piety not sufficiently obedient, but nonetheless authentic.[134]

The choice of objects, and the actors' descriptions of their victims, offer us perhaps the most significant clues about iconoclasm in Zurich. The descriptions provide a popular definition of "idols." Most of the objects the iconoclasts designated as "idols" were not themselves the focus of pious devotion; most were not images of saints, of Mary, of Christ, famous for their efficacy in response to pious prayers and the endowment of masses. It was their relationship to the economy of Christian piety that made them "idols." Although it is almost impossible to discover how the objects came into the churches – whose wealth was originally embodied therein – the conditions of their maintenance in the churches also distinguished them. The maintenance of candles before the retables, the eternal lights, and the care of the altars were not for the most part financed through public or collec-

---

[132] The charge of blasphemy usually included swearing against: God, God's power and might, God's five wounds, God's suffering. Two cases in the 1520s in Zürich involved denying the virgin birth and accusing Joseph of being a cuckold, one of whom was not executed (StAZ, B VI 248, *Liber Baptistalis 1520*, ff. 30r-v, 13r-v).

[133] Chapels were used for community gatherings. See, for example, StAZ, B VI 289, ff. 72r-v.

[134] I have already suggested that Hottinger might have become an Anabaptist and that Ockenfuß expressed a position in keeping with the Anabaptists. Zollikon and Höngg both became centers of rural Anabaptism in 1525–6. On Anabaptist asceticism, see James Stayer, *The German Peasants' War and Anabaptist Community of Goods* (Montreal, 1991).

tive gifts, but through church tithes and rents, through money demanded individually from the laity. All the objects represented not a single gift made at one time in the past, but things that continued to consume candles or tithes for oil, or to contain material, such as wood, that members of the congregation needed for heat, for cooking, and for shelter.

The iconoclasts may have taught the town council to view the images in the churches differently. The council did not, at first, accept the iconoclasts' view of the images as "idols"; but in its prosecution of Meyger, Hochrütiner, and Hottinger it tacitly accepted their essential separation of images from worship – months before it would follow the preachers in citing the biblical injunction against images. In its prosecution of iconoclasts in 1523, the town council distinguished those who attacked the material culture of Christianity, its "images," from those who attacked God Himself. In 1523–4, those who attacked the images were prosecuted primarily for *frävel*, for "riotousness," for a quality inhering in their acting, while blasphemers continued to be prosecuted for attacking God, for the object of their verbal aggression. Thus, in its prosecutions, the council came first to separate the physical presences of Christianity from the person of God. The distance to legislating iconoclasm was thereafter not so great.

Uly Anders's case reminds us that attacks on sacred objects were not, finally, carnivalesque, but done at great personal risk. The Zurich iconoclasts' attacks brought them fines, imprisonment, and even banishment, yet their testimonies gave substance to the label "idol" –made real for the town councilors why it was that the images were so wrong – and they linked iconoclasm not to blasphemy, but to insubordinate piety and to collective ethics. In so doing, the Zurich iconoclasts, with the help of Zwingli and Jud, may have saved their own lives. They also made explicit how well they understood the ways in which Christianity, in all its material forms, was interwoven in the collective life of Zurich – that lamps symbolized the absence of Christian charity, both in that they were not supported through gifts and in that they consumed wealth that could feed the poor.

Strasbourg. *Source:* Georg Braun & Frans Hogenberg, *Civitates orbis terrarum*, vol. I (1572). Beinecke Rare Book and Manuscript Library, Yale University.

3

Strasbourg

In Strasbourg, "Reformation" was less dramatic, its process of longer duration, its effects less defined, and ultimately, less permanent than in Zurich. In Zurich, by 1526, the practice of Christianity was irretrievably altered: The sculpted and painted images had been destroyed, the altars replaced with simple wooden tables, the liturgy reduced to two simple rituals, the practice of charity reformed, pilgrimages halted, processions and the worship of saints stilled. The acts of the iconoclasts had contributed in no small way to that fundamental alteration. In Strasbourg, the pace of reform was more erratic and far slower. As Lorna Jane Abray has argued, in some ways Reformation continued through much of the century, as clergy, commons, and magistrates pursued differing notions of reform with different intensity.[1]

In part, the difference in the process of Reformation in the two towns lies in the greater complexity of Strasbourg's political and social configurations. Strasbourg was some four times larger in population than Zurich. It was also a much larger center of commerce. The Imperial Free City lay along the major corridor of trade between the burgeoning cities of the Low Countries to the north and the Italian cities to the south, as well as along the shifting borderland between the Empire and France. The Ill, which flowed into the Rhine nearby, served Strasbourg's mills and tanneries, and carried goods and the income of custom to the city's ports. Markets, local and international, were a defining feature of

---

[1] Lorna Jane Abray, *The People's Reformation: Magistrates, Clergy, and Commons in Strasbourg, 1500–1598* (Ithaca, 1985).

collective life. Goods and services were located with increasing precision in a matrix of values both social and monetary.

The town council[2] in Strasbourg differed from that in Zurich:[3] Smaller in size, it was also less representative.[4] Strasbourg was governed by a *Stettmeister,* an *Ammeister,* a Great Council or "Senate" (*grosser Rat*), and two privy councils, the XV and the XIII. The *Stettmeister* was patrician; the office rotated every three months among four men. Patricians could not be *Ammeister,* "the real head of the regime," according to Thomas A. Brady; six *Ammeister* were elected from the Great Council and XXI, each of whom served for life, in a rotating rule, one year as *Ammeister* and five years as *Altammeister.* (The XXI, which is often listed with the Great Council, seems to have been, according to Brady, a collective name for the XV and the XIII, along with three or four members simply of the XXI.[5]) The Great Council comprised only thirty men, differing in this way dramatically from that of Zurich: ten patricians and twenty guildsmen selected by the ruling *Schöffen* of each guild, each holding office for two years. Perhaps most significant in understanding the difference between Strasbourg's government and Zurich's is that, by 1500, Strasbourg was ruled much more actively by its two privy councils: the XV, whose jurisdiction was domestic, and the XIII, whose jurisdiction was foreign relations. The *Ammeister, Altammeister,* and members of the XIII were excluded from the XV, yet its jurisdiction embraced "the entire internal life of the city, except for military affairs, including the courts, finance, supervision of the guilds, police, the inspectorates, and the entire system of economic regulation." The XIII, according to Brady, comprised "the inner ruling circle of the city" by 1500; on it sat the

---

[2] Although I take Thomas A. Brady's point, that "regime" better designates the particular constitution in Strasbourg, *Ruling Class, Regime, and Reformation in Strasbourg, 1500–1550* (Leiden, 1978), p. 163, n. 4, its use in this context would suggest greater differences among the three city republics than seem to have existed.

[3] In addition to Abray and Brady, see Adolf Baum, *Magistrat und Reformation in Strassburg bis 1529* (Strasbourg, 1887); Miriam Usher Chrisman, *Strasbourg and the Reform* (New Haven, 1967); and William Stafford, *Domesticating the Clergy: The Inception of the Reformation in Strasbourg 1522–1524* (Missoula, 1976).

[4] The following description is drawn from Brady, *Ruling Class,* pp. 163–8; the quotation is from p. 164.

[5] Ibid., p. 165.

Ammeister, four of the five *Altstettmeister,* four patricians, normally either *Stettmeister* or *Altstettmeister,* and four guildsmen. As we shall see, the *Rat* or town council, sitting together, would promulgate formal rulings on iconoclasm; but our records provide us with no clues as to which level was indeed making the decisions about the practice of Christianity in Strasbourg – the XIII, the XV, or the Great Council and XXI.

Strasbourg was ruled by a pyramidical hierarchy, in which those who achieved offices of rank normally remained in those offices and sat on those councils where the major decisions concerning the economic, legal, military, financial, and even social life of the city were made. That pyramid, moreover, was less open than the government in Zurich: Wealth of significant levels and of certain kinds – mercantile and incomes from property – gave one far greater access to political decision making, whereas artisanal professions found little access to even the most superficial forms of political participation.[6] In Strasbourg, moreover, the emperor was much more than the shadowy presence he was to Zurich: Strasbourg's legal identity, as an Imperial Free City, linked the city republic to the emperor more closely, and imperial authority circumscribed the town council's authority more precisely and explicitly.

Strasbourg's economic and diplomatic concerns both linked it to Zurich and yet led its town council to pursue different policies. So, too, Strasbourg's town council remained much more stable – no dramatic changes in its personnel would alter its direction – its policies much less responsive to the pressures of evangelicals in the 1520s. The years 1523–30 were marked by petitions from the reforming preachers and, occasionally, from burghers independently of the preachers, requesting the right to have the True Word preached, the abolition of the mass, the removal of the images, and the cessation of processions, pilgrimages, and prayers for the dead. The town council's response to each of the requests was invariably ambivalent. As we shall see in the specific case of iconoclasm, it would accord each request a certain validity, yet was hesitant, at times even resistant, to act. In the case of many

[6] Ibid., chap. III.

practices of traditional Christianity – processions, the honoring of saints, the singing of canonical hours, the burning of oil lamps – the town council chose to "suspend" the offending activity, neither eradicating it nor fully supporting its continuation.

This view of the town council serves only in part to explain the pace of reform in Strasbourg. Part of the explanation must also lie in the greater complexity of Strasbourg society and of the organization of religious life within the boundary marked by its canals. While both Strasbourg and Zurich identified themselves as guild regimes, guilds were less prominent a feature of social and political life in Strasbourg. The guild revolt of the fourteenth century had been less successful in permanently restructuring political arrangements in Strasbourg. As Brady has demonstrated, status derived as much from blood, arms, and land as it did from craft;[7] and in Strasbourg, a significant number of the population were not native to the town or its land, and many were not *Bürger* or citizens.

Both size and location may have contributed to Strasbourg's importance as a printing and artistic center. By 1500, Strasbourg already possessed an important printing industry, one that would come to serve the evangelical cause two decades later. Hans Baldung Grien, Nicolaus of Leiden, Nicolaus of Hagenau, and Veit Wagner made Strasbourg their home, if only for a few years, as did dozens of lesser known painters, glasspainters, stonecarvers, engravers, woodcarvers, goldsmiths, and coppersmiths.[8] The crafts of these artisans garnished the public and private spaces of Strasbourg, its churches and guildhalls, as well as the homes of its wealthier citizens. Crafts were also an integral part of the Strasbourg economy, as some practitioners would remind the town council in 1525, when their livelihood was threatened by burgeoning hostility to images and a drop in orders for their products: "since we have learned nothing other than painting, image-carving, and the like, by which work, accorded the status of pious burgher, our wives and children have

---

[7] This is one of his major arguments in *Ruling Class*.

[8] Hans Rott, *Quellen und Forschungen zur Südwestdeutschen und Schweizerischen Kunstgeschichte im XV. und XVI. Jahrhundert*, vol. III: *Der Oberrhein I: Quellen* (Stuttgart, 1936), pp. 185–299.

been nourished, . . . nothing awaits us more certainly than complete ruin and the condition of beggars."[9]

Strasbourg was also an ecclesiastical center.[10] The Cathedral dominated the Strasbourg horizon, its famous rose window visible to travelers at great distance from the city, its scale grander than any other building in Strasbourg, secular or ecclesiastical. The see of the bishopric, Strasbourg was the infrequent residence of the always noble-born bishop, who sought reform of clerical life but not the Reformation of Christian life.[11] He was, moreover, engaged throughout the period in a struggle with the town council over jurisdiction.

Within the boundary formed by the city's canals were housed many more religious than in Zurich.[12] Attached to the Cathedral were monks, canons, and priests. St. Thomas's, Old St. Peter's, and Young St. Peter's churches each had its own chapter. The Knights of St. John and the Teutonic Knights each had a house, whose members were known for their nobility. There were nine monasteries: Augustinian monks were housed in St. Arbogast; Augustinian hermits were in the parish of St. Aurelia; Dominicans and Franciscans each had a large house; Wilhelmite canons had their own church near the eastern border of the town; Antonites from Isenheim established a hospital; and there were Carmelite monks in the parish of St. Nicholas, Penitents in All Saints', and Carthusians. Among the convents, St. Stephen's, reserved for noblewomen since its foundation, was the oldest; it also housed Augustinian canons.[13] Dominicans were housed in five convents: St. Mark, St. Nicholas *in undis*, St. Agnes, St. Margaret, and St. Catherine. By the sixteenth century, only one Franciscan convent still existed, St. Clare am Rossmarkt. Penitents were housed in St. Madeleine convent. Beguines, once so popular in Strasbourg, had suffered under the ridicule of Geiler von Kai-

[9] Ibid., pp. 304–5.

[10] For the following discussion, I have relied primarily upon Francis Rapp, *Réformes et réformation a Strasbourg: Église et société dans le diocèse de Strasbourg (1450–1525)* (Paris, 1974).

[11] On the three bishops who reigned 1440–1541, see Rapp, bk. II, chap. II.

[12] The following description is derived from Luzian Pfleger, *Kirchengeschichte der Stadt Strassburg im Mittelalter* (Colmar, 1941), pp. 68–92.

[13] Ibid., p. 85–6.

sersberg and Sebastian Brant, their numbers and houses decreasing dramatically by the beginning of the sixteenth century.

Strasbourg comprised three times as many parishes as Zurich, nine in number: the Cathedral, St. Stephen, St. Andrew, Young St. Peter, Old St. Peter, St. Aurelia, St. Thomas, St. Nicholas, and St. Martin. Chapters were attached to four of the parish churches. The canons of St. Thomas appointed and paid the salaries of the priests in St. Thomas and St. Aurelia. Young and Old St. Peter each had its own chapter. As we shall see more fully below, preaching was important to the Strasbourgeoise and had been for some time. In 1486, one of them, Peter Schott, had commissioned a carved pulpit in the Cathedral for one of the most forceful and charismatic proponents of reform that the fourteenth and fifteenth centuries had witnessed. For some thirty-odd years, from 1478 to his death in 1510, Johann Geiler von Kaysersberg had preached first against the abuses of the church, then against those of the clergy, and finally against the moral laxity of the laity, in sermons of such rhetorical power and moral presence that he had drawn the same sort of sometimes rapt, sometimes angry, always fully engaged attention as had Bernardino of Siena or Savonarola.[14] Thus, about ten years before the arrival of the first evangelical preacher, Strasbourg had been home to a fiery, austere preacher of extraordinary rhetorical skills and moral vision.

In the 1520s, the city on the Ill would find significant commonalities with Zurich. Both were cities of Roman origin and early Christian settlement. Like Zurich, Strasbourg was an urban commune. Its magistrates, the men who sat on the town council, framed their decisions in terms of the common good, good order, and peace.[15] The two were linked by water and the commerce it carried. Finally, in the 1520s, the two city republics would find their fates increasingly interwoven, as those earlier commercial ties enabled a commerce of ideas: Huldrych Zwin-

---

[14] On peasant reception of Geiler's preaching, see Franziska Conrad, *Reformation in der bäuerlichen Gesellschaft: Zur Rezeption reformatorischer Theologie im Elsass* (Stuttgart, 1984), pp. 29–31.

[15] The structures of the two towns' councils differed, however. For Zurich, see Walter Jacob, *Politische Führungsschicht und Reformation* [Zürcher Beiträge zur Reformationsgeschichte, vol. I] (Zurich, 1970). For Strasbourg, see Brady, *Ruling Class.*

gli corresponded actively with the Strasbourg reformers Wolfgang Capito, Caspar Hedio, and Martin Bucer, and traveled, at
great personal risk, to visit them in 1529. To his death in 1531,
Zwingli considered Bucer one of his closest friends. That friendship was founded in shared theological commitments: the conviction that God's love of humanity took as its expression each
Christian's ability to love his or her neighbor; and the understanding of the Eucharist as a ritual of communion, both between
each Christian and God, and among Christians.

The story of iconoclasm in Strasbourg comes to us differently,
primarily through chronicles.[16] In Strasbourg, none of the judi-
cial or legal records survive: We have no testimonies of iconoclasts before the town council that might allow us to hear their
voices, to glimpse something of their motives; nor do we have
the testimonies of their accusers or of other witnesses to their
acts. We have the accounts of chroniclers, most of whom, like
Sebald Büheler and Jean Wencker, lived and wrote toward the
end of the century, some seventy years after the events.[17] The
accounts of iconoclasm we have for Strasbourg, in other words,
were written by persons most of whom would not have been
present, who may have been removed as much as two or three
times from the event itself.

---

[16] Most of the chronicles have been published as fragments in the series, *Fragments des
Anciennes Chroniques d'Alsace* [hereafter *FACA*], vols. I (1887), III (1892), and IV
(1901), ed. L. Dacheux (Strasbourg): *La Petite Chronique de la Cathédrale (Der kleine
Münsterchronik*), *FACA* I [hereafter *Petite Chronique*]; *Sebald Bühelers Strassburger Chronik*, *FACA* I [hereafter Büheler]; Jacob Trausch, *Strassburgische Chronick*, *FACA* III
[hereafter Trausch]; Johann Wencker, *Summarische Chronik und Zeitregister der Statt
Strassburg* (1637), *FACA* III [hereafter Wencker]. The fullest of these fragments is *Les
Annales de Sebastien Brant*, *FACA* III and IV [hereafter Brant], none of which seems
to have been Brant's own work, but that of Jean Wencker and his family, who com-
posed the chronicle from various sources (Chrisman, *Strasbourg and the Reform*, p.
321). Three other chronicles were published separately: "Strassburg im sechszehn-
ten Jahrhundert, 1500–1591: Auszug aus der Imlin'schen Familienchronik," ed. Ru-
dolphe Reuss, *Alsatia* 10(1873/1874): 363–476 [hereafter "Imlin'schen Familienchronik"]; *Die Strassburger Chronik des Johannes Stedel*, ed. Paul Fritsch (Strasbourg,
1934) [hereafter Stedel]; and *Die Strassburger Chronik des elsässischen Humanisten Hie-
ronymus Gebwiler*, ed. Karl Stenzel (Berlin and Leipzig, 1926) [hereafter Gebwiler].
[17] Büheler's father, "Sebot Buheler, der schriner von Nüremberg," became a citizen of
Strasbourg in 1514, Rott, *Quellen und Forschungen*, p. 303. Büheler's chronicle is
dated 1588. For a description of the Strasbourg chronicles, see Chrisman, *Strasbourg
and the Reform*, pp. 320–2.

The Strasbourg chroniclers did not record who the iconoclasts were. They provide no detail, give no dimension of their identities. Rarely does the narrative present the iconoclasts acting; only twice do we glimpse what precisely the iconoclasts might have been doing and saying. For the most part, the chroniclers record what has happened, has been completed, is closed. They are concerned not with doing, but with results, and convey the effects of iconoclasm, not the acts themselves. Rarely do the chronicles provide more than a generic name for the objects removed and/or destroyed. The details so rich in the Zurich sources are largely unrecorded.

Chronicles are a particularly troubling source. The events they narrate are the product of a process of discernment, of interpretation, by which some dimensions of events are rendered more prominent in the telling and others are excluded. They reflect the sensitivities and concerns of the chroniclers, who may or may not have shared the iconoclasts' perceptions or evaluations of the objects they attacked; indeed, some chroniclers were hostile to the iconoclasts. The very fact that the names of the iconoclasts have disappeared is itself suggestive: This one silence suggests that the chroniclers' configuration of the meaning of the acts of iconoclasm was not the same as the iconoclasts'.

Most of the Strasbourg chronicles come to us even further along in that process of interpretation: They exist no longer in the original, but solely in modern editions based upon the transcriptions of eighteenth- and nineteenth-century scholars.[18] The narrative of events constructed by each chronicler has been interrupted, the relations severed among events he wished (or did not wish) to convey. The accounts upon which we base our investigation, in other words, are framed by a series of redactions and interpretive choices – choices that may not reflect the sensibilities of the iconoclasts, choices that may frame the story of iconoclasm in ways we cannot see.

In exploring iconoclasm in Strasbourg, then, we must take up a different approach. Our analysis begins with the chroniclers' own structuring of the acts of iconoclasm. Like them, we shall

[18] The Brant, *Petite Chronique,* Büheler, Trausch, and Wencker chronicles come to us as such excerpted transcriptions; Chrisman, *Strasbourg and the Reform,* pp. 320–1.

first present the acts of iconoclasm in chronological order, inter-weaving the iconoclastic acts into the larger narrative of reform in Strasbourg. By presenting the acts individually, we shall be able to explore those associations of meaning specific to each act: its individual context. Then we shall step back to a broader perspective, an aggregate view of the acts of iconoclasm, to explore those parts of the story the chroniclers and their transcribers have already rendered more prominent: time, both the specific dates of iconoclasm and its duration; place, the locations of iconoclasm, from chapels in the Cathedral to outlying parish and cloister churches; and, finally, the striking coupling of images and al-tars. In this way, I hope to tease out of those fragments – details of stories of iconoclastic acts provided by the chroniclers – not only the significance sympathetic chroniclers accorded the acts of iconoclasm, but something of the meaning the iconoclasts sought to convey.

One last caveat: Like all sixteenth-century recorders, the chron-iclers used the hagiographical calendar to date the events they narrated. Saints' days serve as temporal references for the attacks against images of saints, relics, and altars dedicated to saints. That convergence, to which we shall return below, gives us one more dimension of meaning for the iconoclasts' acts. It also makes more difficult the task of determining what happened when: The chroniclers usually refer to saints solely by their first names, giving no indication whether a saint was one known in-ternationally or just locally. The dates given in the next section, then, are only so certain as the degree to which their reference can be determined.

Chronological narrative

Iconoclasm in Strasbourg occurred in two waves: February 1524 through the spring of 1525,[19] and from March 1529 to the final resolution of the town council to break up the altars in 1530. The

---

[19] The register [F] in the Municipal Archive in Strasbourg records three incidents of iconoclasm for which I have found no chronicle accounts: on 26 December 1524, iconoclasm (*Bildersturm*) occurred in both Young St. Peter's and St. Martin's churches; and on 8 February 1525, the *Rat* prevented iconoclasm by the coopers.

earliest attack occurred on February 2, 1524, on Candlemas and the Feast of the Purification of the Virgin. Traditionally on that day, relics were carried from the Cathedral to St. Thomas's, where, following terce, the canons of the Cathedral blessed candles for the entire city. Following the consecration of the candles, the Cathedral canons, along with those of St. Thomas and Old St. Peter, returned to the Cathedral, where ceremonies continued,[20] concluding in a mass for the Virgin. Among the relics carried in procession were those of St. Agnes, which were then placed on the altar in the Cathedral dedicated to her. After Bucer's sermon in the Cathedral that day, some of the audience went up to the altar of St. Agnes, took the money from the altar, and stuffed it in the alms box, telling the priest to take himself away with the idols ("mit den götzen heissen hinweg gehn"), or they would throw him over the altar.[21]

The first incident took place, then, on that feast, earlier solely of the Presentation in the Temple, that had by the sixteenth century come to be one of the feasts of the Virgin Mary. It was a feast important in a city where the Cathedral was dedicated to the Virgin. In Strasbourg, this feast was celebrated with elaborate processions and a number of religious ceremonies. The city itself was incorporated into the celebration as the recipient of candles consecrated on its behalf. The first act of iconoclasm took place before an altar dedicated to a saint revered for her purity, who was among the most beloved and best known of the saints, whose name was included in each mass. On one of the feasts of the Virgin Mary, the iconoclasts chose not Mary, but another virgin saint who had her own feast day: Agnes shared Mary's purity, her virginity, but neither her fertility nor her beneficence.

The next incident of iconoclasm took place on Holy Wednesday, March 23, 1524, in Young St. Peter's church. According to legend, Young St. Peter's had received the right from Pope Leo IX to grant indulgences freely;[22] by the sixteenth century, it had

---

[20] Pfleger, *Kirchengeschichte der Stadt Strassburg*, p. 57.

[21] "Imlin'schen Familienchronik," p. 394; Stedel, pp. 91–2. Throughout the notes, the fullest text is cited first, followed by other references. I have also chosen, for the sake of brevity, to provide in the notes only those texts for which no printed edition exists.

[22] Pfleger, *Kirchengeschichte der Stadt Strassburg*, p. 32.

become the custom there to grant indulgences in Passion Week, beginning on Monday and concluding on Wednesday. So, too, it had become customary for the great cross, which stood on the rood screen, to be moved temporarily from its place on Wednesday morning.[23] In the evening of Holy Wednesday in 1524, "some"[24] arrived with axes and hammers and said: "Why should the great idol [*götz*] be lying there? They have prayed to it for more than 400 years and not even reaped a new robe from it. They could just as well have left it standing there, for it would not have stood the embarrassment long." With these "raucous words," they took the money out of the bowls (collection plates), stuffed it in the poor box, snuffed the lights, and asked, "what should the idolatry be doing there?" Fearing an uproar (*ufflauf*), because it was a priestly matter, they closed the church doors, then went out into the church alley, where Herr Heinrich Hertz sat on the corner. There they put weapons on the door as if they had wanted to break in.[25]

The earliest acts of iconoclasm involved no destruction of objects. Both consisted in verbal acts: In both, the iconoclasts verbally attacked the "idols," the *götzen*. In the first incident, the iconoclasts named no particular object; in the second, they designated a cross. In the first, the verbal act took place before an altar dedicated to a saint, Agnes, whose name and perhaps life would have been familiar. In the second, the iconoclasts ridiculed a large wooden cross temporarily moved from its place on the rood screen, above the high altar, as an object falsely accorded the power to answer prayers. In both, the "idols" were linked with the poor as the iconoclasts took money from altars and placed it in alms boxes. In the second act, the cross was attacked in the week spent in reflection upon the Passion of Christ.

During Lent 1524, a number of incidents called the shape and forms of religious life in Strasbourg dramatically into question. In February, Anton Firn read the first mass in German in St.

---

[23] This custom is noted solely by the Imlin'schen family chronicler.

[24] In both accounts, the chroniclers do not indicate whether the iconoclasts were exclusively men.

[25] "Imlin'schen Familienchronik," p. 398. Given how rarely the iconoclasts were quoted, one is led to ask who witnessed and reported this particular incident – how did the chronicler know what they said? Also, Stedel, p. 93.

Thomas's church. On 16 February, Diebold Schwarz, at that time an assistant to the preacher of St. Lawrence chapel in the Cathedral, read the mass in German in the chapel.[26] On 21 February, Martin Bucer preached his inaugural sermon in St. Aurelia's church, marking a victory for the parishioners' right to choose their own preacher. On 2 March, the gardeners of Young St. Peter's, following the precedent of St. Aurelia's, announced the selection of Wolfgang Capito as their preacher.[27] These parish selections would be followed later that spring with the election of Diebold Schwartz to the pastorate of Old St. Peter's.[28] On 13 April, the town council established a committee to oversee the cloisters – their revenues and expenditures, their possessions, and the conduct of their inhabitants – and to inventory their contents. Moreover, throughout that Lent and those following, many people slaughtered and ate oxen.[29]

Many of the challenges to traditional Christian practices did not come during Carnival, that time when the structure of religious authority might be challenged, when the practice of religion, in all its forms and with all its matériel, might be ridiculed or even debased.[30] Though the iconoclastic attacks for which we have records occurred before the beginning of Lent and at its end, during Holy Week, other kinds of attacks – against the Latin mass, against the authority of foundations within parish life, against the autonomy of the clergy, and against the taboos of blood and flesh – took place during Lent. They occurred, that is, in the time of penance, fasting, and purification.

A note for September 5, 1524, in one of the chronicles gives us a glimpse of the increased tension surrounding the images. Images in the streets and in the churches had been "forcefully torn away [*gewaltiglich hinweggerissen*]." The town council mandated that people were not to take or put away the images of their saints

[26] *Petite Chronique*, p. 18.
[27] Stafford, *Domesticating the Clergy*, p. 169.
[28] Ibid., p. 171. In 1525, St. Andrew's church would also petition for an evangelical preacher, Brant nos. 4571–2.
[29] Stedel, p. 92.
[30] Natalie Zemon Davis, "The Reasons of Misrule," *Society and Culture in Early Modern France* (London, 1975), pp. 97–123; Bob Scribner, "Reformation, Carnival and the World Turned Upside-Down," in *Popular Culture and Popular Movements in Reformation Germany* (London & Ronceverte, 1987), pp. 71–102.

on their own authority. It also informed the preachers that a mandate was under consideration, and told them to admonish their congregations. Finally, those whom Claus Ingolt had pointed out – such as the wickmaker, the tailor on Steinstrasse, and their followers, who had torn the images in the churches and on the street away and removed them – were to be placed in the tower and fined.[31]

This note captures the town council's efforts to control iconoclastic violence, both through its own channels of influence and through those of the preachers. The town council would equivocate for six more years, admonishing the preachers to keep their congregations peaceful, promising that it was considering the question of the images and the altars, but being either unable or unwilling to put an end to the attacks. The note also intimates that many more acts of iconoclasm may have been taking place than those the chronicles recount: The cases of the wickmaker, the tailor on Steinstrasse, and their followers appear nowhere else. So, too, the forceful removal of images in the streets is recorded in no other extant narrative. Were these also religious images, of the Virgin, of saints, of Christ, or crucifixes, placed at crossings – another layer of the geography of religion? Brant's note offers us our only glimpse.

The next recorded incidents of iconoclasm took place in October 1524. On Saturday and Monday, October 29 and 31, people removed all the retables, paintings, and relics in the Cathedral and St. Aurelia's church, with the exception of the retable on the altar in the Cathedral, and smashed the holy water basin.[32] The chronicle accounts differ as to the number of people involved and the nature of the violence. The Imlin'schen family chronicler recorded "a great mob at Strasbourg of Lutherans," while Stedel merely notes that "they took away" the images.[33] Both chroniclers record that all the retables, paintings, and relics were removed (although, in the case of both St. Aurelia's church and

---

[31] Brant, no. 4538.
[32] "Imlin'schen Familienchronik," p. 399; Stedel, p. 95. Brant notes that the retable on the high altar in St. Aurelia's was left alone, no. 4545.
[33] "[E]in grosser ufflauf zu Strassburg von den lautterischen," "Imlin'schen Familienchronik," p. 401; "sie ... hinweggethann," Stedel, p. 95.

the Cathedral, as we shall see, objects remained for subsequent iconoclasts); and both connect the attack to St. Luke's Day, the day of that evangelist who, it was believed, had painted the portrait of the Virgin, one of the earliest Christian images[34] and the earliest image of the Virgin.

Traditionally, a procession was held in Strasbourg on St. Luke's Day. In 1524, the *Ammeister* raised the question before the town council "if such a procession and the unnecessary and excessive cost of cloths, candles, eating in inns, etc., ought to be halted, and turned to a better work more pleasing to God."[35] Perhaps he thought the procession would provoke those who had heard Caspar Hedio preach earlier that year that it was better to listen to the Word of God than to go about in the procession for St. Mark,[36] or those who had heard of the preachers' protest against the Passion week procession as "a pagan work, in which God has no pleasure."[37] His question, however, came too late: Too few councillors were present that day, the time was too short, and they did not wish to close anything. The procession was held. (The *Ammeister* would again raise the issue before the town council in 1525; at that time, however, they would agree to halt the procession, and instruct the foundations to set the sacrament on the altar no longer, but otherwise to distribute alms as before.[38])

The next act of iconoclasm took place one month later. On November 22, 1524, the gardeners *unter den Wagnern,* with the support of their preacher, Martin Bucer, opened the grave of St. Aurelia, which lay in the church of her name. They wished to see "whether she lay therein."[39] Finding only a pair of legs, they threw them out in the charnel house with the other legs.[40] This incident is linked to the earlier "Lutheran" iconoclasm by place and by object of attack: In both instances, St. Aurelia's was a locus of iconoclasm; in both, relics were victims of iconoclastic acts.

---

[34] The earliest Christian image was thought to be the veil of Veronica, the *vera icon.*
[35] Brant, no. 4543.
[36] "Imlin'schen Familienchronik," p. 399; Stedel, p. 93.
[37] Stedel, p. 93.
[38] Brant, no. 4644.
[39] Stedel, p. 95.
[40] *Petite Chronique,* p. 19.; also, Büheler, p. 73.

The relics of St. Aurelia were particularly powerful and popular. In July 1199, a soldier of Philip of Swabia, while pillaging the city, had broken into the crypt and sought to break into the sarcophagus of the saint. He was "possessed of an evil spirit," so that he tore apart his hands and feet with his own teeth.[41] In the fourteenth century, the canons of St. Thomas had sought to give the church a new patron saint, St. Mauritius, whom they venerated in their own church. The parishioners never acknowledged the new patron, but remained loyal to Aurelia, continuing to call the church by her name, fixing permanently thereby the name that has endured to this day.[42]

The gardeners of St. Aurelia parish were among the most active of the laity in reforming. They had challenged the right of the powerful chapter of St. Thomas to appoint the pastor of their parish, at last winning the support of the town council to appoint the man they had chosen to preach the True Word, Martin Bucer. After Bucer's arrival, as we have seen, the retables, paintings, and relics in St. Aurelia's church were attacked in October 1524, the relics again in November; and the altars were smashed on February 8, 1525. By Lent, 1525, no retables, no images, and no altars remained in St. Aurelia's church. Even the relics for which the church had been consecrated no longer remained.

As Miriam Chrisman has suggested, the gardeners of St. Aurelia parish offer a rare view into lay and artisanal participation in reform. They also offer a fleeting glimpse of artisanal perceptions of the material culture of Christianity. Their treatment of the relics of St. Aurelia was not only void of deference or wonder, all the more striking given her legendary power: Her remains were adamantly anatomical – the gardeners found legs in the tomb – and, like all bodies, degenerative over time – the bones were thrown in a pile with other leg bones.

The "Lutheran" riot, the smashing of retables, paintings, and relics in the Cathedral and in St. Aurelia's church, occurred in late October. The chroniclers connected it to St. Luke's Day, with its procession. It is also linked, however, to the Feast of All Saints, taking place on the evening before. That evening, All Hallows'

[41] Pfleger, *Kirchengeschichte der Stadt Strassburg*, p. 41.
[42] Ibid., p. 49.

Eve, had, by the sixteenth century, acquired certain rituals of its own, rituals not of inversion, but of sanctioned misdemeanors. The iconoclasts attacked not only images, retables, and paintings that day, but relics. They attacked, in other words, on the evening of the Feast of All Saints, the material remains of saints, throwing them out of the two churches. Three weeks later, the gardeners of St. Aurelia parish opened the saint's grave, to see if she was there, and, finding only legs, threw them on a pile of bones – thus transforming her "relics" into human debris.

The narratives of iconoclasm for the years 1525–6 are even terser than those for earlier acts. *Les Annales de Sebastien Brant* provides two direct accounts.[43] On January 23, 1525, the gardeners of St. Aurelia parish removed the cross that stood before the White Tower, one of the city gates, some 200 meters from their church, removing thereby a major image within the space of their parish. On February 8, the altars in St. Stephen's church, along with those of St. Aurelia's, were smashed. A third note, for February 13, suggests again how much the interpretive choices of the chroniclers and their transcribers have obscured: According to the chronicler, the idolatry (*Abgötterei*) in the Cathedral continued – we do not have any record of what the idolatry comprised – and the stone basin to hold the holy water in St. Thomas had been broken up.

Some evidence for iconoclasm comes to us indirectly, through petitions to the town council.[44] On February 20, 1525, the curates of the Cathedral sought the advice of the town council as to whether, during fasts, they should hang images and the Lenten cloth in the Chapel of the Holy Cross, should sing and play the Salve on the organ, and offer holy water. Iconoclasm had called some, if not all, of these practices into question. The town council advised them to sing the Salve as before, to forgo playing the organ, distributing holy water, and hanging the Lenten veil, and to refrain from prayers to the saints. A second request for the town council's advice is the only evidence for the destruction of altars

---

[43] Respectively, Brant no. 4571 (January 23) and following no. 4584 (February 8). For February 13, following no. 4585.

[44] Respectively, Brant, nos. 4589 (February 20), 4596 (March 15), and 4599 (April 1). See Chapter 2 for a discussion of candles in Zurich.

in St. Martin's church: On March 15, the chaplain asked what he should do, now that the altars had been destroyed. A third exchange with the town council indicates that, as in Zurich, candles were a focus of dispute and possibly iconoclasm in Strasbourg: On April 1, the town council was advised to have all the candles in the Cathedral put away; it agreed to talk to the guilds about candles.

On March 18, the town council again issued an order to "all and each of you Burghers, spiritual and secular, that you on your own authority and by yourself or otherwise should remove or break up nothing, be it small or large, in the churches or on the streets, of images, altars, retables, ivory or stone works, absolutely nothing is to be taken out." It admonished those who were troubled for whatever reason to bring it before the town council, a "legitimate authority."[45] In March 1525, perhaps in immediate response to this order, "six burghers" sought the town council's intervention in issues of Christian worship. Their first concern was "that so many godless masses were held daily." Their second concern:

> how no Christian may endure as well the aggravating idol in the chapel in the Cathedral, which is a grave affront not only to our community but also to the countryside; how one sees daily and unceasingly that people bow before it, pray to it, that those refractory persons take special pains, when the Word of God is preached, to denigrate the same and to provoke those who desire to hear it. The silver idol behind the altar in the choir in the Cathedral causes the same aggravation, as does the idol in the entrance to the Cathedral, for which a lattice porch was recently made. The same can be said of the idolatrous spectre of the Mount of Olives itself, where a lamp is lit and burns now more than ever and during the day, in defiance of God and pious Christians. And of the idols that are more a mockery than an honor to Saint Anne, which is also erected without Scripture. And in conclusion, we see and grasp that all idols are aggravating, in all churches, not to the perfected Christians, but to the weak, and to those who have not yet taken on the Word, whence the great uproar. For all idols

---

[45] Rott, *Quellen und Forschungen*, p. 304.

are against the Word of God and therefore arisen from the devil. They can bring no good fruit. [46]

These six "burghers" provide us with one of the very few statements from the laity of what might constitute an "idol": what objects in the churches might offend, and the nature of their offense. The "idols," for the most part, seem not to have been representative art – those paintings and sculptures that present before the eyes of viewers likenesses of saints, of Mary, of the apostles, or of Jesus. That characteristic does not make an object into an "idol." The "silver idol behind the altar in the choir of the Cathedral" was not distinguished for any likeness it may have carried, but for its substance, silver, and its location. What seems to have distinguished all the idols was their place in the practice of piety: People bowed before them, prayed to them, lit candles before them, allowing those candles to burn ceaselessly day and night. The idols not only were the objects of worship, itself "against the Word of God and therefore arisen from the devil." They also had effect: The people who worshiped them were "weak" as Christians, but found a support in them to oppose the Word of God as it was preached. The idols were "aggravating [*ärgerlich*]" both to perfected Christians, who knew that God had forbidden them, and to weak Christians, for whom the idols were not merely a focus, but a source of false worship.

We do not know if these six burghers number among the iconoclasts. Miriam Chrisman provides some detail for three of

---

[46] "Wir beschwert uns, wie es ouch kein christ duelden mag, der ergerlich götz in der Cappellen im munster, der nit allein unsser gmein, Sonder vil mer denen uff dem Land ein grewelicher anstoss ist, Wie man dann das täglich on vnderloss sicht, das man sich vor im neigt, in anbettet, des sich ettliche wi=derspenstigen besonder beflyssen, wann man das gotts wort prediget, zuo verachtuong des selbigen, und reytzuong deren, die das selbig luost haben zuo hören. Dessglichen ouch erger-nuoss bringt die silberin götz hinder dem altar im chor im münster, ouoch der götz in den eingang des munsters, dem man kürtzlich ein gerembss gemacht hat, Ouoch des götzen gespenst des ölbergs do selb, do man ytz mer dan ander und im tag ein ampell bremend anzindt, zuo eim tratz gottes und frommer christen, Ouch des götzen So sant Anna, mer zuo eim gespött dann zuo eren, ouoch on geschrifft uff= gericht worden ist. Und in summa wir sehen und gryffen das alle götzen örgerlich sind, in allen kirchen, nit den volkommenden christen, aber den schwachen, und die das wort noch nit angenommen haben, wöbcher der grösser huoff ist, dann alle götzen wider das wort gottes und dess halb vom tüfel uff komen, kein guete fruecht bringen kinden." Archives du Chapitre de St. Thomas de Strasbourg (hereafter AST), 87, no. 29.

the authors: Meuchen Jacob der Juong was a fisherman, successful enough to have become one of the *Schöffen*[47] of his guild by
1533; Andres Siferman was the only one to appear in the burgher rolls, as a carpenter, in 1515; Christman Kemlin was a
member of the drapers' guild, and his sympathies with the rebel-
ling peasants in 1525 brought him before the town council.[48]
The other three, Foltzen Hans, Meinolf Dannenföls, and Peter
Sigel, seem to have left no other trace.

The burghers requested that the town council "put the mass to
an end as soon as possible, have the Marian idol in the chapel,
with its cage and birds put away efficiently, place the silver idol
behind the altar in the alms box, and remove all other idols in
the Cathedral and all other churches."[49] The town council did
not heed their request; but for some, specific objects had been designated as "idols." Throughout the following two years, objects
fitting what little description had been articulated in the petition
were attacked in the Cathedral: a "Marian idol" in a chapel before which people bowed and prayed, from which they found
support for traditional Christianity; a "silver" idol behind the altar in the choir; and an "idol" in the entrance for which a lattice
screen had recently been made.

These attacks in the Cathedral, against the "idols," took place
in 1525–6: two during Lent 1525, both on Saturdays, and the
third in Advent 1526. On April 1, the Saturday two weeks before
Easter, the image of the Virgin Mary was removed from her altar in the Cathedral;[50] according to Brant, the iconoclasts put a
crucifix in its place.[51] This image of the Virgin had originated
in Prague and, in 1404, had been placed in the elaborately
carved wooden tabernacle within the chapel of the Virgin, located on the north pier of the nave; in 1483, a new altar had been

---

[47] On the *Schöffen*, see Brady, *Ruling Class*, pp. 166–7.
[48] Chrisman, *Strasbourg and the Reform*, pp. 149–50.
[49] "Sonder das uffs fuorderlichst die messen abgestölt, der mergen götz in der
Cap=pellen mit siner köfig und vöglin genutzlich werd hingethon, Der Silbrin götz
hinder dem althar, in der armn stök werde gelögt, und alle andere götzen im münster, und allen andren kirchen ab gethon," AST, 87, no. 29.
[50] *Petite Chronique*, p. 19; "Imlin'schen Familienchronik," p. 403; Stedel, p. 97.
[51] Brant, no. 4600, who also notes "Erkannt: Das bild by nacht hingweg thun und ein
blotafeln für die kapffs machen und daruff mit guldenen buchstaben schriben:
Allein Gott die Er, oder Gloria in excelsis Deo."

commissioned, and the retable, with its image of the Virgin, placed upon it. Both the image and its tabernacle were noted in the chronicles for the mastery of craft they manifested, for the excellence of their manufacture. That mastery, moreover, had specific monetary value: The tabernacle alone cost more than 60 Strasbourg Pfunde to carve.[52]

The object of attack was integral to the cult of Mary. On it, Mary was represented, her features made visible to the pious; on it, Mary was made "present" again in the minds of her viewers.[53] There is little other evidence that the cult of Mary was particularly attacked by the reformers. Indeed, other images of Mary – sculptures on the exterior of the church, sculptures and paintings in the interior, and stained-glass windows – were not attacked. It may be that other dimensions of this object's significance made it a target. It was located within the major ecclesiastical structure of Strasbourg, a structure, moreover, dedicated to the Virgin. The altar dedicated to Mary was one of the main altars in the Cathedral. In this, the image and its altar would have been particularly visible. The altar to the Virgin had originally been located in the rood screen also dedicated to the Virgin; in 1264, the administrators of the Cathedral's construction had established an altar in a niche in the screen for the Confraternity of Our Lady, which comprised those families who had donated toward the construction of the Cathedral. They endowed the altar with masses for those who had donated: Each Sunday the priest read the names of the donors, and the pious prayed an Our Father and an Ave Maria for each name read. Those masses had been moved along with the altar in 1306 to the small chapel of Mary on the north side of the nave. The masses continued after the new altar was commissioned in 1483, and expanded: For many of the donors, individual masses were held to commemorate the anniversary of their deaths as well.[54] The image, then, was located on an altar in the Cathedral of particular social and liturgical meaning – an altar, moreover, that had been moved and, in recent memory, had replaced an older, perhaps beloved

---

[52] *Petite Chronique*, pp. 11–15.
[53] Cf. Margaret Miles, *Image as Insight* (Boston, 1985).
[54] Pfleger, *Kirchengeschichte der Stadt Strassburg*, p. 65.

altar. It may also have competed with the high altar, that altar at which masses were read for all the laity, not merely those who could donate.

Two weeks later, on April 15, the Saturday before Easter, a lattice porch (*gerembs*) and altar that stood in the entrance to the Cathedral were smashed at night and taken away. The Cathedral servants and the sexton of the chapel of the Virgin claimed that the "lights had been put out in such a way that it could not have happened otherwise."[55] Was the altar, then, the "idol" to which the six burghers had called attention? The altar was in the location they had named, the entrance to the Cathedral, and it had recently acquired a lattice porch. Did people "bow before it, pray to it, . . . take special pains, when the Word of God was preached, to denigrate the same and to provoke those who desire to hear it"? Did those who practiced the old and false Christianity find in it a support for their beliefs?

In 1526, in Advent, on Monday, December 3, the gilded cross that stood behind the high altar in the choir disappeared.[56] The cross was familiar, one of the most prominent sacred objects in the Cathedral. It was believed to have been donated by Charlemagne, the cost of its material and craftsmanship beyond the reach of other men. In some accounts, the great cross was solid gold, in others gilded silver;[57] in all it was a wondrous work of great beauty and grandeur. Itself wondrous in craft and material, it stood behind the "beautiful" retable Nicolaus of Hagenau had carved for the high altar in 1502, a retable noted for both the intricacy of its woodcarving, its craft, and the beauty of its vision, its visual content.[58] Like the image of Mary and its altar, the great cross was especially visible. So, too, its absence would have been visible.

---

[55] Brant, no. 4604.
[56] Büheler, p. 76; *Petite Chronique*, p. 20; "Imlin'schen Familienchronik," p. 407. According to [F], the Sacrament Shrine [*Sakramentshaüschen*] on the high altar was removed from the Cathedral in January 1527.
[57] It may, therefore, be the same "silver cross" to which the six burghers referred in their petition.
[58] The retable was so impressively carved, "daran alle künstler wohl zu sehen haben," Trausch, II, no. 2634 (p. 30). The retable does not survive today, but seems to have been a victim of the sanctioned iconoclasm of 1530 or 1789.

Another incident in 1526, while not of the same kind of violence, is nonetheless significant in a consideration of iconoclasm. On St. George's Day (April 23), the great bell of the Cathedral, made and hung with such ceremony in 1521, was removed from the bell tower and in the following week smashed before the great doors of the Cathedral.[59] This act was neither secret, hidden from public witness, nor directed against representative art. It was, however, directed against an object integral to the traditional liturgy, to the ringing of the hours – a bell, which, moreover, had been a focus of civic pride for its size.

In the early years of iconoclasm in Strasbourg, the poor were connected to the objects in the churches, both explicitly and obliquely. In the first two incidents, the iconoclasts attacked the idols verbally. Their physical acts consisted in removing money left on the altars, probably for the support of church services and possibly for the support of the altars themselves, and placing it in the alms boxes for the poor. So, too, requests made before the town council connected the church decorations to the poor. On January 8, 1526, the caretaker of the common chest requested that a vacated benefice "to the suffering Cross [*zu dem elenden Critz*]" be transformed into alms. On May 2, 1526, the furrier confraternity demanded that their ornaments, gems, and possessions, previously used in the mass, be divided and half given to alms, half to the smallpox house; the town council granted their demand.[60] The great cross in the Cathedral also may well have been connected to the poor, if obliquely. In their petition of 1525, the six burghers had requested the town council place the "silver idol" in the alms box; in 1526, the great cross was not smashed, its remains left for others to find, but "disappeared," never to be seen again in the form of a cross – probably melted down, perhaps into alms.

The surviving narratives do not mention any acts for 1527 and only one for 1528, when stones reserved for nobles and citizens in the churchyard, "against tradition [*wider das herkommen*]" (gravestones?), were being taken away. The town council admonished "work people" not to remove any stones other than those that were given to them. Iconoclasm may have waned in

[59] Büheler, pp. 69, 75–6.
[60] These two instances are from Brant, nos. 4653 and 4675.

those years, or it may be simply that no records of acts of iconoclasm have survived. We do have evidence, however, that the
conflict over images and altars did not subside: On March 21,
1528, another six burghers petitioned the town council that the
mass, the altars, and also the images, be taken forcefully away
and the honor of God be furthered.[61]

The years 1529–30 marked the culmination of iconoclasm in
Strasbourg. Two acts of physical iconoclasm are recorded for
1529: The first took place during Lent, the second, during the
summer. On Tuesday, March 23, the parishioners of Old St.
Peter's, along with their pastor, Diebold Schwarz, broke up all the
altars and images, removed them from the church, whitewashed
the walls, and "covered the walls with writing, in the place of
the images of the saints."[62] On August 2, Schwarz, who seems to
have been the most actively iconoclastic of the preachers, "of his
own power" struck an image in the Dominican churchyard.[63]

During 1529, the reform preachers pressed with increasing
forcefulness, based quite possibly on greater public support, for the
reformation of Christian practices. Twice in the spring of 1529,
they called for the removal of images from the churches, always
coupling the images with the altars, always framing their discussion of both in terms of idolatry:

> Fifth: There still remain altars and idols at hand, before which
> many carry on idolatry. Since this is very much against God's
> law, we request that you abolish it and put the oil lamps away, so
> that one gives oneself up entirely to God. (May 12, 1529)

> Second: Since it is recognized that the idolatrous images are not to
> be suffered, and in Scripture it is also forbidden to have idols and
> images in those places where one is to honor God, it is our re-
> quest, to remove these, as well as the altar lattice work [*gerems*],
> and also the shield (coats-of-arms), that of pagan craft, which one
> hung there out of worldly desire. (Mittwoch post Florentii XXI)[64]

---

[61] For these events of 1528 see Brant, nos. 4711 and 4721, respectively.
[62] Büheler, p. 78. See also "Imlin'schen Familienchronik," p. 411; Stedel, p. 99; and
Trausch, II, no. 2681.
[63] Brant, no. 4790.
[64] Ibid., nos. 4781 and 4820, respectively.

We shall return below to the linkage of images and altars, and what it meant to label them both idolatrous.

In 1529, the town council responded to the iconoclasts and the preachers. In direct response to the preachers' second petition, the town council ordered the removal

> of all images of false worship and before which one had paid reverence; let stand, however, whatever is not an idolatrous image, but a representation of the suffering of our Lord Jesus Christ. Concerning the altars that still exist at this time, let them remain until another time; so command the alms officers. Concerning the shields and banners: leave them hanging for the time being.[65]

This mandate was followed by another, which underlined one of the difficulties inherent in the position the town council had adopted: "Inform the alms officers which images are idolatrous and which are not, so that they can fulfill their mandate."[66] The preachers had not distinguished between idolatrous and nonidolatrous images in the churches. In words and in acts, the preachers and the iconoclasts had designated *all* images in the churches as idolatrous – for them, there was no distinction between image, *Bild* or *Bildnüss,* and representation, *Bedeutung.* If the town council was seeking with this mandate a middle way – a compromise between those who sought to rid the churches of all images and objects, and those who sought to protect the traditional practice of Christianity and all the objects upon which it depended – it failed: Either images were idolatrous or they were not.

In early 1530, the town council requested the alms officers to remove the idols and the altars from the churches "as previously requested," apparently from churches that had become Protestant.[67] In its directives on images, the town council linked images to altars, as the preachers and some of the iconoclasts had done, and both to the poor, requesting that the alms officers take charge of the removal of images and altars. The town council's choice of alms officers to oversee the removal of images echoes

---

[65] Ibid., no. 4821.
[66] Ibid., no. 4824.
[67] Ibid., no. 4849.

arrangements in Zurich.[68] Other civic officers, such as those in charge of the cloisters, would have been more likely candidates; but the Strasbourg town council had linked the administration of alms with the images and the altars, first turning church ornaments, excluding their silver and gold, over to the alms office; then placing alms officers in charge of the removal of images and altars. In part, it may have been that the town council intended to supply the alms officers with a new source of income; in part, though, it intimates a shift in the basis on which images and altars were evaluated.

At last, on Monday, February 14, 1530, the town council issued a mandate:

> Since the images are completely against God and his order, the images and retables everywhere, along with the altars, should be removed. And in the Cathedral, the Chapter should be shown in a friendly way, that they must also remove the retable in the choir. If they do not wish that the choir be closed, and also the screens be removed, and the retable be returned to whomever it belongs, when they wish it, and that all curates, in the places in the cloisters and the churches where they are curates, ensure that it takes place. If they do not wish to do it, the designated alms officers will do it and ensure compliance with the order in all cloisters, churches, foundations, and pastorates, so that all the retables and altars in all places are removed.[69]

People began soon thereafter to destroy the images. The canons of Young St. Peter complained to the town council that on March 2, 1530, a retable, valued at 500 Gulden, had been smashed. In order to protect another retable in the choir, valued at 1,000 Gulden, along with a number of smaller items, they wished to close the choir. So, too, did the canons of Old St. Peter. The town council denied their requests:

> [S]ince the sermons that have been given frequently up to now inform one sufficiently of the bright and illumined Word of God, that such images are idolatrous, that Scripture is opposed to and angry toward them, the town council announces [*wisst*], in order

---

[68] See my *Always Among Us: Images of the Poor in Zwingli's Zurich* (Cambridge, 1990), esp. chap. 4.
[69] Brant, no. 4849.

that this issue anger no one any further, to bear them no longer, and therefore commands, to remove them in good order.[70]

As noted by Sebald Büheler,

Also in this year they began to break up the altars in Young St. Peter's and in St. Thomas's, as well as the retables, and in the Cathedral, they broke up, completely smashed, and ripped away the retables and other additional objects throughout the night.[71]

The removal of images and altars was neither peaceful nor orderly. Many objects were smashed or torn apart, violently destroyed, before their removal, often without the cooperation of any authority, secular or religious. "That very day [*uff hüt*]," the secular priest in St. Claus monastery took a few soldiers into the church and smashed all the retables and altars, even though the steward was seeking to remove them "that day [*uff hüt*]."[72] According to one chronicler, a retable and other stone images, valued at more than 400 Gulden, were smashed in Young St. Peter's.[73] According to another, the altars and images there were "mischievously thrown out, smashed, and handled to great offense."[74] The Herren zum Spiegel had the massive sculpture of Christ on the Mount of Olives in St. Thomas walled up.[75] The canons of the Cathedral, seeking to protect the choir, asked the town council to forbid anyone to "remove, smash, or throw away any image or other picture in windows or anything else, or to genuflect or burn lights before it."[76]

The town council, however, was no longer willing to protect the objects in the churches. On April 28, 1530, the XXI ordered the Cathedral painted over on the inside, "from top to bottom." On July 6 or 20 (*Mittwoch post Ulrici*), 1530, it denied another request to leave the choir undisturbed and ordered instead that the tabernacle, along with the altar, be removed.[77] The town council

---

[70] Ibid., no. 4853.
[71] Büheler, p. 79.
[72] Brant, no. 4853.
[73] "Imlin'schen Familienchronik," p. 417.
[74] Brant, no. 4853.
[75] This sculpture survived the Reformation and is now located in the Cathedral.
[76] Brant, no. 4853.
[77] Ibid., no. 4878.

agreed that tabernacles and altars were to be removed from the churches; unlike the iconoclasts and the preachers, however, the council did not include banners and coats of arms among those things banished from the churches. That difference is telling, and marks a boundary: The town council distinguished images of false worship from other images in the churches; the preachers and the iconoclasts did not. For them, the interiors of churches needed to be purified of all symbols of "worldly desire," whether they were an immediate component of worship or not: The entire space of the church was to be pure.

The time of iconoclasm

What patterns emerge among the acts of iconoclasm in Strasbourg? Here, too, the chroniclers' interpretive decisions can be our guide. Their structuring of events in temporal sequence, their location of objects within the interiors of specific churches, and their designation of a few of the objects of attack provide us with frames of meaning we may apply in order to discern what the iconoclasts' acts may have meant to their contemporaries – perhaps even to glimpse what meaning the iconoclasts may have sought to convey through their acts.

The most visible frame of meaning, the one with which the chroniclers invariably began, is time. By designating the date of each act, they enable us to see if any patterns of temporal meaning emerge and at what levels: the marking of saints' time, the liturgical divisions of the calendar year into season and week, the secular rhythms of the year of harvest and market times. For example, no particular saints' days anchor the acts of iconoclasm, although celebrations of various saints do provide the occasion for iconoclasm. The acts of iconoclasm offer no pattern within either the secular or the liturgical division of the week: They took place from Sunday evening through Saturday. Nor do particular months appear more prominently in the accounts. It is only at the level of liturgical seasons that iconoclasm acquires temporal pattern: Of fourteen separate incidents, most took place near or during the Lenten season, in February, March, or April; two occurred in late October and November; one during Advent. These were seasons of particular physical reference – the coming and culmination of the Incarnation and the celebration of saints. They were also agricultural seasons, planting and harvest; the latter may have even brought more people into Strasbourg for markets.

Iconoclasm in Strasbourg occurred throughout a six-year period. The very fact of its duration suggests something else about iconoclasm – not so much its inherent meaning, but the contemporary reactions to it. The coincidence of the earlier acts of iconoclasm with the geographically and socially broad violence of the Peasants' War has led some to connect iconoclastic violence to that war. The later incidents of iconoclasm in Strasbourg, however, coincide with no broader political or social violence. In Strasbourg, the fact that attacks against crucifixes, retables, and altars continued persistently over a period of six years suggests little or no decisive opposition on the part of authorities – the absence of legal sources notwithstanding. While we do not have their records, their judgments, the town councilors' ambivalence is visible in the chronicles.

That ambivalence suggests something about the place of iconoclasm within the social and political dynamics of the town: first, that the town councilors may have been unclear how to evaluate the images in the churches. Should the images' characteristic as property, their characteristic as church art, or their function in the liturgy be given precedence in deciding what to do with them? It also suggests that no clear majority – or, as in Zurich, no decisive minority – had emerged. Images were an issue of sustained and substantial debate in Strasbourg. Those who remained loyal to the authority of the bishop and of traditional Christianity sought their protection and, in a number of instances, removed the more portable images, ornaments, liturgical objects, vestments, and altarcloths from the city in order to prevent their destruction. The evangelical preachers sought their removal: Hedio, Capito, and Bucer sought the town council's intervention to have the images removed from the churches;[78] Bucer and Schwarz actively helped their parishioners and audience to remove the

---

[78] See, for example, Brant, nos. 4538 and 4547.

idols from the churches.[79] Throughout, the council neither supported the iconoclasts nor prosecuted them with sufficient force to prevent further acts.

The places of iconoclasm

In Strasbourg, the locations of many of the incidents of iconoclasm correspond with the locations of evangelical preaching. By the summer of 1524, Mattheus Zell was preaching in the St. Lawrence chapel in the Cathedral; Wolfgang Capito was provost of the Chapter at St. Thomas; Caspar Hedio was preaching in the Cathedral; Theobald Schwarz was the preacher in Old St. Peter's; and Martin Bucer, who had preached in the Cathedral, was the pastor of St. Aurelia's. That is not to argue for preachers provoking iconoclasm: In Young St. Peter's, St. Aurelia's, St. Stephen's, and Old St. Peter's, the parishioners had petitioned the town council to appoint the preachers. Rather, it suggests something of a predisposition for evangelicalism in those parishes: Iconoclasts may well have numbered among those seeking an evangelical preacher.

The correspondence of evangelical preaching and iconoclasm suggests a pattern of reform configured to lay religious borders, not clerical. All but one of the acts took place, as in Zurich, in those churches used by the laity:[80] The great majority of acts occurred in the Cathedral; others were in the parish churches of Young St. Peter, St. Aurelia, St. Stephen, St. Martin, and Old St.

---

[79] On the activities of the parishioners of St. Aurelia, whose preacher after 1525 was Martin Bucer, see Brant, nos. 4436, 4545, and 4584; *Petite Chronique*, p. 19; "Imlin'schen Familienchronik," p. 401; Stedel, p. 95. On the activities of the parishioners of Old St. Peter's church, whose preacher after April 1524 was Theobald Schwarz, see Büheler, p. 78; Stedel, p. 99; "Imlin'schen Familienchronik," p. 411; Trausch, II, no. 2681.

[80] In two of the three attacks on the cloisters, first, against the Carthusian house and St. Arbogast in 1524, and third, against the Carthusians again in 1525, the crowd drank all the cloisters' wine and ate their food. In the second, in 1524, a crowd stormed one of the Dominican houses, the parish church of St. Andrew, and the Augustinian house, captured a Dominican preacher and monk, the pastor and his assistant at St. Andrew, and the provincial in the Augustinian house, and turned them over to the town council. In none of these instances were any objects attacked or destroyed, in none were the persons of the religious attacked, Büheler, pp. 73–4.

Peter.[81] Moreover, the reformation of the liturgy – the transformation of the mass, the removal of images, liturgical objects, altarpieces, and altars, the reorganization of the liturgical calendar and week, the cessation of processions both in the parish and within the walls of the churches – took place at the parish level. One by one, the churches that were sites of iconoclasm became evangelical, "reformed."

The spatial pattern of iconoclasm configures to those churches the laity frequented. These churches were not, however, exclusively lay; indeed, for the most part, the sites of iconoclasm were not exclusively lay churches. Only one of the churches was exclusively for the laity: St. Martin's. Iconoclasm mostly took place in churches of mixed domain, lay and religious.[82] All the churches regulated by chapters – the Cathedral, St. Thomas's, St. Aurelia's, Old St. Peter's, Young St. Peter's, and St. Stephen's – were sites of iconoclasm. It may be that iconoclasm was part of a larger pattern of lay conflict with religious. As we have seen in the cases of St. Aurelia's and Old and Young St. Peter's, the parishioners rejected the authority of their chapters to choose priests for them. The parishioners of St. Aurelia, moreover, refused to pay tithes to their chapter; as late as 1529, the town council was still seeking to enforce the chapter's right of tithing and rents.[83] It may be that iconoclasm belongs to a larger effort on the part of the laity to acquire greater independence from religious regulation of parish life. Again, however, the chronicles are silent.

---

[81] Indeed, the churches otherwise were markedly different, varying in age and the size of both the building and its users. Old St. Peter's, according to the Konigshoeven chronicler, was the oldest church; however, its structure dated from 1199, when it was rebuilt in its present location, Lucien Hell, "Zur Baugeschichte der Alt-St. Peterskirche in Strassburg in Mittelalter," *Archiv für Elsässische Kirchengeschichte* 13(1938), p. 356. Its choir was built only in 1455, Büheler, p. 62. Gebwiler places the date of Old St. Peter's move at 1398, p. 60. St. Martin's church, built in 513, may have been the oldest structure, Büheler, p. 45. The Cathedral was the newest structure, not yet complete in 1524. Young St. Peter's was founded in 1031, but its buildings were older, Gebwiler, p. 59.

[82] In this section, I have chosen to use the term "religious" rather than "clerical," in order to underline what separated the clergy from the laity: They lived under a rule, *regula*.

[83] Brant, no. 4791.

It may be that some of the churches themselves fell victim to reform. On January 25, 1529, the town council ordered the demolition of St. Martin's church, "in order that the day laborers earn something in the winter."[84] This church had been one of the parish churches whose parishioners had been active iconoclasts early on, smashing all their altars sometime in March 1524. In 1525, it had been closed, its lay priest sent to St. Stephen's, its parish boundaries redrawn, and its parishioners incorporated into other parishes.[85] Other churches would be demolished as well: the Franciscan cloister in 1529;[86] the cloister St. Arbogast in 1530;[87] Elena church in 1531.[88] By midcentury, the map of religious spaces in Strasbourg was redrawn, the parishes reduced in number, many of the cloisters effaced, transformed into houses for the poor, for orphans, for the sick, for those with smallpox, and one, into a school for poor children.[89]

The configuration of parishes, the geography of religious life within the town, provides one layer of definition for iconoclasm. Another level of spatial organization – the map of sacred and religious spaces within the churches – provides another layer. Iconoclasts did not attack any of the exterior sculpture of the churches, although figures of saints, of Christ, and of the Virgin could be found in abundance on church tympana, façades, and portals. Throughout Strasbourg, church exteriors were undisturbed; nor did they come under consideration by the town council or the preachers for the removal of their sculptural programs. In the great majority of accounts, iconoclasm was enacted *inside* the churches; the only exceptions are the oblique reference to attacks against images in the streets and the case of the cross in St. Aurelia parish. The objects attacked by the iconoclasts belonged to the interiors of churches: Their context was that space, the primary use of which was the worship of God, the division of which sepa-

---

[84] Ibid., no. 4764 (see also no. 4808); also *Petite Chronique*, p. 20; Büheler, p. 78; "Imlin'schen Familienchronik," p. 417; Stedel, pp. 100–1.
[85] Brant, no. 4624.
[86] Büheler puts the date of the demolition of the Franciscan cloister at 1532, p. 47.
[87] Ibid., pp. 50, 79; Stedel, p. 101.
[88] Büheler, p. 79.
[89] Brant, no. 4814; see also the map of parishes in 1570 in Jean-Pierre Kintz, *La société strasbourgeoise 1560–1650* (Paris, 1984), p. 104.

rated lay and clerical modes of worship. Insofar as it is possible, let us seek to envision that context, the population of particular objects and the particular spaces they helped to define.

One church, the Cathedral, must serve us for this exercise: Only for the Cathedral did the chroniclers identify most of the objects the iconoclasts attacked, what they were and where they were located. In part, it speaks of the greater familiarity of the Cathedral to the people of Strasbourg. The Cathedral was the "maior ecclesia Argentinensis civitatis," the preeminent church of the city of Strasbourg. It was known in ways the parish churches were not, its interior familiar to many Strasbourgeois. We have already glimpsed its centrality in the religious life of Strasbourg: Relics were carried from there and returned there in processions in celebration of the Purification of the Virgin; the St. Lux procession brought the people of Strasbourg to its doors. Processions on other feast days, Palm Sunday, St. Mark's Day, and on three days of Rogation Week in celebration of the Ascension, linked the Cathedral to other churches, reinforcing its place as the center of religious life in the city.[90] The objects within the Cathedral, too, would have been familiar. Many had been the pious gifts of the Strasbourgeois to their church.[91] Their location, their visual characteristics, their significance within religious and social frames of meaning would have been known more widely: The geographic boundaries of the Cathedral's population were of different scope and different nature from those of the parishes – in theory, the Cathedral belonged to everyone.

Objects from the Cathedral survive in the Musée de l'Oeuvre Nôtre Dame in Strasbourg, suggesting the density of images within the walls, as well as their subject matter and the variety of their media.[92] Chronicles give some indication of the original location within the structure of the church of altars and chapels, as well as some of the major objects, both surviving and no longer extant.[93] Let us, then, seek to imagine the interior of the Ca-

---

[90] Pfleger, *Kirchengeschichte der Stadt Strassburg*, p. 57.
[91] Ibid., pp. 65–7.
[92] The majority of objects in the Musée are from the exterior of the Cathedral.
[93] For the following description, I have drawn primarily upon *Petite Chronique*, supplemented by various guidebooks to the Cathedral.

thedral of Our Lady of Strasbourg, that most public context for acts
of iconoclasm.

As one entered the nave from the west portal, one might well
see first the rood screen. In place since at least 1252, ancient and
stable, the rood screen served to delineate space. Extending across
the nave from western to eastern piers, just to the west of the transept and fully in the nave, it divided the Cathedral into that area
open to the laity (the nave and its aisles) and that reserved for the
clergy (the choir and apse). Elaborately and intricately carved, it
consisted in seven bays, each topped with sculpture, between
which were fourteen statues of saints and New Testament figures.[94] Like the altar next to which it stood, the rood screen was
dedicated to the Virgin. Recorded first in 1252 and then in an
engraving by I. Braun in 1630, it survived the iconoclasm of
1524–30 only to be torn down, along with the altar to the Virgin,
in 1683.[95] The rood screen was visible from the moment one
entered the church from the west, marking the division of the
religious and liturgical space of the church into that for the laity
and that reserved for the clergy.

To the left of this screen, on the north pier of the nave, was the
chapel of the Virgin, its altar, constructed and dedicated in 1483,
and its elaborately carved and beautifully painted retable, carved
and painted in 1404 and also dedicated in 1483. Set within the
screen was the "front" or high altar, with its important retable,
made by Nicolaus of Hagenau. Behind that altar was the great
cross. As one looked up within the Cathedral, one could see the
dome of the apse, repainted and its woodwork renovated in 1480.
As one entered the nave, one would see the great wooden crucifix, commissioned by a citizen, Hans Vetter, in 1410, and carved
and painted(?) by Michael Böehm.[96] One would also see the altar, with its lattice porch, that stood at the entrance to the Cathedral. To the side, on a column near the Cathedral tower, one
would see the image of Christ, as he carried his cross. To either
side as one walked down the nave were smaller altars, dedicated

---

[94] For the description of the rood screen, I have relied upon Madeleine Klein-
Ehrminger, *Our Lady of Strasbourg Cathedral-Church* (Lyon, 1986), pp. 45–6.
[95] Ibid., p. 7.
[96] Büheler, p. 55.

to those saints who were "lesser" in the Cathedral's hagiography. Perhaps among them was the altar of St. Agnes. Just before the rood screen, on the north wall, one could see the Chapel of St. Michael, built in 1515–21. To the south was the Chapel of the Holy Cross, sometimes called the Chapel of St. Catherine, consecrated in 1338, with its statuary on the pillars. Located throughout the Cathedral – sometimes at altars dedicated to the saints, sometimes elsewhere – were the remains of sacred persons, relics. The Chronicle of the Cathedral lists among the sacred possessions the right hand of John Chrysostom, part of the arm of St. Arbogast, and a finger of St. Peter.[97]

Behind the screen were the transept, the choir, and the apse. To the north of the crossing was the baptismal font, in front of the old St. Lawrence altar, first mentioned in 1181. To the south was the Doomsday pillar, a column upon which were mounted three tiers each of four sculptures, of angels, of the four evangelists, and of Christ. On either side of the apse were the chapels of St. John the Baptist to the north, first noted in 1181, where the baptismal font had originally been located, and of St. Andrew to the south.

One last object needs to be placed within the interior of the Cathedral: the great organ, located on the north side of the nave. Like the choir screen and the columns of the Cathedral, it bore images, plastic and painted. Like the altars and retables, it was essential to the practice of worship in the Cathedral. Like so many of the objects in the Cathedral, it was generated and maintained through pious gift giving: The people of Strasbourg were able to renovate the main organ in 1385, replace it in 1433 and again, in 1489–91, when the great organ was built.[98] It, too, was an object of reverence in the fifteenth century. It, too, was the subject of debate during the reform: In 1529, the town council was advised to demolish it; in 1531, the town council agreed to consider if it should be preserved "for the psalms."[99]

This exercise enables us to imagine that the iconoclasts made choices of what they would attack. The interior of the Cathedral

---

[97] Gebwiler, p. 58
[98] *Petite Chronique*, pp. 10–18. They also built a smaller organ in 1402.
[99] Brant, nos. 4770, 4910.

was dense with images: at least forty altars;[100] multiple retables; a cross and a crucifix; the Doomsday pillar; dozens of carved and painted images; multiple sculptures, some incorporated into larger structures such as the choir screen or the columns; stained-glass windows; the great organ, and a smaller one. There were dozens of "images" in the Cathedral, and each conveyed meaning on multiple layers: as representations of particular saints, or of particular events in the life of Christ; as objects donated by specific persons within the social map of Strasbourg; as places endowed by Strasbourg's pious with special enactments of worship;[101] according to their function within the liturgy; according to their location within the space of the church. The interior of the Cathedral was crowded with images of multiple meaning. Many of them may well have been likely targets, but some among them were successfully attacked. To put it another way, the iconoclasts succeeded in calling to the attention of others, including us, certain of the objects within the Cathedral.

The objects attacked in the Cathedral subsequent to the first violence against "images and altars" – the image of the Virgin, the lattice porch and the altar, and the cross – had specific location in the church's interior space. These objects were located along a central axis of the Cathedral, the nave and crossing, in that part of the Cathedral accessible to the laity. They were also located so as to be visible soon after one entered the Cathedral. At least two of the three served to mark important locations: the altar to the Virgin and the high altar. The altar at the entrance and its lattice porch may have been important as well. In seeing at least two, and perhaps all three of them, one located major altars in the church; one located, in other words, foci of worship – places where the pious would turn their gaze, toward which their attention would be directed. These were places where the laity worshiped God most frequently and publicly.

---

[100] Klein-Ehrminger, *Our Lady of Strasbourg Cathedral-Church,* notes that forty altars were removed in 1529–30, p. 7.

[101] See Rott, *Quellen und Forschungen,* pp. 302–3, on the kinds and numbers of pious bequests for the endowment of masses and the creation of new altars, retables, and images for the churches.

The objects of iconoclasm served to direct the pious eye. Some were also themselves symbols of specific dimensions of that worship. The image of Mary, as it was revealed or enclosed within the retable on the altar to the Virgin, would have helped to mark sacred time: the feasts of the Virgin – her Birth, Presentation, Purification, the Immaculate Conception, the Annunciation, the Visit to Elizabeth, her Motherhood, Sorrows, and Assumption – and the liturgical calendar – Advent, Christmas, Epiphany, Lent, Easter, and Pentecost. The cross, standing "behind" the high altar, was at once connected to the liturgy that took place at the altar and itself a symbol of particular meaning. It served to reinforce the mass's invocation of Christ's passion and the traditional church's reading of that event as a sacrifice. By the sixteenth century, the cross had become an epigram connoting not only the physical destruction of Christ, but the theological interpretations of Christ's pain-filled death. It meant the atonement for human sinfulness; it connoted that essential function as sacrifice that traditional Christian theologians had defined for Christ.

In all, three crosses were attacked in Strasbourg before the official cleansing of the churches: one in Young St. Peter's church in 1524; one near the White Tower gate in St. Aurelia parish in 1525; and the great cross in the Cathedral. The three were of different workmanship and materials; all, however, were striking and visible. The two crosses in the two churches were of "grand" scale, and their locations made them "visible": The cross in Young St. Peter's stood on the rood screen above the main altar, and that in the Cathedral behind the high altar; thus they were at center, both within the interiors of the churches and in the liturgical use of the space. The cross in St. Aurelia parish may have been "visible," too, standing as it did before one of the town gates. All symbolized a particular understanding of the meaning of Christ's life, one that was enacted with each reading of the mass.

The records do not permit the same imagining of the interiors of the other churches, nor the same location of the objects in the geography of piety within the churches. Imagining the interior of the Cathedral, however, helps us glimpse how the interiors of other churches may have looked. Parish churches were of a different scale, their length, width, and height smaller, their interiors slightly closer to human scale. Since we know so little of the population of objects within the churches, we can only speculate on the density of images. They would have had fewer altars – Old St. Peter's, for instance, in 1501 had five altars in addition to the high altar[102] – and fewer retables. As in the Cathedral, sculptures would have adorned columns and niches, carved images hung on walls and rested on shelves, and murals decorated the ceilings of apses and the walls of naves. Fewer of these objects, however, would have been of grand scale. Also, the interiors of the parish churches, unlike that of the Cathedral, were not populated with objects of special renown. We cannot place specific images within the interiors, nor map them with the same detail.

Images and altars

For the most part, the objects attacked in Strasbourg were not designated beyond "image" or "altar." The chroniclers' narratives of iconoclasm in the parish churches point toward another reading of iconoclasm. No longer located with precision within the interior of the churches, nor, for the most part, directed against objects of particular identity, the acts of iconoclasm are accorded broader reference: The iconoclasts attacked neither specific individual images, nor altars to specific saints, but "images and altars" together, of no specific association. For the chroniclers the focus of attack was significant not through reference to particular saints, donors, moments in the life of Christ, nor through its location within the particular map of religious space within an individual church. It was not what they represented, but what objects themselves were, qua objects – their genus, not their species – that was significant.

Thus we move to a level of abstraction, to speak of "images and altars" in general. In this, the chroniclers echo the language of the town council and the preachers: They, too, did not distinguish among the images and objects. We have some evidence that the iconoclasts may have shared this view of the images as

[102] Hell, "Zur Baugeschichte der Alt-St. Peterskirche," p. 372.

generically wrong: The earliest physical acts of iconoclasm, in the Cathedral and St. Aurelia's church in October 1524, were directed against "all" the altars and images (and, presumably, many were in fact damaged or destroyed). The objects of this early attack represented nothing in particular, they had no specific meaning. It is what they represented in general – what they were to the iconoclasts – to which we now turn.

From the start in Strasbourg, iconoclasm was linked to altars: The first invocation of the idols occurred before an altar; the earliest physical attacks against images were simultaneously directed against altars. Subsequent acts of iconoclasm physically attacked altars as well as images. In linking images to altars, iconoclasts emphasized one particular frame of meaning for their acts: the liturgy.

At the same time that retables, images, and altars were subject to physical attacks, the evangelicals were calling for the reform of the mass. On the Tuesday before Ash Wednesday, February 16, 1524, in the St. Lawrence Chapel of the Cathedral, Diebold Schwarz read the mass in German.[103] During Lent, in the crypt of the Cathedral, he read the mass in German, which was also done in St. Martin's and St. Thomas's churches, and offered the sacrament in both kinds to the laity.[104] In 1525, the town council forbade the images to be hung or bedecked in any way, the Lenten veil to be hung, palms or baptismal oil to be blessed, and ordered "the sacramentals [*sacramenta*] to be removed during Lent."[105] In this same time, the German mass was halted, the reformed service of the Lord's Supper begun,[106] and the town council forbade anyone to drape or serve the altars, images, and crucifixes, or to hang the Lenten veil. On April 6, almost three weeks after Easter, the town council forbade all the cloisters to sing or read masses; thereafter, only the four chapters were to be allowed to read the mass, and then only once daily.[107] The

---

[103] Stedel, pp. 92–3.
[104] *Petite Chronique*, pp. 18–19.
[105] Büheler, p. 75.
[106] This service, which replaced the mass, sought to reenact the Last Supper: The preacher stood before a simple wooden table; the bread (no longer on the paten) and wine were served in simple containers, plate and cup, to all the congregation.
[107] "Imlin'schen Familienchronik," p. 402.

canonical hours were no longer to be observed: Masses would no longer serve to mark sacred time. Furthermore, the Salve was no longer to be sung in the Cathedral and other churches.[108]

> Now gracious Lords, sworn and eminent, may it be not entirely bearable to you as Christians, that so many godless masses are held daily, which are grimly adorned [*grümlich geschmucht*] through the suffering of Christ. For the mass makers, without any command or word of God having been given, sacrifice the body and blood of Christ for living and dead, for the favor of their sins, everything that Christ had offered one time on the cross for all believers. . . . there is not, however, one word in all of divine scripture of such a mass. Therefore must it certainly come from the devil, that one may take of the fruits so well, for through the mass the most shameful whores and knaves and hypocrites, to the depravity of the poor in soul and body, have lived in all violation and mischievousness until now, are increased and maintained, as your gracious Lords not only hear in sermons, but also must know yourselves in your hearts. (Petition of Six Burghers, March 1525)[109]

The evangelicals did not seek the right to hold the Lord's Supper according to the Gospel. This they had accomplished in 1525. They sought instead the unity of worship: the eradication of any enactment of the traditional mass, by any person, lay or clerical, in any location, religious or secular, public or private. For them,

> masses are such an abomination before God and false worship, that no greater abomination or stronger blasphemy has ever been found on the earth or ever will be found, for they are a perversi-

---

[108] Ibid., p. 407; Stedel, p. 98.

[109] "[N]uon gnedigen herren, beschwert und höchlich, und mag E.g. So ir christen gantz nit lidlich sin, das man so vil gottloser messen täglich haltet, da duerch das liden christi gruom=lich geschmucht würt, dann so die Messmacher on allen befelch und wort gottes fürgeben, den lib und blout Christi für lebendig und todten zuo oepfern, zuo guengchuen irer sünd, das alles Christus ein al am craitz für alle glouebigen hat uoss gericht, . . . so hat man doch in aller göttlicher geschrifft von solcehn messen ein wort nit, Doruomb es gewislich vom tüfel muoss her komen das man wol an den fruechten abneme mag, dann duerch das messen, die schentlichen huoren und buoben und glyssner zuo verdörbnüss der armen an seel und lib in allem bracht und muotwillen lbebn bissher uff komen, gemert, und erhalten sind, wie E. g. das nit allein täglich prödigen hört, sonder selb im hertzen also sin erkennen muoss." AST 87, no. 29.

ty and a public defamation of all the most holy worship and greatest honor, that men have ever created or might create, namely the most holy death of Our Lord Jesus Christ, His most beloved Son, who alone is so pleasing to God, that for that reason he is blessed [*gnedig*] (Preachers' Supplication Concerning the Mass, 1527)[110]

Again and again, the reformers spoke of the mass as a "great blasphemy."[111] It did not merely fail to please God, it was an affront, an active assault against God. It was not sufficient for the reformers to have gained the right to practice their own form of worship. It was necessary for those forms of worship that actively dishonored God to be eradicated.

It was difficult for the reformers to convince the town council of the necessity of the unity of the practice of Christianity throughout the town. Unlike in Zurich, where the reform of the liturgy had been swift and complete, the Strasbourg town councilors addressed the practices of traditional Christianity piecemeal. In 1525, the town council acted, perhaps in the wake of the iconoclasm in the Cathedral during Lent, to stop various practices of the traditional church. On April 3, the council agreed to halt all ceremonies, "namely Palmday, [no longer] to lay our Lord God in the grave on Good Friday, to wave no palms, [to have] no foot-washing, also no baptism with holy oil, throughout Lent." On April 10, they forbade the cloistered to hear any confessions or to give the people the sacrament. The cloistered were allowed to read or sing only one mass each day, for which the churches were to be held open to the people. Otherwise the churches were to be kept closed: Even if they wished to sing or read the hours, the doors were to be closed.[112]

As late as 1527, the town council's legislation remained within traditional delimitations of lay authority in the practice of reli-

---

[110] "Praedikantsupplik der Messe halben," *Martin Bucers Deutsche Schriften*, vol. 2, *Schriften der Jahre 1524–1528*, ed. Robert Stupperich (Gütersloh/Paris, 1962), p. 506.

[111] This language appears in a number of petitions the preachers presented to the town council during the years 1525–9. See *Martin Bucers Deutsche Schriften*, vol. 2: sec. 3. This language is echoed in Brant, no. 4721, another supplication of six burghers, this time against the mass, March 21, 1528.

[112] Stedel), p. 97.

gion: On April 1, the town council forbade any burgher to hear any confession in the choir of the Cathedral or give any sacrament, any woman to enter the choir, or anyone to burn any lights before the sacrament, under penalty of a fine.[113] Not until 1529 did the town council forbid the mass to be read in those four chapter churches that had retained the privilege since 1525, although it provided that "nonetheless, if it could be proven with Holy Scripture, that it was right, it should be reinstituted as before."[114] Even in 1529, as the evangelicals recognized, the possibility that the people of Strasbourg might return to traditional Christian practices remained real.

In Strasbourg, as elsewhere, the people did not wait for the magistrates to legislate reform. The demands of their theology were too pressing. They acted early on to alter the form and place of worship.

> 1525 the German mass was put away in Strasbourg and the Lord's Supper begun for which specific altars in the churches were made over. In the same fasttime, my Lords forbid in all churches and cloisters anyone to bedeck [*aufbutzen*] or serve at the altars and crucifixes, or to hang up the Lenten veil as had been done in the past. . . . In this time the Sacrament was removed from all of the churches. (Johannes Stedel) [115]
>
> Sixth, they complain that we have erected special altars: to which we say no. We need no altars, for we sacrifice no outward sacrifice than our own body. . . . [W]e have had a comfortable table and footing made for this and turn ourselves directly to the people, because we will talk with them and in order that the prayer be in common and they should understand every word. (The Preachers' Response, February 13, 1525)[116]

On December 16, 1525, a wooden altar was built to replace the city's altar at the rood screen in the Cathedral. All the liturgical objects and clothes were removed from it and put away, and the Lord's Supper was offered.[117] For the reformers, the altars were not merely a symbol of the mass; they were its locus, its base.

[113] "Imlin'schen Familienchronik," p. 408.
[114] Stedel, pp. 98–9.
[115] Ibid., p. 97.
[116] "Der predicanten verantworten," *Martin Bucers Deutsche Schriften*, vol. 2, p. 446.
[117] *Petite Chronique*, p. 19.

The mass took place before and upon the altars. They were its physical foundation, the surface upon which the implements of the mass rested – the paten, the chalice, the monstrance, the host, and the wine. The stone and marble carved and hewn into this particular form had been consecrated to this one function. At altars, the traditional church's reenactment of Christ's sacrifice was performed again and again. As early as 1525, the reformers had built a different locus for their reformed liturgy: a wooden table at which no objects of the mass were to have a place. As early as 1525, the reformers had recognized the interdependence of mass and altar, the dependence of false worship upon a particular physical context.

The images belonged to the old altars: They rested upon them or hung near them. Some images were integrated into the sacred rhythms that were marked at the altars. Images of Christ, Mary, or the saints were hung with cloths, retables opened or closed to mark religious seasons. Images helped mark those places within the churches where old forms of worship were enacted.

The images' *Abgötterei,* their idolatry, lay not in drawing men's eyes away from God. The burghers, the preachers, and the iconoclasts did not speak of the images in these terms. The images' idolatry was of a different kind, linked to the mass, to its "blasphemy," its denigration of Christ's sacrifice "one time at the cross for all believers." Standing upon the altars and integrated into the mass, the images helped reaffirm a particular conception of Christ's life, a particular interpretation of the meaning of His life and, more disturbingly, his death. Like the mass and the altars, the images did not commemorate Christ's life and death for their wonder and the grace they bestowed; the altars participated in that ritual that reenacted Christ's death again and again, as though that one great sacrifice had not sufficed for all humankind for all time.

The idolatry of the images and the altars was also linked to the multiplicity of altars. It was linked to the plurality of places at which people called upon God, places that had been instituted out of private interests and private desires. In order to regain this dimension of the reformers' conception of idolatry, we must imagine how the interiors of the churches were transformed in 1530:

Anno domini 1530. All the painted retables, images, and crucifixes, as well as the altars were taken away and the places where
they stood all painted over in stone-color, so that one did not see
where they had stood.[118]

The destruction of the altars in 1530 shattered the locations for
the practice of the traditional mass. Equally significant, it reduced the numbers of altars in each of the churches: No one was
to know anymore "where they had stood." The destruction of
the altars ensured that the worship of God would no longer occur
in ever more places within the churches in ever greater frequen-
cy. It brought to a halt the centuries-old tradition of the endowment of altars and masses, endowments that accrued over time.
In the fourteenth century alone, 140 benefices had been endowed for the reading of masses; in the Cathedral, more than
thirty altars had been endowed with even more daily masses.
Many of these endowments created positions, prebends, the sole
function of which was to read a mass once a day. By the middle
of the fifteenth century, there were 116 chaplains and prebends
in the Cathedral, 31 in St. Peter's, and 26 in St. Thomas's, the
function of each of whom was the reading of masses.[119] By the
beginning of the sixteenth century, each of the churches
possessed multiple altars, built at considerable expense,[120] at
which masses were read, at some more than once a day. Moreover, much of that worship had a kind of specificity: The masses
were read, for the most part, for specific persons within the parish, families or guilds, and not for the entire community, parish,
city, or the body of Christian believers.

... we should acknowledge and set all our hope on it, for which
the Lord instituted his Supper, that is to say, that he gave us his
body and blood for the eternal redemption and righteousness [*er-
loesung und uffrichtong*], the New covenant and eternal Testament,
that we are the children and heirs of God, which we should, as
we gather together, observe and, as we eat the bread in common,
as Paul says, and drink from the chalice, proclaim and praise his

[118] Ibid., p. 20.
[119] Pfleger, *Kirchengeschichte der Stadt Strassburg*, pp. 123–4.
[120] An altar the canons of Old St. Peter's commissioned for the choir from Veit
Wagner cost "200R," Trausch, I, no. 2633.

death, that we would be strengthened in belief in Him and love for our neighbor in all zeal and patience. (Preachers' Supplication Concerning the Mass, 1527)[121]

The multiplicity of private chapels, of altars belonging to various families or guilds, were not merely to be removed; they were to be erased. There would no longer be multiple and separate loci for worship. The spaces in the reformed churches had as their center one table, to which the entire congregation would turn. The eyes of the faithful would not be distracted by images in the nave, the aisles, on tabernacles; the body of the faithful would not be fragmented by multiple foci of worship, by multiple masses offered for individuals, families, or specific guilds. In 1530, with the removal of all the altars, the crucifixes, and the images, the geography of piety within the church, with all its reference points, was redrawn.

The interiors of the churches were transformed: No longer would the eyes of the faithful encounter the exquisite choir screens, the elaborately carved and delicately painted retables, the massive and expensive altars, the beautifully crafted altarcloths, monstrances, patens, and chalices. Rood screens would no longer divide the churches into spaces for two kinds of use, lay and clerical. Retables and images would no longer mark the rhythms of traditional Christian liturgy. Crucifixes would no longer contribute to the interpretation of the liturgy; they had no place in the Lord's Supper. Altars would no longer provide the foundation for the traditional liturgy, nor mark the many places it was enacted; and the objects of that liturgy, the patens, chalices, monstrances, would no longer have a resting place, a location to which they belonged. These objects, rood screen, retables and images, and altars had no place in reformed churches.

No longer visible, these things would no longer shape the reception of the Eucharist. They would not reinforce visually the division of Christians into lay and clerical, the cadences of liturgical time, the multiplicity of the mass. Indeed, the mass itself no longer had a place. It could not be enacted without its base or

---

[121] "Praedikantsupplik der Messe halben," *Martin Bucers Deutsche Schriften*, vol. 2, p. 506.

146

its implements. Nor could its false meaning be disseminated: No symbols remained in the churches to convey its traditional reading. In eliminating the old context of the mass – the screens, the retables, the images, and the altars – the reformers enabled a new conception of the central event of Christian liturgy. When the faithful entered the reformed churches, their eyes encountered walls painted with words of the Bible and saw simple tables. Their minds were offered images not of sacrifice, but of disciples patiently recording the words of their Lord, and of a simple meal shared among a circle of believers.

Iconoclasm in Strasbourg did not have closure, as it did in Zurich. The town council's decree did not mark a moment of relative consensus. There was not, as there had been in Zurich, a clear and unitary vision of the reformed Christian community.[122] The removal of objects was not complete in 1530: Certain objects survived to rest, finally, in the Musée de l'Oeuvre de Nôtre Dame. Nor did removal cease at that time: In 1534, the gravestones were removed from the Cathedral, their places erased with the placement of smooth stones.[123] Moreover, unlike Zurich, which lay peacefully within the Swiss Confederation, Strasbourg was a border city, resting on the ever-shifting boundary between two states of differing confessions. Its religious life not only followed the smaller currents of internal divergences, but was swept by larger political tides as the French king and the Habsburg emperor pursued the "natural" borders of their states. In 1681, Strasbourg would be annexed to France by Louis XIV, a monarch who successfully pursued a policy of religious uniformity. The churches in Strasbourg, mute witnesses to its history, were "recatholicized" under Louis, the Cathedral's interior once again embellished with multiple elaborate altars and retables; and when France herself became iconoclastic in 1792–3, they were attacked again, this time in the name of the Cult of Reason.

[122] This is Jane Abray's compelling argument in *The People's Reformation*.
[123] Büheler, p. 81; also Stedel, p. 117.

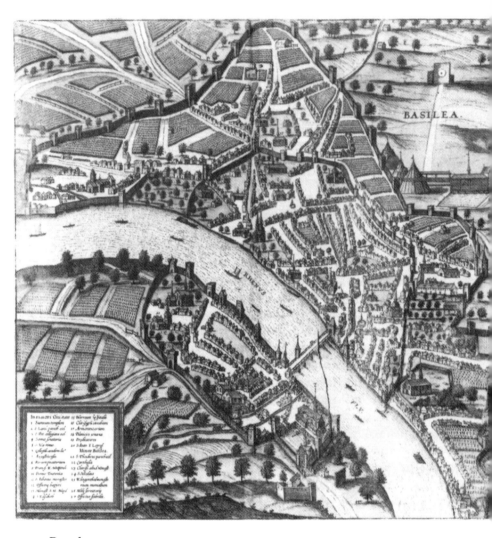

Basel. *Source:* Georg Braun & Frans Hogenberg, *Civitates orbis terrarum,* vol. II (1575). Beinecke Rare Book and Manuscript Library, Yale University.

4

Basel

Sometime after noon on Tuesday, February 9, 1529, residents of Basel, numbering some two hundred according to most accounts, mounted the hill on which the Cathedral stood, entered the church, chopped up the rood screen, altarpieces, and panel paintings, and smashed statues, crucifixes, reliquaries, monstrances, patens, chalices, and lights. From the Cathedral, the iconoclasts moved to the parish churches of St. Ulrich's, St. Alban's, and St. Peter's, smashing the objects in each of these churches in Grossbasel.[1] They were finally persuaded to stop about four in the afternoon, before crossing the Rhine to Kleinbasel, but after some three hours of iconoclasm. On the following day, the town council oversaw the completion of the iconoclasm: Stone and ivory objects were smashed into pieces; everything made out of wood – retables, screens, panel paintings, sculpture – was burned in fires before the churches. By Wednesday evening, almost all the objects in the churches had fallen either to the iconoclasts' axes and hammers or to the fire.[2]

The iconoclasm that took place in Basel on February 9, 1529, was among the most dramatic: in the number of iconoclasts, in breadth of destruction, and in its violence against the objects in

[1] Grossbasel is to the south of the Rhine, and Kleinbasel, to the north.
[2] "Chronik des Fridolin Ryff 1514–1541," printed in *Basler Chroniken* [hereafter *BC*], vol. I, ed. Wilhelm Vischer & Alfred Stern (Leipzig, 1872), pp. 80–9; "Die Chronik des Konrad Schnitts 1518–1533," *BC* vol. VI, ed. August Bernoulli (Leipzig, 1902), pp. 115–17; *Johannes Kesslers Sabbata*, ed. Emil Egli & Rudolf Schoch (St. Gall, 1902), pp. 301–3; Oecolampad to Wolfgang Capito, 13 February 1529, *Briefe und Akten zum Leben Oekolampads*, ed. Ernst Staehelin, vol. II (Leipzig, 1934), no. 636.

the churches. Basel differed, moreover, in one way from other broad acts of destruction in the early years of the Reformation, such as took place in Bern: No authority, secular or ecclesiastical, sanctioned it – it was illegal. Thanks, perhaps, in part to famous witnesses such as Erasmus of Rotterdam, it became the most famous of all the iconoclasms that occurred before midcentury. Only Huguenot riots in France in 1560–1 and the Wonder Year in the Netherlands of 1566–7 matched in intensity the reverberations among those witnesses both local and distant who recorded their observations. With Basel, we have come from a handful of iconoclasts to a crowd of two hundred or more, from attacks on single objects to iconoclasm against all the objects, from one church at a time to all those as yet unreformed. Even though, by 1529, contemporary observers had heard of dozens of incidents of iconoclasm, they were, for the most part, astonished and unprepared for the violence they witnessed at Basel: It had, for them, no precedent. Even though the Basel iconoclasm came near the end of all iconoclastic incidents in the early years of reform in German-speaking Europe, its violence was still unfamiliar, forbidden, taboo.[3]

Perhaps even more than other incidents of iconoclasm, the Basel iconoclasm offers no easy access to interpretation. The contemporaries' astonishment suggests that they, at least, saw no preceding events that could explain it. Dozens of incidents of blasphemy had been recorded. Many individuals had attacked and sometimes destroyed single images: Fridlin Yberger had struck the crucifix he carried from a chapel in St. Alban's church; Urban Schwarz had attacked the crucifix before St. Johanntor; Hans Stucki had demolished a number of saints' images; Hanns Bertschi had shattered stained-glass windows in the Cathedral; Hans Ludi of Waldenberg had attacked the relics and images in St. Peter's church; Jacob Hurling had verbally attacked a crucifix, candles, Marian worship, and described the mass as cannibal-

---

[3] *Aktensammlung zur Geschichte der Basler Reformation in den Jahren 1519 bis Anfang 1534* [hereafter ABR], 5 vols.; vol. III: *1528 bis Juni 1529*, ed. Paul Roth (Basel, 1537), nos. 374–6, 381–7 [all citations in ABR refer first to volumes, then to document nos.]. Most of my source citations are drawn from ABR, which contains most of the pertinent documents accurately transcribed.

ism.[4] There had been widespread destruction of images and objects in St. Martin's and the Augustinian churches, and subsequent calls for the elimination of the "idols" in all the other churches by Pentecost. All these incidents and the increasingly insistent and forceful demands of the evangelical citizens for the abolition of the mass and the institution of evangelical preaching in all the churches did not seem, at least to most local chroniclers or distant observers, to foreshadow iconoclasm of such force, such complete destruction, such widespread participation. Those who offer some narrative of explanation do not agree on the background to the iconoclasm or its catalyst: The chronicler Fridolin Ryff argues that the town council had provoked the citizens of Basel to action; the chronicler Konrad Schnitt suggests that evangelical preaching had moved the people of Basel to such violence; and the more distant observer, Johannes Kessler, places Basel iconoclasm within larger movements of reform, inexorable in their progress toward reformation.

That iconoclasm left few clues in its wake. The "mob" remains faceless; no one was willing to admit that he or she had participated in it, even though the council would issue a blanket pardon for all iconoclasts on February 12, only three days after the event. No single object, with its own location and context, was its focus. The iconoclasm occurred on the day of Shrove Tuesday for many towns, but Basel traditionally celebrated Carnival six days later, following the old method of reckoning the length of Lent. To contemporaries, it seemed unprecedented; to us, like so many other incidents of iconoclasm, it offers only its location and the date on which it took place as initial entrées into its meaning.

Both location and time are rich in meaning, as we shall see, if first we accord them a "thickness" of their own. The following section seeks, therefore, to sketch in detail the "place" of the iconoclasm of February 9: the town of Basel and within it, the Cathedral. The Cathedral signified a great deal to sixteenth-century

---

[4] ABR, vol. I: *1519 bis Juni 1525,* ed. Emil Durr (Basel, 1921), 192, 336; vol. II: *Juli 1515 bis Ende 1527,* ed. Emil Durr & Paul Roth (Basel, 1933), 197, 439, 725; vol. III, 209.

residents of Basel – not only the primary church, with its specific organization, but also a clergy whose practices had troubled for a very long time. The subsequent section takes up the narrative of one witness, to locate the iconoclasm within the human dynamics of Basel: between laity and clergy, "commons" and magistrates, evangelicals and those still loyal to Rome. The final section takes up the timing, and explores what meaning that one chronicler might wish to have invoked, to have attached to the iconoclasm of February 9.

The setting

The violence of the Basel iconoclasm was famous in part because it was so pronounced. Set against a background of settlement and learned civility, the iconoclastic hands, raising axes and hammers, were all the more prominent; the fires the following day, consuming the shattered remains of hundreds of beloved images and treasured objects, all the more shocking. To most contemporaries, from the town council to that shrewd and articulate observer, Erasmus, Basel was not a place of violence or conflict, but an ancient, settled place that had become one of the most civilized towns in the early sixteenth century. Something about the place where the Rhine turns from its westward course northward, heading toward the North Sea, and where the Birs, Birsig, and Wiese flow from the surrounding mountains into the Rhine, had drawn people to settle there earlier than in Strasbourg or Zurich. The Celts had domiciled there long before Rome would establish an outpost, even longer before the Christian diocese would claim Basel as its see.[5] Even as the Rhine rhythmically reasserted its fierce power, flooding its banks, washing away the bridge, making evident how precarious human settlement at Basel was, people would build a chapel at the bridge, honoring those who survived and stayed. By 1500, some nine thousand people lived in Basel proper – less than half the population of

---

[5] René Teuteberg, *Basler Geschichte* (Basel, 1986), chaps. 5 and 6, provides a brief summary of this early history.

Strasbourg, but nearly double that of Zurich – once again on the rise from the drop a half-century earlier.[6]

In the years immediately preceding the Reformation, Basel drew men of wondrous talent and dazzling learning, some to put down roots, all to remain for a while and contribute to the town's reputation. The humanist Aeneas Silvius Piccolimini had been enchanted by the town during his stay there; as Pope Pius II, he chartered a university that would itself draw scholars to teach or merely to partake of the intellectual life the university enabled.[7] Sebastian Brant traveled from his home in Strasbourg to Basel in 1475, where he would stay for some twenty-five years, write and first publish the *Ship of Fools* in 1494. In particular, Basel drew a luminous circle of humanists to live within its walls, to work intimately with its book industry, its internationally famous publishers, Amerbach, Petri, and Froben, its book printers, some seventy in the early years of the sixteenth century, and the dozens of talented engravers and woodcarvers who supplied its beautiful fonts and illustrations.[8] The quality of the publishing house of Froben had drawn Erasmus there in 1514;[9] and he, in turn, became the pole toward which other humanists, many already in residence, would turn: Glareanus, Reuchlin, Beatus Rhenanus, Hutten, and Erasmus's friend and collaborator on the New Testament, Johannes Oecolampad. So, too, artists, such as Hans Holbein the Younger from Augsburg and Urs Graf, would come to work for the presses, the town council, and the religious, designing title-page prints and illustrations, murals, and portraits. Hol-

---

[6] Hektor Ammann, "Die Bevölkerung von Stadt und Landschaft Basel am Ausgang des Mittelalters," *Basler Zeitschrift für Geschichte und Altertumskunde* 49 (1950): 37.

[7] The fullest history of Basel to 1529 is Rudolf Wackernagel, *Geschichte der Stadt Basel*, 3 vols. (Basel, 1907–24). Paul Roth provides a narrative of the years 1528–9 in *Durchbruch und Festsetzung der Reformation in Basel; Eine Darstellung der Politik der Stadt Basel im Jahre 1529 auf Grund der öffentlichen Akten* [Basler Beiträge zur Geschichtswissenschaft, vol. VIII] (Basel, 1942). Hans Guggisberg's *Basel in the Sixteenth Century: Aspects of the City Republic before, during, and after the Reformation* (St. Louis, 1982) provides a brief but excellent study of Reformation Basel in English, with extensive notes.

[8] Guggisberg, *Basel in the Sixteenth Century*, chap. 1.

[9] In 1514, Erasmus remained for about a year and a half; in 1521, he moved to Basel, calling it then his home. He left in February 1529, but returned, to die there in 1536. No place else offered him the density of friendship (England offered his dearest friendship, More), and no place else offered him a publisher as understanding as Froben.

bein was resident in Basel for most of his early years of artistic production, working for Froben, providing illustrations for Erasmus's *Praise of Folly*, the Bible, and other works, as well as paintings commissioned by secular and religious patrons.[10] Huldrych Zwingli came to Basel to study, first as a young man sometime before 1498, again in 1502–6, to matriculate at the 40-year-old university, and again sometime in 1514–16, when he would meet Erasmus. In September 1529 he returned to Basel, this time as the prominent and hunted reformer of Zurich, on his way to the Marburg Colloquy, who was to be joined by his trusted friends, Oecolampad in Basel and then Martin Bucer in Strasbourg.[11] The Zurich iconoclast and later Anabaptist, Lorentz Hochrütiner, would turn up in Basel in August 1525 and July 1526;[12] and others, such as John Calvin, who would publish the first edition of the *Institutes of the Christian Religion* in Basel, would be drawn to a city that was seeking to distinguish between accommodation and compromise in its pursuit of reform.

In the early years of the sixteenth century, the preeminent political identity of Basel was civic: It considered itself first a city republic. Like Zurich, Basel was governed by a town council of two chambers: the Small Council (*kleiner Rat*) and Great Council (*großer Rat*).[13] The Small Council was the final arbiter of all political decisions. From it the *Bürgermeister* and the *Oberzunftmeister,* the Master of Guilds, were chosen. Each of Basel's fifteen guilds contributed two guildmasters and two councilors to the Small Council, one of each was to sit each year, the "new," while the other was emeritus, the "old"; in fact, by the sixteenth century, both new and old guildmasters and councilors sat together in order to ensure continuity of policy. The members of the Small Council belonged automatically to the Great Council, which

---

[10] Holbein arrived in Basel by 1515, departed briefly for France and for two years in England in 1526, returned in 1528 and purchased a house in Basel, only to return to England in 1532, where he would die eleven years later, *Contemporaries of Erasmus: A Biographical Register of the Renaissance and Reformation*, ed. Peter G. Bietenholz & Thomas Deutscher, vol. 2 (Toronto, 1986), pp. 194–5.

[11] G. R. Potter, *Huldrych Zwingli* (New York, 1977), pp. 1–2, 92–3.

[12] ABR II, 46 & 455.

[13] For the political constitution of Basel, I have relied upon Hans Füglister, *Handwerksregiment: Untersuchungen und Materialien zur sozialen und politischen Struktur der Stadt Basel in der ersten Hälfte des 16. Jahrhunderts* (Basel & Frankfurt a.M., 1981).

comprised the "Six" (*Sechser*) of the guild regiments, four of the Kleinbasel patricians, the *Schultheißen* of the two civic courts, as well as a changing number of men elected from the guild commons or *Zunftgemeinde,* for a normal total of about 250 members. The Great Council was usually called to sanction decisions of the Small Council or, "in times of social or political tension, to ensure [the Small Council] of the loyalty of the guild commons."[14] Thus, the practice of politics in Basel more closely approximated that of Strasbourg: A much smaller circle of men, drawn from a narrower range of professions, were in fact making decisions concerning the economic, financial, commercial, social, and political life of the town. Indeed, by the end of the fifteenth century, according to Füglister, the ruling elites of Basel had moved to a system even closer to that of Strasbourg, in which less public organs of government, such as privy councils and smaller offices, were the location for many of the most significant decisions concerning public life in Basel. Parallel to Strasbourg, though not identical, was the social composition of those smaller organs: The most prosperous guildsmen were also the most prominent politically, serving frequently and for long duration in the Small Council and in those offices that had acquired great authority by the sixteenth century. In Basel, as in Strasbourg, it was possible, moreover, for a man to belong to more than one guild: in practice, the guild of his father, as well as a poorer guild, through which he had easier access to political office. Thus, the "guild regime" of Basel more closely approximated the stratified political life of Strasbourg than the more fluid arrangement in Zurich.

Basel had not always been a city republic. Like Strasbourg, Basel was the see of a bishopric, an ecclesiastical administrative center with suzerainty over extensive lands.[15] For some thousand years, along with Strasbourg, Basel had floated in the ebbing and flowing of different dynastic powers: Carolingian, Burgundian,

---

[14] Ibid., p. 138.

[15] On the many ties, administrative and cultural, between Strasbourg and Basel, see Hans R. Guggisberg, "Strasbourg et Bâle dans la Réforme," in *Strasbourg au cœur religieux du XVIe siècle,* ed. Georges Livet & Francis Rapp (Strasbourg, 1977), pp. 333–40.

Habsburg. It had never been fully integrated into any one of these domains, always retaining an autonomy, a clear political and economic identity as urban commune. It would not be until 1501, when Basel chose to join the Swiss Confederation, that its political boundaries would be set, its political identity anchored in all the Confederation would come to symbolize in the early sixteenth century.[16]

The beneficiaries of that shifting political boundary were the churches and religious in Basel. In their efforts to hold Basel's loyalties, the kings of Burgundy, especially Rudolf II and III, had bestowed chapels and altars in its churches and privileges and benefices on its clergy. The emperor, Henry II, who had formally assumed rule over Basel from his childless uncle, Rudolf III, in the eleventh century, had been even more generous. The golden altarpiece, treasured by people of Basel and now in the Cluny Museum in Paris, was one of his gifts to the city. The residents of Basel had commemorated what they believed was his greatest gift to their town in a statue, dating from roughly 1290, that stands on the west portal of the Cathedral. The emperor, elegant and sinewy in the high gothic style, his power and dominion signaled by his crown and scepter, holds in his right hand a miniature of the Cathedral: His gift had been the construction of the current Cathedral, less grand than the one in Strasbourg, but sharing its exuberant Rhine Gothic style, its delicate stonework, its airiness and technical mastery. Completed in less than twenty years, consecrated on October 11, 1019, the church had been a physical reminder to all people of Basel of imperial power and the imperial patronage of the bishops of Basel.[17]

It is not clear when the bishopric was first established in Basel: We know only that from 740 onward, Basel had served continuously as the seat of its diocese. The bishopric was an office linked by patronage to the emperor and by birth to the nobility of surrounding lands. The medieval bishops of Basel seem to have been less a force for religious reform and less autonomous of the emperor than their counterparts in Strasbourg. The bishops of

---

[16] Thomas A. Brady, Jr., *Turning Swiss: Cities and Empire 1450–1550* (New York, 1984).
[17] After the earthquake of 1356, the pope would promulgate indulgences, and the people of Basel would donate to repair the damage and to complete the west tower.

Basel formed a nexus in a web of connections of privilege, receiving from kings and then emperors lands, incomes, and exemptions from local taxes and duties. At the same time they were acquiring, up to the early fourteenth century, greater authority over the life of the town. That authority was less and less circumscribed, even as the bishops themselves became less and less connected to the town: Four bishops of the late thirteenth century spoke only French and could not make themselves understood to the town council or many of the town's religious.[18] By the sixteenth century, the bishops were more solidly linked to imperial nobility than they were to the town that was moving to sever the Holy Roman Empire's dominion over it.

The Cathedral of Basel was home to a chapter of particular arrogance.[19] The chapter overlooked the town, but its canons were not of the town: The oldest foundation in Basel,[20] the Cathedral chapter had refused all citizens of Basel entrance into its ranks since 22 March 1337. Over the following two centuries, it would fight not only the Basel town council, but the bishop and even the Pope to ensure that each of its twenty-four canons was noble in birth – preferably from noble houses far removed from Basel – and that each would have few familial or personal ties to the predominantly mercantile and artisanal town populace. Indeed, in 1470, the canons would tighten the regulations for entrance into the chapter: Even those people of Basel who attained prominence through study at their newly chartered university, who achieved a Magister or Doctor's degree, were not to be admitted into the chapter. For some thirteen years, from 1512 to 1525, the chapter would fight the town council to prevent the admission of the native scholar and friend of Erasmus, Ludwig Bär, capitulating only to the combined pressure of council and Pope Julius II.

This distance was symbolized in its rite of initiation. The canons chose their next colleague and came to his home to inform him of his calling. The following day, the new canon took his oath before the assembled chapter in the Cathedral. A prelate

[18] Teuteberg, *Basler Geschichte*, p. 112.
[19] For this and the description that follows, Wackernagel, *Geschichte der Stadt Basel*, vol. 2, pt. II, chap. 6.
[20] Ibid., vol. 1, p. 117.

would then take him by the hand, lead him into that most sacrosanct and restricted space of the church, the choir, and show
him that stall that would be his for life, or until he relinquished
it. The new canon was then led into the chapter room, where he
received possession of his benefice and all the privileges and
benefits pertaining. At the end of his initiation, the canon would
find himself deep within the Cathedral, in an area inaccessible
to the laity, surrounded by men who were his social peers, some
of whom may well have been kin, and endowed with privileges
no other clergy in Basel enjoyed and wealth both ancient and
extensive.[21]

The chapter was self-selecting and, for the most part, self-
regulating. They fought to protect the autonomy of their selection of membership and to protect the nobility and dynasties of
their ranks. They had also been granted privileges early in their
history: not only exemption from all secular jurisdiction, both
civil and imperial, but exemption from local custom duties, taxes,
and other obligations of labor and payment. Legally under the
jurisdiction of bishop and pope, the chapter was willing to oppose
both in determining their membership, suggesting something
of the conflicts that frequently arose over the extent of the bishop's authority and the chapter's autonomy. Moreover, the canons
had been given lands, with all their attached incomes, throughout the Basel countryside. Thus, they were landlords, while not
being of the land, rentiers who did not participate in the commercial life of the town. They received income from religious
endowments within the town, yet gave little of it back to the local
community.[22] Their incomes from those lands were among the
richest in Basel; some of the individual canons received incomes greater than that of the popular parish church, St. Martin's.

---

[21] In 1525, of the thirteen canons present, two shared the appellation, perhaps pat-
ronymic, "von Rinach" (a third was named "von Rynach"), and two "von Pfirt"; one
of the resident canons, the cantor, and one of those nonresident were "von And-
low"; and another nonresident canon shared with a canon the name "von Hallwil,"
ABR I, 501e.

[22] In March 1526, the guilds of Basel lodged a formal complaint against all religious in
Basel, that they did not employ local guildsmen, but did the craftwork and other
manual trades themselves; ABR II, 258.

Like the worst examples of clerical abuse, the canons frequently left Basel: to visit their other benefices, to study at distant uni-
versities, some to visit Rome, one on a pilgrimage; at no time
in the records were all twenty-four canons present in Basel. In
1474, Pope Sixtus IV found it necessary to command the canons
to remain in residence at the Cathedral, so famous were their absences. As late as 1525, however, only thirteen of the canons
were in residence, occupying their benefices, and using them;
another six had taken possession of their benefices, but were not
in residence, and four had never taken possession of their benefices.[23] Perhaps most bitterly, they had been designated leaders
of the town's religious community: The archdeacon of the chapter listed among his official duties responsibility for protecting
the civic peace among the clergy; and in 1512 the chapter appeared before the town council in its hall as representative of all
resident priesthood – this though they themselves neither fully
resided in the town nor fully administered the duties of priest to
the people of Basel.

Far less powerful than the Cathedral chapter, the chaplains of
the Cathedral were also far less exclusive in their membership,
frequently forming alliances with the local citizenry against
the chapter. They were greater in number: In 1525, there were
seventy-two.[24] Their responsibilities, however, like those of the
canons, were exclusively to the Cathedral, and not to the people
of Basel: Each chaplain attended to an altar within the Cathedral
or its cloister; each was responsible primarily, if not exclusively,
for saying mass the number of times stipulated in the altar's endowment that paid his prebend. Some of the chaplains heard
confessions and administered the sacrament, but the care of
souls, living souls – unlike service to the chapter and to the altars
– was not a formal responsibility.

Among the Cathedral clergy, only the preachers seemed to
serve laypersons directly. There were two preaching offices in
the Cathedral. The first the pope had authorized in 1438, for the
education of diocesan clergy and the illumination of the laity,
in recognition of the need to "increase worship in the Cathe-

[23] ABR I, 501e.
[24] Ibid., 501a.

dral."[25] The next free canon's benefice was to be used for this position; in Basel, that position opened in 1456 and concerned not the general care of souls, but preaching – in German to the laity Sunday, Monday, Wednesday, and Friday every week, daily during Advent and Lent; in Latin to the clergy once or twice a year. This first Cathedral preacher was also periodically to offer the clergy lectures on theology. The second preaching office, *Leutpriester* (the People's Priest), was established at the Cathedral in 1471. He, too, was to be learned. Unlike the Cathedral preacher, the *Leutpriester* seems to have had as his intended audience primarily the resident clergy of the Cathedral. Still, the position was not filled by the kind of men typical of the Cathedral chapter: Among the men who preached to the Cathedral clergy were Professor Michael Wildbeck, the reformer Jacob Götz, and Johann Geiler von Kaysersberg.

In 1525, the position of Cathedral preacher was empty.[26] By 1525, laypersons of Basel did not protest, perhaps because the chapter was unlikely to appoint a preacher sympathetic to the growing desire for reform, perhaps because the laity no longer looked to the Cathedral clergy for leadership in its religious life. Traditionally, the Cathedral clergy's links to lay religious life were oblique: Its provost held patronage over St. Peter's church, the canons participated as preaching rectors at St. Martin's, and the Curate of St. Peter's and the *Pleban* of St. Martin's participated in matins of Christmas Eve. In 1259, the pope had confirmed an earlier arrangement the bishop had made: The Cathedral chapter would have no parish function within the town. In 1525, the Cathedral clergy were responsible for the care of no souls in either the town or the diocese.

By the sixteenth century, six other churches in Basel would serve laypersons. St. Martin's was the oldest church in Basel and its first parish church. In the eleventh century, the Bishop of Basel had founded St. Alban's cloister and turned over all the parish obligations of the Cathedral to it – an awkward arrangement, since the cloister lay outside the town walls until a new wall was built in 1200. It was St. Alban's right to serve as a parish church

---

[25] Wackernagel, *Geschichte der Stadt Basel*, vol. 2, pt. II, p. 855.
[26] ABR I, 501e.

that the pope confirmed in 1259. In the thirteenth century, the bishop and then the pope had granted full rights to administer the sacrament and the care of souls to St. Leonhard's church and St. Peter's collegiate church. Subsequently, St. Ulrich's church had been founded to serve the outer city and St. Theodore's to serve Kleinbasel. By 1497, St. Leonhard's seems to have been the largest parish, followed by St. Alban and Ulrich's combined, then St. Peter's.[27] These churches served the spiritual needs of the people of Basel, baptised their children, blessed and buried their dead, preached to them and offered them the Holy Eucharist.

The Cathedral itself was more fully a participant in lay religious life than was its clergy. More lay confraternities were attached to altars within it than to those of any other church. The Cathedral housed many beloved objects, more than any other church in Basel, even the well-endowed St. Peter's. Among the best known were a splinter from the holy cross – housed in its own beautiful reliquary that the Cathedral's founder, Emperor Henry II, had given the Cathedral in addition to the golden altar-piece[28] – and relics of Henry himself, kept in another reliquary in the church. The increase in devotion to the canonized emperor engendered gifts of stained-glass windows, monstrances, images, and other objects for the Cathedral. Indeed, so great was the town's devotion to the builder of the Cathedral that it chose his saint's day for formalizing its entrance into the Swiss Confederation. The people of Basel willingly gave to complete the reconstruction of the Cathedral after the earthquake of 1356, though their donations decreased over the fifteenth century. They were proud of the Cathedral, its beauty, its artistic and aesthetic sophistication, and they long honored the building as symbolizing a collective Christianity, even as they opposed those clergy who served in it.

By the 1520s, even Bishop Christoph von Utenheim (bishop 1502–27), who had the town council's enthusiastic support, could not, in his attempts at clerical reform, overcome the distance his predecessors and the chapter had built over centuries between

[27] Ammann, "Die Bevölkerung," p. 37.
[28] The splinter was stolen sometime before 1529.

themselves and the urban laity. His efforts to reform the behavior of the religious failed: The chapter was too autonomous, too arrogant, and the clergy of the town, both monastic and pastoral, were too suspicious of an office long indifferent to them. However, Bishop Christoph's efforts, even had they been successful, centered not on the practice of religion, but on the behavior of the clergy, such issues as celibacy and humility. The cultural and social distance between the Cathedral's clergy and its town – the clergy's foreign and noble birth, their disengagement from lay religious life, their exemption from civic duties of all kinds, made physical with their frequent absences from the town – this distance was too deeply established for reform to uproot it easily.

Increasingly, from the fifteenth century onward, the town council sought to bridge the Cathedral clergy's isolation from the town by curtailing the bishop's authority within the town and bringing the chapter under the suzerainty of the council.[29] In the course of the fifteenth century, the membership of this group of laymen had become increasingly mercantile and artisanal, less and less noble.[30] The contrast was not lost on the people of Basel: The Cathedral chapter remained intransigently noble at a time when the leadership of lay Basel was almost exclusively drawn from the guilds. The specific points on which the town council aggressively and increasingly successfully opposed the noble and foreign Cathedral chapter and bishop were urban and local. In 1521, the council repudiated its oath of obedience to the bishop, ending its subjection to episcopal rule. In May 1528, Bishop Phillip complained formally to the town council: It had made citizens of the other religious in the town, drawing them under the town council's suzerainty and away from the bishop's; the town council had extended its jurisdiction, its right to indict and prosecute, to include the religious, even canons; it had seized the income of St. Alban's monastery, which the bishop had founded,

---

[29] On the relations between the town council and the bishop, see Hans Berner, *"die gute correspondenz": Die Politik der Stadt Basel gegenüber dem Fürstbistum Basel in den Jahren 1525–1585* (Basel, 1989), esp. pp. 13–41, for the years 1525–30.

[30] On the later history of the Basel town council, its composition and competences, see Alfred Müller, "Die Ratsverfassung der Stadt Basel von 1521 bis 1798," *Basler Zeitschrift für Geschichte und Altertumskunde* 53(1954): 5–98; on the reorganization of the selection process for town councillors in 1529, see esp. pp. 7, 16–17.

endowed, and built; it had inventoried the possessions of clergy throughout the town; it had seized the property of those who died; it had allowed the people to ridicule the clergy. Perhaps more significant to us, the bishop also complained that the town council had allowed the alteration of worship and the destruction of altars in parish churches; and it had transgressed the freedom of the Cathedral chapter.[31] The town council had successfully influenced the choice of a bishop, Christoph von Utenheim, in 1502, and forced the Cathedral chapter to accept Ludwig Bär in 1525; by 1529, following a policy of moderate reform, it had moved significantly to participate in decisions traditionally made by the bishop and chapter.

One narrative of iconoclasm: The chronicler Fridolin Ryff

So successful was the town council in its encroachment on the rights and authority of the bishop and chapter that evangelicals in Basel turned to it in their pursuit of the reform of religious life. The chronicler Fridolin Ryff would cast the narrative of that iconoclasm as an encounter between the town council and the *Gemeinde,* those citizens of Basel who were not magistrates, who might never qualify for decision-making offices, but who had purchased membership in the political community of the town.[32] Ryff was himself an active supporter of evangelical reform: In 1527, two witnesses had testified that "Fridlin Ryffen," a weaver from Basel, had excused coarse language for the saints because "it was not about the Mother of God, she was a woman like any other woman."[33] Ryff may have been a participant in the iconoclasm of February 9. For him, the destruction of that Tuesday afternoon was the culmination of popular frustration with a magistracy that would not move to reform.

---

[31] ABR III, 110a.

[32] On the social stratification of Basel's government, see Füglister's excellent study, *Handwerksregiment,* esp. pts. 2 and 3.

[33] July 29, 1527, "es sye nut umb die muoter gottes, sy sye ein frow wie ein andre frow; und mit züchten ze reden oder ze lesen, er schyss sant Pettern uf den glatzeten kopf," ABR II, 696.

There had been in Basel a cadence of increasing movement, restlessness, among laypersons, an increasingly forceful and insistent call for reform. Up to 1528, the town council sought a balance that proved in town after town impossible to preserve: Masses were to be maintained at altars in accord with the wishes of the original endowment; each was to worship "according to his own conscience"; and the priests, of all kinds – not the lay parishioners – were to determine the nature and practice of the mass.[34] By 1528, however, evangelicals were becoming increasingly impatient. On April 10, Good Friday of that year, members of the Spinnwetter guild[35] had removed all the images in St. Martin's church. On Easter Monday, April 13, they had then done the same in the Augustinian church. When the town council had sought to prosecute four of the Easter iconoclasts – a stove fitter, a cooper, a joiner, and a carpenter – who had been discovered and caught, more than a hundred guildsmen had gathered in the marketplace early April 15.[36] The town council, noting that it could not negotiate with so many, demanded that they send a delegation. The result of that delegation's day-long negotiation was a mandate calling for all the images in St. Martin's, the Augustinian, and the Franciscan churches, as well as in the Spital, to be put aside.[37]

On May 16, 1528, the wine agent Hans Beck was required to swear an oath (*Urfehde*) that he would no longer go about demanding that all the holy images (*heiligen*) and altars in the Cathedral be removed before Pentecost, as well as those in the churches that had been "disturbed" (*gesturmpten*). On May 20, Steffan Ferrer and Hans Byrri, from the village of Liesberg, were also required to swear that they would no longer storm the holy images (*heiligen*) and assistants in the churches, but remain obedient to authorities. On September 1, Hans Ludi of the village of

---

[34] ABR II, 733, 735, & 740.
[35] This guild comprised some of the less profitable crafts: "Maurer und Steinmetzen, Hafner, Ziegler, Zimmerleute, Tischmacher, Wagner, Schindler, Dreher, Küfer, Kübler, Wannenmacher, Siebmacher, Bildschnitzer, Holzleute," Füglister, *Handwerksregiment*, p. 2.
[36] Testimony of the iconoclasts, ABR III, 86; testimony of witnesses, ibid., 155. See also Wackernagel, *Geschichte der Stadt Basel*, vol. 3, pp. 496–7.
[37] ABR III, 87.

Waldenburg had to swear he would no longer disturb, throw out, strike, or break holy images (*heiligen*) and pictures in St. Peter's parish church, despite the town council's prohibition of iconoclasm.[38] On the fourth Sunday in Advent that year, as the guilds gathered to celebrate the Ember Day, the members of various guilds voiced their impatience with the slowness of reform in the town and their determination to push for it, to allow no more hesitation. On December 23, 1528, some two hundred evangelical citizens[39] met in the gardeners' guild house and drafted a petition to the town council, formally requesting that it end the false preaching that was dividing the town, leading the innocent and ignorant to false faith, and unify the town under evangelical reformed Christianity.[40]

In each of these exchanges, the distance between the town council's policy and the evangelical position was evident. The evangelicals found the diversity of Christian faiths intolerable: There was but one true faith, and false faith too easily led the innocent, the ill-informed, the illiterate astray. The evangelicals spoke of *abgötterei*, idolatry, the drawing away of the Christian from true worship. For them, the choice of religious practice and belief was treacherous; for them, false worship was seductive where true worship was not. Multiple readings of Scripture would lead not to true faith but to confusion. Too many voices would confuse laypersons, who needed to be able to trust the guidance of their preachers.

For our purposes, the most striking slippage between the town council and the evangelicals is in their choice of terms to describe the images in the churches. In its record of the oaths (*Urfehden*), the town council attributes to Hans Beck the term *heiligen*, holy objects, relics, perhaps images of saints; in its own mandate, it names the objects in the churches *bylder*, pictures or images. Fridolin Ryff, the only evangelical whose voice we hear directly, calls the objects that the iconoclasts destroyed in St. Martin's and the Augustinian churches "idols or images [*götzen*

[38] These events of May–September are from ABR III, 117, 123, 209, respectively.
[39] The number is from Teuteberg, *Basler Geschichte*, p. 212.
[40] ABR III, 291.

oder bilder]."[41] The town council did not see the problem of the images in terms of idolatry; for it, the objects inside the churches were *heiligen, bylder,* holy images, pictures of beloved holy persons. For evangelicals, they were something quite different.

Again, the town council sought peace through mediation.[42] On December 26, it summoned delegations from the evangelicals and from the clergy still loyal to Rome. Not surprisingly in hindsight, but perhaps unexpectedly for the council, the two sides could reach no agreement. The town council had copies of the guild petition sent to those of the "old faith," who, on December 29, gave their formal response. Throughout the negotiations, the town remained in a state of watchfulness: The gates closed, the watch increased. The product of this tension was the town council's ordinance of January 5, 1529, read in the Franciscan and Dominican churches:

> [A]ll and every preacher, parish priest, curate, people's priest, and religious [*ordenslut*], who assume the office of preaching in either part of Basel, shall proclaim and preach nothing other than solely the pure, clear gospel, the holy divine word, comprehended in biblical writ, along with whatever they might wish to protect and arm it, without recourse to other interpreters [*lerern*], human sentences, confluently [*einmundigklich*], freely, openly, and unconcealed, as the first mandate wished and indicated, to the revelation of the honor of God, to the planting brotherly trust, love, and the common peace.[43]

The town council postponed the decision whether to abolish the mass permanently until the Sunday after Trinity, when a disputation would be held in the Franciscan church. The two sides were each to prepare their positions based solely on Scripture, and each citizen was to examine his conscience as to whether the mass should be held or eliminated entirely. Until that disputation, masses were to be suspended, with three exceptions: no more than one mass daily in the Cathedral, one office in St. Peter's church, and one in St. Theodore's.

---

[41] "Chronik des Fridolin Ryff," p. 57.
[42] Wackernagel, *Geschichte der Stadt Basel,* vol. 3, pp. 504–5.
[43] This and the following excerpt are from ABR III, 333.

And with that our common citizenry should calm the schism, which they had carried on recently, be satisfied with one another, none pursue anything unfriendly against another, but rather live in brotherly and civic peace next to and with one another, virtuously and in friendship, wait out the designated time, and not rouse themselves nor behave intemperately.

Again, the town council called for peace and order in the face of "intemperate" Christians.

A month before the great iconoclasm in Basel, the town council had acceded to one of the evangelicals' demands – preaching from Scripture alone – but it had not agreed to evangelical preachers in all the churches, nor to the permanent abolition of the mass. Once again it had postponed the decision on that rite that divided the Christian community in Basel. The town council itself could not move: Twelve of its members, some among the most powerful and influential, remained faithful to Rome. They sought, even after the ordinance of January 5, to prevent the dismantling of traditional Christianity in Basel. In the weeks preceding the iconoclasm, both evangelicals and town council invoked communal peace and unity, but the two had opposing visions of what those terms meant. The evangelicals believed that peace and unity lay in a uniformly reformed Christianity, in which preaching and clergy no longer divided laypersons but unified them in a single understanding of the true faith. The town council, on the other hand, was willing to curtail the authority of the bishop and the privileges of the chapter, but not to adjudicate religious life and practice. Itself divided, it could only envision peace and unity through harmonious accommodation: "[I]f the learned themselves are not unified, why should we take on the burden of deciding?"[44]

According to Ryff, popular support for the evangelical position and the numbers of those dissatisfied with the town council's position of moderation grew audible in the forty-eight hours preceding the iconoclasm.[45] Beginning Sunday evening, February 7, and continuing through Monday, what Ryff called the *Ge-*

[44] ABR III, 338.
[45] The following is drawn primarily from the "Chronik des Fridolin Ryff," pp. 80–90, with additions as noted; all quotations are from Ryff, unless otherwise indicated.

meinde gathered in increasing numbers. To the town council it stated its unity, its confidence that its position was the morally correct one, and the strength it derived from that knowledge. Early Monday morning, it sent a delegation to the town council. The *Gemeinde* very likely included some if not all of those citizens who had signed the petition of December 23, as the demands it sent to the town council echoed theirs: an end to the religious schism in the town and evangelical preaching in all the pulpits. Ryff and the extant records both suggest that the town council temporized over these for two days, promising to respond to the *Gemeinde*'s demands, yet reasserting its principle of toleration of multiple faiths. As the town council temporized, the *Gemeinde*'s demands increased: The town council must excise the "papal party" within it, those twelve councilors still sympathetic to the Roman church, who were closely allied among themselves and "friendly to priests"; and the entire guild membership, not just those who had a seat in the council, was to elect guild masters and *Sechser,* those six members from each guild, all of whom were seated in the town council.

The *Gemeinde* was also becoming in a real sense visible. Citizens gathered first on Sunday at the guild house of the gardeners, where "thirty articulate citizens" decided to assemble the following morning at six at the Franciscan house. According to Ryff, some eight hundred citizens gathered that morning and prayed to God for help and grace, that "we might further the honor of God and have His Word among us [*handhaben*]." From 6 A.M. onward, the *Gemeinde* would be present, starting in the Franciscan house; later, while the town councilors were at dinner, the citizens went home, armed themselves, and gathered in the Kornmarkt, or grain market,[46] where peasants would come to sell their grain.[47] There the citizens took over all the streets from below the town hall, where the town council had been meeting, to the Kornmarkt, securing all doors and fastening iron chains across a number of the streets.[48] On the day before the icono-

---

[46] Today the Marktplatz.
[47] Ryff explicitly names the place Kornmerckt (p. 86), while Wackernagel designates it Marktplatz (*Geschichte der Stadt Basel,* vol. 3, p. 512).
[48] ABR III, 374.

clasm, the *Gemeinde* was acting to secure the town, performing one of the civic duties that the Cathedral clergy had refused to accept.

The *Gemeinde* did so when there was no external threat, when its perceived threat was internal to the town: the town council and the clergy. Still, the town council did not feel itself so threatened that it agreed to come to a decision, but again bade the *Gemeinde* keep the peace and harm no one.[49] Unease continued to grow on both sides. The *Gemeinde,* according to Ryff, recognized that they would be individually vulnerable and secure only as a group, as *Gemeinde.* They remained together that night, some returning to the gardeners' guild house, some to other guild houses, of the Saffran guild or the vintners, and some to the Rhine bridge. Sometime during the night members of the town council fled down the Rhine.[50] Lights were lit in all the streets, and all the citizens held a great watch.

By the following morning, Tuesday, February 9, according to Ryff, the *Gemeinde* had come to believe that the town council would do nothing; the priests' faction was too strong; God's Word would have no effect.[51] Sometime after noon on Tuesday, the *Gemeinde,* who had been standing for one full day in their armor in the Kornmarkt, became restless. Anxious to see what might be happening, some forty of them went to the Cathedral plaza, to the quarters where many of the clergy lived, then finally into the Cathedral, "to walk around." Echoing the narrative of the Zurich iconoclast, Lorentz Meyger, Ryff continues: One opened a retable with his gun; it fell over and broke, "so they left." These forty soon returned to the Cathedral hill, however, with two hundred more who had joined them from the Kornmarkt. Some suggested approaching the town council. One proposed that instead they go into the Cathedral again and "smash the idols, petitioning the

[49] See, in addition to Ryff's account, ABR III, 368.
[50] Ryff claims these were two *Junker* who had opposed evangelical reform, whereas Hügis names the "bürgermeister Meltiger unnd jünckher Egly Offenbürg unnd sunst noch einer der raeten," ABR III, 374. Johannes Kessler names "Hainrich Meltinger, burgermaister, junker Egle von Offenburg, herr Andres Bischoff und herr Hans Oberriet," pp. 302–3.
[51] Some of the *Gemeinde's* demands were met before the iconoclasm, according to Josef Rosen, *Chronik von Basel: Hauptdaten der Geschichte* (Basel, 1971), pp. 103–4.

idols first to see if they would decide" the issue of religious reform in Basel.

In the meantime, in response to the destruction of the retable,
the Cathedral clergy had locked all the church doors. The two
hundred citizens broke into the Cathedral, shattering the doors.
They chopped up the rood screen, the retables, "the idols, stone
and wood." Everything, every ornament, every precious object
that would have been inside the church was smashed into little
pieces. Only those things that were made of gold or silver, or
other small items, were untouched and preserved, "for no one
sought to take anything, only to smash, nor did anyone dare to
put on anything that he might wear." Iconoclasts came not to
steal, nor even to "take away" as Zurich iconoclasts had done, but
"to smash."

The delegation that had been sent to the town council returned
with the council's request for more time. By the time they arrived with their commission to stop the violence, the iconoclasts
had completed their work in the Cathedral and had moved on to
St. Ulrich's, St. Alban's, and St. Peter's churches, from one to the
next, until they had smashed the "idols" in all the churches in
Grossbasel. (St. Martin's, St. Leonhard's, and the Augustinian
and Franciscan churches had already been "cleansed.") When
it caught up with the iconoclasts, the delegation sought to stop
them; but the iconoclasts would not stop until there were no more
"idols or retables" in Basel. The destruction continued until four
in the afternoon (again, according to Ryff's estimation), when
the citizens reassembled in the Kornmarkt and decided to cross
the Rhine into Kleinbasel, there to do away with the "idols" as
well. Some spoke of going to the town hall to get an answer from
the council, so that the conflict might come to an end. One,
whose words were recorded by Oecolampad, cried out "in three
years of deliberations, you effected nothing; in this one hour we
resolve everything."[52] Thus confronted, its desire for time for
deliberation thwarted, the town council requested but one hour
more to give them its decision, and bid them be peaceful. They

[52] "'Vos intra triennium deliberando nihil effecistis; nos intra horam hec omnia
absolvemus,'" Oecolampad to Wolfgang Capito, 13 February 1529, *Briefe und Akten
zum Leben Oekolampads*, no.636.

were stilled, and within an hour the town council conceded all their demands, from reform of religious life to restructuring of the town council.[53] "With this the *Gemeinde* came to good peace and quiet, and each went home."

Ryff's account is important to us for a number of reasons. It is, by far, the fullest account of February 7–10 and the iconoclasm of February 9. Ryff identifies the participants, significantly, as "citizens." It was important to him to convey the character of the iconoclasts: This was no "mob," no "riot," but the gathering of men who had been granted membership in the political life of the town. "Citizens" could not be adolescents, or apprentices, but responsible and adult members of an urban commune. They were good Christian citizens: They sought neither rebellion nor the overthrow of legitimate authority; to the end, they accorded the town council's decisions authority, even as they sought to change the means by which its members were chosen and to dictate the content of those decisions. They sought to reconstitute the council's membership to represent their religion, not that of the clergy. They negotiated with the town council in the language it had left them. Iconoclastic violence was the choice of a group who saw themselves as devout and responsible Christians, whose choices for moral action had narrowed in the preceding months and weeks, as other efforts to move the council to enact true Christian practices – the sole morally correct decision – failed.[54]

Ryff sought to locate the iconoclasm of February 9 in the dynamic between the town council and the *Gemeinde*. According to

[53] The town council rescinded some of its promises as early as February 12: Although it was willing to restructure, it did not grant the entire guild rights to elect *Bürgermeister* or *Sechser*. ABR III, 387.

[54] On the moral intent of popular action, I have found most useful John Cashmere, "The Social Uses of Violence in Ritual: *Charivari* or Religious Persecution," *European History Quarterly* 21(1991): 291–319; Natalie Zemon Davis, "Charivari, Honor, and Community in Seventeenth-Century Lyon and Geneva," in *Rite, Drama, Festival, Spectacle: Rehearsals Toward a Theory of Cultural Performance*, ed. John J. MacAloon (Philadelphia, 1984), pp. 42–57; and "The Rites of Violence," *Society and Culture in Early Modern France* (London, 1975), pp. 152–87; E.P. Thompson, "The Moral Economy of the English Crowd in the Eighteenth Century," *Past and Present* 50(1971): 77–136; and "'Rough Music': Le Charivari anglais," *Annales* 27(1972), 285–312. I have also learned from Jim Scott's weekly seminar in Agrarian Studies and the conversations that seminar has engendered.

his account, the evangelical iconoclasts of that date forced an unwilling town council to seize direction of lay religious life. By setting the iconoclasm of February 9 within a political context, Ryff also suggested something of the changing popular perception of the relation between political authority and the practice of religion among laypersons. Along with the petitioners of 1528, Ryff accepted tacitly the town council's authority, still disputed by the bishop and canons, to change fundamentally the practice of religion in Basel. For him, the council was weak in its faith, its policy the expression of a willful resistance to true reform. For him, ironically, the council's "failure" to pursue reform arose not from any limitation of its authority in issues religious, but from a lack of will to enact the practice of true religion – so successful had the council been in the expansion of its reputed authority.

If, as Ryff argues, the iconoclasts were seeking primarily to move the town council to take up the reform of religious practice, then they were successful. That evening, the council agreed to evangelical preachers in all parish churches and took over supervision of the religious houses and their possessions, even of the Cathedral chapter.[55] It abolished the mass. On Wednesday, February 10 – Ash Wednesday according to Ryff – it oversaw the completion of iconoclasm from the Cathedral, where it was meeting.[56] It granted people permission to chop up all the retables, the other forms of images, all those objects made of wood in the churches. At first, people sought to distribute this wood to the poor, in order that they might have fuel for fires; but because fights broke out over the fair distribution of the wood, the town council ordered all objects be burned. "Many great Carnival fires were seen on this day; in the Cathedral square alone twelve fires were made, and fires burned before every other church." According to the modern Basel historian Rudolf Wackernagel, there were so many objects that some had to be burned inside the Cathedral, in that most sacrosanct and reserved part of the

---

[55] ABR III, 371–2, 382, 384. Wackernagel presents a chronology different from Ryff's, placing the town council's acquiesence after the fires on Ash Wednesday (*Geschichte der Stadt Basel*, vol. 3, pp. 513–17). Since he otherwise relies on Ryff for his chronology, I find this puzzling and have been inclined to accept Ryff's structuring of events.

[56] ABR III, 383.

church, the choir, where the chapter had for so many years reaffirmed its remove from the laity of Basel.[57] Everything of stone or ivory was smashed. All the churches were whitewashed. "Thus, on this day burned many expensive retables and screens and works of art, which had been made with such expense, but there was nothing so beautiful that it did not go into the fire. Thus the idolatry in Basel, in all areas and offices came to an end in the churches; I do not know, if in all hearts."

Other accounts differ from Ryff's on issues from the small to the significant. They differ as to time of day: The other chronicler, Konrad Schnitt, set the time at about 5 P.M.; Dürs Hügis, the bailiff at Dornach, set the time sometime after 2 P.M. More significantly, the accounts vary as to how they designated the iconoclasts: Some named them "Lutherans"; the secretary of the Cathedral chapter, not surprisingly, referred to them as *herren werckleuth,* artisans or workers, in his report to another canon; the town council, affirming Ryff's description, chose to call the iconoclasts *ein gemein burgerschafft,* a common citizenry, in its formal report. In designating the iconoclasts as "Lutherans," moreover, those accounts implied an explanation for the iconoclasm that differed from, but did not contradict, Ryff's, whereas Schnitt expressly attributed the iconoclasm to evangelical preaching.[58]

Fridolin Ryff's account warrants our close attention: Its detail suggests that he may himself have been a participant in the iconoclasm of February 9, may have had as direct access to the motives of the iconoclasts as anyone could have had; and yet, his narrative offers details that do not fit comfortably in his story, clues that other issues were at play. The violence took place not within a civic domain – at least, not yet a civic domain – but within the public and sacred spaces of the churches. It was not directed against objects primarily symbolic of political authority's expression and articulation, but toward objects whose primary significance was religious. Both the place of the original iconoclasm, the Cathedral, and the time, Carnival for other places, suggest other dimensions of meaning, suggest that Ryff's expla-

[57] Wackernagel, *Geschichte der Stadt Basel,* vol. 3, p. 516.
[58] See ABR III, 374–6, 381–8; "Die Chronik des Konrad Schnitts 1518–1533," pp. 88–90.

nation is not exhaustive, but only partial. We have seen why the Cathedral itself might have been the focus of lay anger: Its clergy had actively maintained a cultural and social distance from the townspeople. Before we turn to why the objects themselves in the Cathedral were attacked, let us take up the other clue Ryff offers: his location of the iconoclasm of that Tuesday and Wednesday in Carnival.[59]

The time of Carnival

The time of the iconoclasm in Basel may have been "Carnival," but it did not fall in the two to three days immediately preceding the beginning of Lent as the people of Basel observed it. In Basel, the beginning of Lent fell that year in the following week.[60] Ryff's allusion to Carnival may not signal an express intention on the part of the iconoclasts to connect their acts with the temporal frame of Carnival and all its meaning; but his invocation of Carnival may lead us, albeit tentatively, to other layers of meaning for that iconoclasm of February 9, and to another understanding of the images in the churches and their meaning for the people of Basel. The following explores Carnival generally for what light it might shed upon the acts of the iconoclasts and the meaning the images held for them.

For some four hundred years, there had been two different methods of reckoning the length of Lent. Lent commemorated the forty days and forty nights that Jesus spent fasting in the wilderness or desert (Matthew 4:2). The earliest reckoning of its length counted forty days back from Easter (not including Easter itself) and included the six Sundays that fell within the forty days.[61] Under that system, Lent began on the Tuesday *following*

---

[59] The most thorough discussion of the meaning and origins of the German word *Fastnacht* is Werner Mezger, *Narrenidee und Fastnachtbrauch: Studien zum Fortleben des Mittelalters in der europäischen Festkultur* (Constance, 1991), pp. 9–15. For the origins of the latinate term *carne vale*, see Julio Caro Baroja, *El Carnaval* (Madrid, 1979), pp. 30–42. In the following discussion, I have chosen to use "Carnival," the term English speakers now use to name those days before Ash Wednesday.

[60] Theo Gantner, "Die Katholiken und die Basler Fastnacht," *Schweizerisches Archiv für Volkskunde* 65(1969): 26.

[61] For the following discussion, see Dietz-Rüdiger Moser, *Fastnacht-Fasching-Karneval. Das Fest der "Verkehrten Welt"* (Graz, Vienna, Cologne, 1986), pp. 19–20.

Invocavit Sunday, and Carnival concluded on Monday. The number of days people celebrated Carnival seems to have varied from region to region, from three days to a number of weeks. In 1091, however, Pope Gregory the Great ruled that Sundays were not to be counted among the forty days of Lent: As the "Lord's Day," they served to commemorate the mystery of the Resurrection – to link, in other words, the fasting of Lent rhythmically to Easter. Thus, the forty days of Lent became forty-six days, forty days plus the six Sundays, beginning the Wednesday *before* Invocavit Sunday, Ash Wednesday.

By the fourteenth century, the two different times of Carnival were distinguished in the popular parlance as "Bauernfastnacht," Peasants' Carnival, or the old date of Carnival, and "Herrenfastnacht," or the Lords' Carnival, that Carnival whose date had been set by noble clergy. Either could be an indefinite number of days in length, but the one ended six days later than the other. Basel followed "the old manner" of reckoning the date of Carnival. We do not know how many days in length Carnival was in Basel, but the bonfires of Wednesday, February 10, were certainly premature: In Basel, Carnival ought to have concluded the following week. What did Ryff, a resident of Basel and presumably familiar with its local tradition of celebrating Carnival after the "old fashion," wish to signal? Why did he connect the iconoclasm to Carnival?

Here, too, the relation of the Cathedral clergy to the town may provide us with a clue. The Bishop of Basel would have chosen the date on which Lent was to begin; indirectly, then, he set the time of Carnival. Thus, the time of Carnival, itself not sanctioned by the clergy in Basel, was nonetheless set by their head, the bishop (even though the bishop's choice of time left the older, originally popular Bauernfastnacht, intact). In keeping to the older date, moreover, Basel distinguished itself from most of its neighbors, who quickly adapted Gregory's "reform." The town's maintenance of the older date may have signaled a more traditional and conservative calendar to men such as Ryff, who perhaps were seeking to recover lay authority to set the time of Carnival, to take from the bishop the right to determine the date for one of the most popular of lay religious festivals.

For Carnival was a popular, a lay holiday.[62] It was not supported by the Church, financially or dogmatically: In Basel, the Cathedral provost's list of expenses for the subvention of religious feast days did not include Carnival.[63] The obscurity of Carnival's origins confirm that it had no clerical sanction in its beginnings: There is no formal record of recognition or institution. It had begun as a lay celebration, and the many failed efforts of religious and secular authorities to suppress various dimensions of it spoke to its resiliency, its significance for laypersons, and their autonomy in the celebration of Carnival. In Basel alone, the records speak eloquently of the variety of lay practices during Carnival and the authorities' opposition to them.[64] In 1432, laypersons were forbidden to go about in "the devil's skin" during either Christmastime or Carnival. In 1440 and again in 1488, the journeymen were forbidden either to force their fellows, journeymen or guildsmen, to drink with them on Ash Wednesday, or to throw anyone into the fountains. In 1484, the authorities condemned but could not prevent the mock battle of the young men in the plaza behind the Cathedral, which frequently escalated into a riot; they would reiterate their prohibition in 1488 and 1497. In 1516, young men were forbidden to strike others

---

[62] The literature on Carnival is enormous. In addition to studies cited elsewhere, I have relied upon Caro Baroja, *El Carnaval*; Eduard Hoffmann-Krayer, "Die Fastnachtsgebräuche in der Schweiz," in *Kleine Schriften zur Volkskunde*, ed. Paul Geiger (Basel, 1946), pp. 24–94; Norbert Humberg, *Städtisches Fastnachtsbrauchtum in West- und Ostfalen. Die Entwicklung vom Mittelalter bis ins 19. Jahrhundert* (Münster, 1976); Samuel Kinser, "Presentation and Representation: Carnival at Nuremberg, 1450–1550," *Representations* 13(1986), 1–41; *Masken Zwischen Spiel und Ernst. Beiträge des Tübinger Arbeitskreis für Fastnachtsforschung* (Tübingen, 1967), esp. the article by Hans Moser, "Städtische Fastnacht des Mittelalters," pp. 135–202; Wolfgang F. Michael, *Das deutsche Drama des Mittelaters* (Berlin & New York, 1971), sec. II; Dietz-Rüdiger Moser, *Fastnacht-Fasching-Karneval*; Hans-Ulrich Roller, *Der Nürnberger Schembartlauf: Studien zum Fest- und Maskenwesen des späten Mittelalters* (Tübingen, 1965); Bob Scribner, "Reformation, Carnival, and the World Turned Upside-Down," *Social History* 3(1978), 234–64, reprinted in *Popular Culture and Popular Movements in Reformation Germany* (London & Ronceverte, 1987), pp. 71–101; Adolf Spamer, *Deutsche Fastnachtsbräuche* (Jena, 1936); and Bianka Stahl, *Formen und Funktionen des Fastnachtfeierns in Geschichte und Gegenwart, dargestellt an den wichtigsten Aktivitäten der Mainzer Fastnachtsvereine und -garden* (Bielefeld, 1981). Less helpful is the collection of essays in *Le Carnaval, le fête et la communication* (Nice, 1985), in which the essays' brevity leads to distorting generalities.

[63] ABR I, 521.

[64] The following incidents are all from Hoffmann-Krayer, "Die Fastnachtsgebräuche in der Schweiz," pp. 28, 57, 59, 82, 86.

with bags of ashes, covering and "laying waste" to their clothes. In 1526, the town council called for an end to the songs, sung during Carnival processions, that ridiculed, slandered, even dishonored both spiritual and secular persons; the town council found it necessary to reiterate this demand only seven years later. The Basel town council sought as well to limit lay festivity to those days before Lent: In Basel, an edict of 1418 forbade mumming during Christmastime and restricted it solely to Carnival.

Both secular and ecclesiastical authorities found it difficult, nay impossible, to regulate Carnival. There was something too fluid, too permeable about the festival: They could seek to regulate its time and specific activities within it, but they could not control the entirety of its content or its participants – those were too elusive, too ephemeral, too fluxive. Carnival was open in a way other festivals were not. Anyone could participate. Even the town councilors, who sought to restrict certain activities in Carnival, took part in some of its mockeries, its play: In 1507–8, they stole the Fritschi puppet, a Carnival puppet, of Luzern, invited the Luzern town council to retrieve it, and hosted a mock diplomatic reception for the delegation sent on that mission. The individual guilds sponsored processions on different days in Carnival. So, too, did journeymen and apprentices have their own mode of play. Various *Junker* orders would host mock battles. Apprentices and magistrates, old men and young women, all might play a role in its festivities.

Carnival was also a time of social fluidity. The social and political arrangements of persons, the hierarchies of status and authority in which each person in Basel found his or her "place," became less determinate; they might be temporarily displaced, even lifted.[65] Masks altered status and the relation of their wear-

---

[65] See especially Roberto DaMatta, "Carnival in Multiple Planes," in *Rite, Drama, Festival, Spectacle,* pp. 208–40. Also Victor Turner, "Carnaval in Rio: Dionysian Drama in an Industrializing Society," in *The Anthropology of Performance* (New York, 1986), pp. 123–38. I am more persuaded of DaMatta's view of Carnival as a time of dislocation, in which social relations become more fluid, than the more predominant view of Carnival as a time of inversion. My thinking on social fluidity has benefited from Linda Seligmann's work on Peruvian market women, and the conversations that ensued.

ers to others. The mask itself, an elaborately carved and crafted object, made explicit an important social perception: that the person and the "mask," his outward appearance, were separable. In calling attention to that separation, the mask made all the more tenuous the connection between each "player" and his "mask." Carnival plays turned on that fluidity.[66] The different roles within society were represented in the plays, but the men who "played" them did not hold them normally, in non-Carnival time.[67] Like the masks people wore on the streets, Carnival plays made explicit that the person could be separated from his "role," the place he held and fulfilled within society. In those plays, moreover, principles other than birth or wealth determined one's status, one's social place. Most often, relations among men were defined by either character, the willingness or ability to abide by a simple and accessible moral code, or wit; by these, one could alter one's place in the stratified society of the town. Moreover, as the plays made explicit, wit and character could be found in a wife, in an apprentice, in a weaver or shoemaker, as well as in a miller or a merchant; indeed, in the plays, the wife, the apprentice, and the weaver or shoemaker were more likely to possess mental and moral gifts than were the miller or merchant.

The people of Basel understood that dimension of Carnival. In 1376, in what became known as "Böse Fastnacht," Basel artisans – in response to arrows and horses that nobles from the household of the Habsburg Duke Leopold III had let loose in the crowd – themselves donned armor, attacked, and arrested some fifty counts, canons, knights, and their retinues.[68] The town council was forced to restore the peace that had been so badly breached by its residents, but artisans had reminded the lords how quickly armor and arms transform relations among men of differing status, how they make that status meaningless. So, too, on Februa-

---

[66] *Fastnachtspiele aus dem fünfzehnten Jahrhundert*, pts. I–III [ed. A. von Keller] [Bibliothek des Literarische Vereins in Stuttgart, vols. 28–30] (Stuttgart, 1853); and *Fastnachtspiele des 15. und 16. Jahrhunderts*, 3 vols., ed. Walter Wuttke (Stuttgart, 1973).

[67] Richard Hornby, *Drama, Metadrama, and Perception* (Cranbury, N.J., 1986), esp. pt. I.

[68] Wackernagel, *Geschichte der Stadt Basel*, vol. 1, pp. 295–6.

ry 8, 1529 – which was being celebrated as Carnival elsewhere – when the *Gemeinde* declared its moral stature to the town council, it invoked what the Carnival plays would have made manifest: that its moral strength gave the *Gemeinde* a basis to assume roles it normally did not "play."

The days of Carnival were denoted by movement, individual and collective. People moved about – in processions, in dances, in mock battles, wandering the streets. Processions made Carnival's fluidity both visible and spatial: the movement of journeymen and apprentices through parts of Basel in which they were not resident; the wagons that carried symbols of lay life to parts of the town where the clergy lived; the processions of men bearing the arms of their order or house, their war banners and weapons, through the town in times of peace.[69] During Carnival, the town was spatially open, socially fluid, and physically in motion: Dances and battles, drama and processions, mumming and masks, spoofs and mockeries all marked the days preceding the beginning of Lent. In 1529, artisans armed themselves in a time of peace, moved from their own quarter to that of the Cathedral, and, for a space of three hours or so, assumed the role of reforming authority.

Another important aspect of Carnival was that people ate: chickens, beef, sausages, pork. They feasted. They drank – wildly – ale, wine, spirits. Here, too, Carnival was inclusive: All people ate in some way; most laypersons ate precisely the foods distinguished at Carnival. Many also marked Carnival with special meals and wild drinking. Various orders and guilds would host meals for their members during this period. Carnival was thus the occasion for sharing a meal among a group, for knitting particular men or women together through this significant social activity. Such meals, however, were not marked by decorum, were not "ritualistic" in this sense: They were marked by a lack of decorum and by excess, too much food, too much drink, gluttony and drunkenness. It was their excess that made them Carnival meals.

---

[69] Hoffmann-Krayer, "Die Fastnachtsgebräuche in der Schweiz," pp. 67–8, 70–1.

Carnival was a time of social fluidity, but it was not a social or secular festival. It was a lay religious festival.[70] It had a place within the rhythms of the Christian year: Incarnation, Epiphany, Carnival, Lent, Easter, Pentecost. For laypersons, various activities linked Carnival to other religious holidays. In some areas of the empire, St. Martin's Day, November 11, was known as "Kleine Fastnacht," "Little Carnival."[71] In Basel, mumming linked Christmas and Carnival, until it was forbidden at Christmastime. In Rapperswil on Lake Zurich, a particular dance of women and their daughters began the Monday following Candlemas and continued four times a week to the end of Carnival; as with so many other lay practices, this dance was eventually restricted to "Schmutzigen Donnerstag" and the two last days of Carnival.[72]

As Carnival plays themselves enacted, Carnival was most directly linked to Lent.[73] The timing of Carnival was set most immediately by the beginning of Lent, which in turn was established by the date of Easter. Without Lent, there would be no Carnival: Without fasting, feasting would lose its definition; without fish, meat, its special connotation; without austerity, excess, its exuberance. The austerity of Lent made meaningful the excesses of Carnival; likewise, Carnival, with its excessive eating and drinking, its colors, its masks, underlined Lenten austerities – its fasting, its celibacy, its covered altars and closed altarpieces, its colorlessness, its motionlessness, its silences.[74] As Brueghel made visible in *The Battle of Carnival and Lent* (1559), laypersons knew well the essential interdependence of the two, the gluttony of the one and the emaciation of the other, the sensuality of the one and the deathly deprivation of the other: the heightened

[70] Werner Mezger, Dietz-Rüdiger Moser, and Samuel Kinser argue for such an understanding of Carnival, Moser for its location in the Christian calendar, both Moser and Kinser for its essential interdependence with Lent, and Mezger for its deeper connections to questions of foolishness and physicality.
[71] Dietz-Rüdiger Moser, *Fastnacht-Fasching-Karneval*, p. 26.
[72] Hoffmann-Krayer, "Die Fastnachtsgebräuche in der Schweiz," p. 77.
[73] The most direct connection is made in "Das Spil von der Vasnacht und Vasten Recht, von Sulczen und Broten," *Fastnachtspiele*, vol. II, pp. 628–31 (no. 73), which Wuttke attributes to Hans Rosenblüt (p. 326, text, pp. 3–7).
[74] Martine Grinberg & Sam Kinser, "Les combats de Carnaval et de Carême: Trajets d'une métaphore," *Annales* 38(1983), 65–98.

meaning each acquired through contrast, its "battle" with its opposite.[75]

Lent was the reassertion of those values by which the clergy identified itself, the particular conception of asceticism that had been specified under Benedict and had itself come to define what constituted the best Christian life. Thus it was the reassertion of the line that divided religious and lay during the rest of the year. During Lent, laypersons enacted the celibacy and asceticism that normally distinguished the clergy, the monks, priests, canons, friars, bishops, all the clerical hierarchy, from the laity. During Lent, moreover, the clergy reasserted their regulation of Christian practice: They covered the altars, closed the altarpieces, withheld Communion, the Eucharist, silenced those dimensions of Christian practice to which laypersons had access.

Its opposite, Carnival, was thus the celebration of the condition of being "lay." It was *carne vale*, goodbye to flesh; Fastnacht, the night before the Fast. In it, the "flesh"[76] was celebrated, in preparation for the austerities, the asceticism of Lent. In celebrating the "flesh," Carnival defined it: the eating of meat, sexuality in its many manifestations, dancing, singing, exuberance and mockery – the wantonness of lay life in contrast to the control and regulation (at least in theory) of the religious. The days of Carnival were not marked by monastic hours, by the liturgical structuring of the day, but tumbled over, one into the next, as men and women danced, ate, drank, out of their normal routines. The world of laypersons was a world of the "flesh," as it had been defined by monks since the earliest years of the Church. All those dimensions that defined lay life over against the religious were celebrated during Carnival: sexuality, feasting on the flesh of animals, violence, warfare, sensuality, a kind of

---

[75] Claude Gaignebet, "Le combat de Carnaval et de Carême de P. Bruegel (1559)," *Annales* 27(1972), 313–45.

[76] The German name for the days preceding Lent is not as explicit in its reference to "flesh" as are the Latin, Italian, Spanish, French, and English names, but the activities I explore for their definition of "flesh" belong to *Fastnacht* as it was celebrated in German-speaking Europe. In the following discussion, I have tried to maintain the distinction between flesh in its simple reference and the "flesh" of Carnival, with its multiple levels of meaning and its mystical dimension, by enclosing the latter in quotation marks.

wantonness, a chaos. Carnival, a celebration of the world of "flesh," was the laity's holiday.

The separation of Carnival and Lent had been breached twice in Basel: with the "Butterbriefe," letters releasing laymen or -women during Lent to eat meat that could be purchased from the bishop; and on Palm Sunday, 1522, when some evangelicals ate sausage. Each of these breaches signified. In the first, the laity protested so strenuously that the letters were withdrawn. The second was a familiar signal of reformation. Evangelicals chose to break the Lenten fast in Wittemberg, in Zurich, in Strasbourg, again and again, because that breach had such powerful reverberations. It was important that they had eaten "flesh" during Lent: They had broken not only a traditional taboo, but transgressed a significant border that traditional Christianity maintained. In medieval Christianity, "flesh" belonged not to Lent, but to Carnival.

Ash Wednesday, the threshold between Carnival and Lent, was that moment when the clarity of the opposition between the two began to dissolve. On that day, many places, apparently also Basel, traditionally concluded Carnival with fires.[77] These blazed the death of Carnival and all it signified; their ashes marked the beginning of Lent and, as the peasants would know, of growth. Fires were a particularly complex signal for the beginning of Lent: They transformed matter into heat, objects into an essential need in Basel in February. Carnival fires may also have signaled a sacrifice, the destruction of something – sometimes an effigy, other times beloved objects – to honor God. Ryff called "Carnival fires" those fires that consumed all that was left of the objects in the churches, that concluded the great iconoclasm in Basel. He linked, thereby, the pyric conclusion of iconoclasm to Carnival elsewhere. Ashes marked the point of contact between Carnival and Lent, turning the "flesh" of Carnival, its matter, into the ashes of Lent. Perhaps we may now connect the objects that the fires consumed in Basel on February 10 with the "flesh" of Carnival.

---

[77] Spamer, *Deutsche Fastnachtsbräuche*, pp. 64–6.

Images and the "flesh"

The records from the decade preceding the iconoclasm of 1529 present a marked pattern of the exchange of property: between lay donors and religious beneficiaries, between chapters and their canons, and, increasingly, between clergy leaving their orders and the town council. This exchange concerns us here only insofar as it suggests something of how people were perceiving the objects in the churches, those thousands of pious gifts donated to the churches to honor them, bestowed upon the religious who served those churches to ensure that masses would be said, that monks and canons would be present for eternity to remember the dead in their celebration of the Eucharist – the monstrances, the reliquaries, the crucifixes, the land, the rents, tithes, monies. As the inventory of the Cathedral chapter's and St. Peter's chapter's "precious objects, treasures, and ornaments" indicates, the religious had come to possess all those gifts.[78] Some twelve monstrances, eight other reliquaries; the heads of St. Panthal (the first bishop of Basel), St. Ursula, and St. Eustace; six crucifixes (not including two smaller crosses), silver pictures of St. John the Baptist and St. Christopher, three chalices, and dozens of other liturgical objects were listed as belonging to the chapters of the Cathedral and St. Peter's.[79] Included as well were the relics those monstrances and reliquaries housed: of Peter, Paul, Andrew, Lawrence, Nicholas, Christopher, Apollonius, Benedict, Catherine, and Dorothy; of Henry II, the Cathedral's beloved founder; the milk of the Virgin; the finger of St. John the Baptist; the arms of Saints Philip, Veltnis, and Walpert, as well as relics unspecified in the inventory of the two chapters.

This situation, which had become normative by the sixteenth century, intimated a troubling shift in the perception of the objects in the churches. The man-made objects therein had been given – through endowments or outright as gifts – with the intention to link laypersons to the religious concretely, in the cur-

---

[78] ". . . propst und cappittel der Hohenn styfft Basel nachbeschriben derselben styfft cleynat, gezierdt und ornatten," ABR I, 462.
[79] Ibid.

rency of the secular world.[80] Material and artificial, physical
and man-made, the monstrances, reliquaries, altarpieces, crosses,
crucifixes, statues, chalices, patens, and candles were gifts, most
made or purchased by laypersons.[81] "Property," the possession of
physical objects and their enjoyment, represented a particular
conception of the relation between an object and persons. "Property" did not link person to person in a relation of obligation and
reverence, but person to object, to the physical world, to the world
of the flesh. "Gifts" indicated a very different relationship, linking persons through objects that were not themselves the focus.

Something had happened to the objects in the churches: They
had become property that could be sold, stolen, exchanged, and,
finally, inventoried. This meaning was amplified in the case of
the objects in the Cathedral: The chapter did not acknowledge
that those objects linked them to the community, but claimed
them as their own as they sought to maintain a rigid distance between themselves and the people of Basel. In becoming something that the religious could "own" – in that increasingly precise sense that sixteenth-century merchants and artisans would
know – the gifts in the churches had lost something, their embodiment of connections between laypersons and the clergy.

There were other ways to conceive of the relationship of the
objects to their churches, and to the parishioners who honored
those objects for so long; there were other ways to conceive of
"flesh." Here, too, Carnival can be our guide, as we delve into a
deeper level of its meaning. Carnival not only had a place within the rhythms of the Christian year, but also belonged to that
year, to the cadences of Christ's greater and lesser presence
among men as Himself human. It was right that the festival celebrating "flesh" should occur after Epiphany, after Theophany,
the appearance of God before humankind. It belonged in the

---

[80] On gift giving, the classic study of gift exchange and its significance in different
cultures remains Marcel Mauss, *The Gift*, trans. Ian Cunnison (New York, 1967).
More recently, Annette B. Weiner has posed a more complex interplay in gift giving, which more closely approximates what I believe was the perception regarding
the objects in the churches, in *Inalienable Possessions: The Paradox of Keeping-While-
Giving* (Berkeley, 1992). See also Mary Douglas & Baron Isherwood, *The World of
Goods: Toward an Anthropology of Consumption* (New York, 1978).

[81] As opposed to the production of manuscripts, which was, as far as we know, almost
exclusively the domain of the religious.

cycle of Christ's embodiment: from Incarnation, to Epiphany, to Carnival, to Lent, to Easter, at once Death and Resurrection. The cadences of Christ's presence on earth had been so powerful that another feast, Corpus Christi, came to be celebrated in Basel since the fourteenth century, in the long months between Easter and Advent.[82]

In their contrasts, these two festivals, Carnival and Corpus Christi, suggest something of the cadences laypersons accorded to Christ's "presence" on earth. Carnival was much older than Corpus Christi, muddier in its origins, more multifaceted in its connotations, more multivocal in its resonances. Its connection to Christ's embodiment was less direct, and also less defined. Corpus Christi occurred during the Pentecost season, when Christ would have returned from His Resurrection to walk among the living, to breathe the spirit into His apostles. Carnival held a different place in the cycle of Christ's embodiment: It occurred before Lent, those days commemorating Christ's days in the desert, the asceticism of Christianity. It was located on the opposite side of Lent from Easter.

Carnival may have had Lent as its reference point, but it was implicitly linked to (and its date ultimately determined by) Easter,[83] that anchor for both Lent and Carnival. On Easter, laypersons would break their fast, would feast. During Carnival, they feasted on the flesh of animals; on Easter they feasted on the body of Christ by partaking of the Eucharist. On that day, they would confront again the multiplicity of meanings that "flesh" had for Christians: The body of Christ bore no sensible relation to the bodies of animals, His flesh and theirs differed. Carnival thus underlined not only the austerities of Lent, but also the mystery of Easter: It made evident the secular meaning of "flesh" and, by contrast, made distinct and unique the "flesh" of Christ. Easter was the resolution of the tension between Lent and Carnival. On Easter, both spirit and body were celebrated, God and

---

[82] On the feast of Corpus Christi, see the work most recently of Miri Rubin, *Corpus Christi: The Eucharist in Late Medieval Culture* (Cambridge, 1991), who attributes the origins of Corpus Christi to Beguines in Liège (chap. 3).

[83] A number of plays connected the two feasts explicitly. See Michael, *Das deutsche Drama des Mittelaters*, pp. 182–4.

man reconciled; spirit was embodied, and the body was resurrected.

On Easter, the altarpieces would be opened, the images uncovered. People would see images they could last have seen during Carnival. They would see again how God had taken on human form, become man through His birth into a human family. They would see in the Passion cycles how God had come to suffer physically and to die as man, and they would meditate on the mystery of the Resurrection. Images participated in Easter's representation of the mystery of Christ, and as they were covered, then opened, their participation was emphasized. Within the cycle of Christ's embodiment, images held a delicate balance. The matter of which they were made belonged to the "flesh" of the world of Carnival; what they represented, Christ, belonged to the "flesh" of Easter. Open in Carnival, the images may have been its kind of "flesh"; open in Easter, they revealed the mystery of Christ.

In Basel, iconoclasm itself obliquely linked Carnival and Easter. On Good Friday, April 10, 1528, a handful of iconoclasts, most of whom belonged to the Spinnwetter guild, had attacked the images in St. Martin's church; on Easter Monday, April 13, the same group had attacked the images in the Augustinian church.[84] They had attacked the images not on Easter itself, but on Good Friday, when Christ's body died on the cross, and on Easter Monday, after the miracle of the Resurrection. In 1529, the iconoclasts, who had been fasting since Sunday night, according to Ryff, attacked the images on the Tuesday that other towns marked as Carnival. None of the incidents occurred on Easter or Carnival in Basel, yet they touched upon them, played against them, invoked them and their dialogue on the nature of flesh. What does the time of iconoclasm tell us about its meaning?

First, the iconoclasts called attention to the nature of the images' "flesh." In both 1528 and 1529, the iconoclasts attacked neither single representations of specific saints or Christ, nor images in a particular location, images over altars. In 1528, they

[84] ABR III, 86, 115.

attacked images in churches that were moving toward reform – one, St. Martin's, under the leadership of Oecolampad. In 1529, the iconoclasts attacked all the images in those churches that had yet to reform – objects that had been inventoried by clergy who had refused to accede to the desires of the great majority of lay-persons in Basel to become evangelical and cleansed – and they began with that church whose clergy had been most aggressive in the assertion of its distance from the laity. Many if not all the objects had once been gifts linking the religious to the laity, gifts whose original purpose was to ensure that the religious served the spiritual needs of laypersons: said masses for them, baptized their children, buried their dead, and offered them communion with the body of Christ. As something the religious could list on their inventories of property, the images could not represent the "flesh" of Christ: That flesh had no owner other than God.

The Basel iconoclasts of 1529 attacked the objects in the churches while Strasbourg was still celebrating Carnival. They smashed them into their component matter, returned them to their original substances: wood, stone, ivory, gold, silver, precious stones. They turned them over first to the poor, as firewood and clothing, substances that served physical human needs, as did the feasts of Carnival. Then they surrendered them to fires like those that concluded Carnival, transforming them into smoke and ashes, the beginning of Lent.

As Carnival did for the human body, the iconoclasts trans-formed the perception of the images' "flesh." Themselves fast-ing, they smashed the "idols" into matter, the stuff of which mundane things were made. They demolished them all, never distinguishing among them, never according the images indi-viduality, differing content or meaning. The evangelicals did not see in the churches all the many objects with their multiple functions and meanings, their differing locations within the spaces of the churches and within the organization of sacred space; they saw *götzen* (idols) and *bilder* (images). For the icono-clasts, the objects were all essentially the same. When others en-tered the churches on Wednesday morning, their vision of the images was permanently changed: Before their eyes were the severed arms and heads of reliquaries and statues, the shattered panels of retables, the scraped and dented precious metals, the stones that had decorated them knocked out. Witnesses saw no more "images," but fragments whose form no longer concealed the matter of which they were made.

The Basel iconoclasts, moreover, reclaimed the objects in the churches for laypersons. As contemporaries decried, they took from the clergy their valuable property and destroyed its religious value. The iconoclasts smashed the physical links between clergy and laity, the hundreds of pious gifts that had knit the two together over centuries in mutual obligation and service. They redeemed the objects' matter first for the lay poor's use, then to be consumed in Carnival fires. They reclaimed them in terms of their physicality: their substance, their ownership, and their use. They also asserted laypersons' right to determine the religious meaning of those objects in the churches. In smashing them all into their component substances, the iconoclasts destroyed the means by which the images conveyed meaning: their form, the representations they bore, the particular interplay of color and line that intact the objects had presented. The iconoclasts denied representation to the images, and in smashing them ensured that they would represent nothing to any other eyes.

For most chroniclers and modern historians, the iconoclasm of February 9, 1529, was the catalyst for reformation in Basel. On April 1, the town council issued its Reform Ordinance, and the practice of religion in Basel was reorganized according to the evangelical principles Oecolampad had delineated.[85] The iconoclasm of February 9 seems to have had another, more curious consequence as well: Basel is one of the few cities that celebrates a Protestant Carnival or Fasnacht.[86] Elsewhere, "Reformation" entailed the elimination of Carnival, the pagan festivities Rome had condoned for so long. In Basel, the opposite is true: "Reformation" engendered a second Carnival. Protestant Carnival did not replace the older one, but coexists with it, "Protestant" or new alongside "Catholic" or old Carnival. Catholics celebrate on those

---

[85] Ibid., 473.
[86] Peter Weidkuhn, "Ideologiekritisches zum Streit zwischen Fastnacht und Protestantismus in Basel," *Schweizerisches Archiv für Volkskunde* 65(1969): 36–74.

days designated by Rome to precede Ash Wednesday: the "new" date, set by Gregory in 1091, before Invocavit Sunday. Protestants, however, celebrate on the older date of Carnival in Basel, a week later, on the Monday and Tuesday after Ash Wednesday. Protestant Carnival possesses a moving dignity, as pipers and drummers move slowly and rhythmically through the old town, invoking that military Carnival of the fourteenth century, leading their lighted lanterns along narrow *Gassen* and across *Höfen,* and marking the "traditional" date of Carnival with sober, even melancholy beauty.

There is little religious to Basel Fasnacht: Its date is set by the Catholic calendar and its determination of Lent – but, in repudiation of that determination, a week later; and some of its "lanterns," illuminated wagons pulled during the Morgestraich, bear antipapal motifs. Perhaps the clearest echo of that earlier "Carnival" comes at the end of the first day of Protestant Carnival, Monday, when the so-called lanterns – the product of year-long efforts on the part of artists, designers, and painters – are parked in the plaza before the Münster, their exuberant and colorful forms contrasting with its austere exterior, not in the church, but in that public space before it. Yet the modern Fasnacht resists easy interpretation, its meaning by no means transparent, its masks and costumes at once garish and stunning in their artistic mastery, its decorum all the more elusive for its lack of formality: Here is no "inversion," nor jubilant "popular culture," but movement and color, the fantasy of pipes and drums and masks of infinite variety, and the dramatic cohesion of perhaps twenty thousand people in the old town for one day and one night. In some ways, the modern Fasnacht stands in stark contrast to that earlier Carnival, its propriety opposite the earlier violence, its music contrasting with the sounds of smashing hammers and burning wood, its elegance and artistry opposite the anarchy and destruction of that earlier "festival." Yet it serves to remind us both of the complexity of that earlier Carnival, its multiple layers of meaning, and of that time the evangelical laity set for themselves to define the world of the flesh and its connection to the spirit.

Conclusion

For the iconoclasts, all the objects in the churches – candlesticks, monstrances, lamps, chalices, rood screens, as well as the carved retables, panel paintings, freestanding sculpture, and crucifixes – were "idols." It was not sufficient to leave the images in the churches alone; indeed, they would disobey their magistrates' express orders to do so. Why did the images have to go? Why were iconoclasts willing to risk fines, imprisonment, even death to rid the churches of all the "images"? Each of the case studies offers a partial answer to that question; together they help to explain why so many Europeans, from so many different communities, over a half-century's time would risk so much to cleanse their churches of the material culture of traditional Christianity.

In Zurich, iconoclasts called attention to the ways in which the images consumed: Monies spent on lighting and the maintenance of images could be used to feed human beings; wood, frozen in the false form of a crucifix, could be used to warm the poor. In Zurich, the "idols" were voracious, stealing food and heat from needy human beings, the "true images of God." Of all the iconoclasts we have studied, those in Zurich most fully delineated a Christian economy, in which the material culture of Christianity was to be circulated for the maintenance of the human community and not the stone and wooden, the inanimate and artificial, cold and fixed images in the churches.

In Strasbourg, iconoclasts called attention to the location of images within the geography of worship – that geography in which the laity had a place. Most iconoclastic acts in Strasbourg linked images and altars, attacking both and signaling the essential connection among all the objects in proximity to the ritual – chalices, patens, monstrances, candlesticks, representations of Christ, Mary, the Apostles, and Saints, but especially altars, altarpieces, and crucifixes – and the mass. The acts underlined that images and altars together were the setting for a ritual that evangelical preachers and citizens had labeled "idolatrous" and "blasphemous." One kind of Christian material culture, images, was not severable from the other, altars: Together they provided the setting for, and thereby gave visual meaning to, the ritual at the center of a Christianity that had gone profoundly wrong. They were the means by which the "sacrifice" of the medieval mass was enacted, the place, the visual referents, the visual clues and interpretations for a human reenactment of – and therefore blasphemy against – God's single, all-encompassing, and eternal sacrifice.

In Basel, the iconoclasm of February 9, 1529, calls our attention to a particular configuration of the Christian community, with its fundamental division of lay from clerical, and its attribution to the clergy – a group to which the laity had less and less access – of a life of piety, a piety inhering in the entire lived experiences of the clergy. If we follow the timing the chronicler Ryff attributed to their acts, those acts suggested as well that images helped to anchor that division of humanity between the "spiritual" clergy and the "carnal" laity, a division that denied the status of laity the same quality of piety it attributed to clergy, just as it denied to physical existence the potential for piety, which could inhere only in a life of ascetic denial of physicality.

The iconoclasts' acts indicated the multiplicity of relations – between man and God, between clergy and laity, between the world of the spirit and the world of the body – that images embodied. The focus of their attacks, their timing, and their locations also signal the place of the images in the laity's experience of Christian theology. These acts pointed to particular locations for the images within traditional practices of Christianity, intimating connections between the images and the theology that underlay those practices.

191

With their acts, iconoclasts signaled something of their understanding of "representation" and "presence," entering with their acts into dialogue with medieval theologians' discussions of the relation between images and divinity. For the iconoclasts, what was "present" through all the images in the churches made them "idols." With their acts, they invoked ways in which Christ was indeed present: in the practice of Christian brotherly love, in the Eucharist, in the cadences of the Christian year, and in the proper attitude of secular and ecclesiastical leaders to their congregations. With their acts, the iconoclasts signaled exactly how Christ was absent from the images, and made those absences perceptible for others. When framed in the ethics of Christian brotherly love, the images' voracity became manifest. When connected to altars, images' participation in the enactment and definition of the mass became explicit. When iconoclastic acts pointed, albeit obliquely, to the objects' participation in the human culture of Christianity, with its separation of clergy from their congregations, the images' role in that division of the Christian community became perceptible. As contemporaries recognized, those acts also destroyed material links between the laity and the clergy, whose pastoral obligations the images had not secured. Iconoclasts' acts framed the images in those places Christ was most "present" among humanity: the practice of Christian brotherly love toward one's "neighbor," the communion of the Eucharist, and the pastoral activity of the priesthood. In so doing, they highlighted how images – as they currently were understood, as they currently functioned, as they currently represented – were in conflict with, and even in opposition to, Christ's presence in the world.

The images were no longer a place where God's "presence" might be evoked. They had come to embody so much: that place where the wealth of Christians was frozen, kept from needy human beings; the material links between laity and clergy. They had come to participate in the ritual, the mass, that represented an understanding of the moment of union between laity and God, which had become "blasphemous" in the eyes of pious laity. All the objects in the churches had come to embody so much that opposed God's presence in the world. For the iconoclasts, objects that drew human charity from the poor, embodied an unrequited gift giving, or participated in the division of the body of Christians at their moment of communion could not be places where Christ was "present," even if they bore his face, his form, representations of his person, as in the case of crucifixes. Moreover, the pious must no longer address any image in the hope of addressing God or even Christ. It was impossible that either Father or Son might be reached through any object in which what God was – charity, mercy, love – was so perceptibly absent.

All the objects in the churches were "idols," but not because they represented God. For iconoclasts, the issue was not the biblical injunctions against representing God that Karlstadt, Haetzer, and even Luther would invoke. It was not what the idols depicted: Even oil lamps were "idols." The issue was at the very center of Christian life: Where was God or Christ "present"? For the iconoclasts, the answer was compelling: God and Christ could not be "present" through the images in the churches.

> ... and in this year [1529] on Ash Wednesday those of Basel have broken up their holy things [*heiligen*] and all the images in the churches and had them dragged onto the Kornmarkt, the same they had their hangman burn, as though they had been public [*offentliche*] heretics. (*Sébald Bühelers Strassburger Chronik*)[1]

The acts of the iconoclasts enabled others to discern what was so very wrong with all the objects in the churches. They framed the images in terms that made it clear why it was imperative to destroy them in the churches. The images were not adiaphora. They were not even "the books of the illiterate," a notion that enabled Luther ultimately to keep them. "Images," the iconoclasts' acts pointed out, encompassed far more than narrative art, those pictures the pious could imitate, or even representative art, those portraits of Mary, the apostles, and the saints. "Images" were that means by which a religion that was voracious, divisive – not merely un-Christian but anti-Christian – was itself made present in the lives of ordinary people.

---

[1] *Fragments des Anciennes Chroniques d'Alsace*, vol. I, ed. L. Dacheux (Strasbourg, 1887), p. 78.

The violence of iconoclastic acts and their dramatic restructuring of the spaces of the churches may have also taught people to see in ways they had not before. It seems likely that iconoclastic violence enabled those preachers like Zwingli, who were too nearsighted to notice, or like Bucer, who were more concerned with other dimensions of reform, to see more clearly the images and their place within Christianity as it was practiced by ordinary people. In the wake of iconoclasm, the images' physicality, their materiality, was explicit. As Lorentz Meyger showed, images were subject to decay and deterioration. As the Basel iconoclasts demonstrated, form and matter were severable. Once the forms of images were destroyed, their content and their "representing" were no longer perceptible. That violence – the smashing, shattering, breaking, pulling and pushing down, and the burning – removed the images from their familiar matrices of association, abstracted them from the networks of connections, both human and ideal, that had given them their "place." It transformed the "images" from a place of complex meaning and interaction into rubble, wood for the poor, matériel for sale, cobblestones.

What did the iconoclasts create? Before iconoclasm, Zwingli would not have known the "beauty" of a whitewashed wall in a church: No Christian church presented such an "image" to the eyes of its congregation. The iconoclasts made "visible" a new aesthetic: the whitewashed wall, the church interior in which the walls themselves were visible, and not the panels, sculptures, tabernacles, and candlesticks. If we follow the communication of the Basel iconoclasts, these white walls did not represent a transcendent ascetic, but a realignment of the relation between the world of the flesh and the world of the spirit, a realignment that rejected the asceticism of the traditional religious as false and accepted the world of the laity as itself religious. As Carnival celebrated the world of the flesh, obliquely, it insisted upon Christ's embodiment and all that that meant. In Zurich, other "images," the poor, were to be the true images of God: They best captured what an "image of God" was to be.[2]

---

[2] See my *Always Among Us: Images of the Poor in Reformation Zurich* (Cambridge, 1990).

Also, the space of the churches itself was redrawn. Those markers by which sacred and profane, religious and lay, were distinguished – the altars, screens, standing crucifixes, and altarpieces – had been destroyed. The space of the churches itself was open again to definition. Most Protestants, Lutheran, Reformed, and Calvinist, reconceived the space in the churches as a single, communal place.[3] The pulpit was recognized as a place of central importance within the church, and in some Protestant traditions would become increasingly elaborate artistically, but it would not be a location of sanctity. For most Protestants, churches no longer offered a geography of holiness, but a place in which the faithful gathered to worship.

Iconoclasts called attention to the ways the objects in the churches enabled a certain form and manner of worship and participated in a particular conception of divinity: Images were an essential medium of medieval Roman theology. With their acts, the iconoclasts destroyed that medium: In all the churches where the "idols" were smashed, the images gone, the visual dimension of traditional Christianity was silenced in the whitewashed walls. The iconoclasts' acts altered the environment in which they worshiped. They had initiated the removal of the physical setting of the mass, the visual referents of one theology, and the medium for one way of conceiving of an incarnate God. In so doing, they made traditional worship impossible: They altered how others would worship, how they would approach God. Worship was radically re-formed, its location, its physical anchors, its visual referents, its material expression irretrievably altered; and for the iconoclasts, how one worshiped could not be separated from what one worshiped. They also removed those means by which ordinary people may have meditated on the Incarnation. In the churches, the white walls signaled a different conception of "presence."

At stake, for the iconoclasts, in Reformation was "presence": How was God to be present in the world? For the iconoclasts, that presence centered not upon the question of two natures that theologians had discussed since the beginning of Christianity. For

---

[3] Anglicans would keep Catholic divisions of the space of the churches and reinstitute rood screens and other physical signals of those divisions.

them, the theological question of "presence" centered upon relations, between God and human beings and between one human
being and another. In each town, iconoclasts played upon the relation of "flesh" and "spirit" so central to Christianity – in Basel,
perhaps most explicitly, but in Zurich and in Strasbourg as well.
In each place, iconoclasts' acts pointed toward where Christ
might be "present": not in things, but in acts of brotherly love,
gestures, relations, behavior, and in the culture that would structure the lives of evangelical Christians – the Reformed communion service, the cadences of the Christian year, and preaching.

With their acts, iconoclasts had also suggested what they believed worship to be. In Zurich, the iconoclasts turned the objects
in the churches into food for the poor, transformed church art into substances that could warm human beings or enable them to
purchase food. In Strasbourg, the iconoclasts removed the images
by which the mass had been envisioned; without the visual referents for the words of the mass, those words lost essential associations of meaning, the most elusive part of their content. Without
images and altar, the mass had no place, no material context. The
Eucharist was freed both from "idolatrous" visual referents and
associations, and from its anchoring in a particular physical context – it could be enacted anywhere Christians gathered. In Basel, the iconoclasts destroyed the material links between the laity
and the clergy. They smashed the concrete expression of lay gift
giving, which had supported the clergy, who had laid claim for
centuries to a greater proximity to Christ than any layperson
could enjoy. In so doing, they smashed a particular configuration of the relations between "lay" and "clerical": For the Basel
iconoclasts, the laity were no longer to be second to the clergy in
piety or in proximity to Christ. This, then, was their vision of true
Christianity.

Evangelical iconoclasts participated, through their own "language" of acts, in "Reformation." In choosing to destroy those
images, the iconoclasts suggested something about how they
conceived the role of ordinary people in the formation and practice of Christianity. With their acts iconoclasts spoke to theologians and other members of their communities, emphasizing

why it was that all the "images" were "idols": their participation both in false practices and, more important, in a wrong theology. "Images" were not merely implements in false worship; they were a central medium of ordinary people's theology. They were "idols" because they participated in a wrong understanding of the nature of divine "presence" in the world. In destroying the "idols," iconoclasm contributed to a reconceptualization of Christianity's presence in the world. With their acts, iconoclasts also helped to create a space in which God's presence was aural – the Word – and expressed in the liturgy and in the relations of the faithful to one another. They created a place in which they might worship God as *they* conceived Him.

Finally, the acts of the iconoclasts teach us something about that larger abstraction, "culture." Most visibly, they underline its fragility, its openness to destruction. Images, texts, cultural objects disappear; the cleansed churches offer few clues to the presences they formerly contained, their visual dimension so altered that the language of images that formerly adorned their walls, their chapels, their columns, their clerestories, their naves, choirs, apses, and ambulatories, is no longer discernible. The acts of the iconoclasts also underline culture's dynamism. They belong to that culture, are fully intelligible only within it, and call attention to dimensions of that culture that are otherwise less visible. In destroying, the acts of the iconoclasts have told us something about late medieval Christian culture that we might otherwise not know – in this way, they are a constituent element of that culture. In the end, their legacy might be said to extend into our modern world. In decrying the loss of so much beauty and so many objects of aesthetic and material wealth, art historians partake of a view of images Reformation iconoclasts made possible: For those art historians, images have lost any higher reason that would justify their destruction – they have lost their numinous power – and become fully part of the material world and its values.

Iconoclasts risked a great deal to "honor God." Uly Anders lost his life. Claus Hottinger was banished, subsequently captured by the Lucerne government, still entirely loyal to Rome, and executed for various blasphemies, including iconoclasm. Others suffered imprisonment and fines. The Basel iconoclasts were unwilling to identify themselves, even with a promise of pardon, and the chronicler who was sympathetic to them was careful not to identify any of them by name. These were not small gestures of resistance, moments of drunken rebellion. They were acts of piety, illegal at first, destructive of objects others considered their "property," far more raucous than saints' asceticism. They were no less "Christian," however, and more tangibly and immediately concerned with "the betterment of one's neighbor."

Index

Index

Calvin, John, 2, 21, 154
Campenhausen, Hans Freiherr von, 7
candles
  in Strasbourg, 112, 119–20
  in Zurich, 70
Capito, Wolfgang, 109, 131
  and removal of images, 130
  and Young St. Peter's church, 114
Carnival, 71–2, 114, 173–4
  and Christian year, 180–2
  and Corpus Christi, 185
  and Easter, 185–6
  feasting, 178, 181
  fires, 172–3, 182, 187, 188
  "flesh" defined by, 181–2, 184–8, 194
  lay religious festival, 176–80, 181
  and Lent, 180–2
  literature on, 174n59–61, 176n62, 177n65
  plays, 177–8
  processions, 179
  and Reformation, 188
  social fluidity, 177–9
  timing, 174–5, 188–9
Cathedral, Basel, 151–2, 174
  bishop and Carnival, 175
  bishopric, 155–7, 161–3
  building, 161
  chapter, 157–9, 160, 161–3, 173
  inventory, 183, 184
  masses in, 166
  preachers, 159–60
  site of iconoclasm, 149, 169–70, 172–3
Cathedral of Our Lady, Strasbourg, 132
  benefices, 145
  building, 107
  and candles, 119–20
  crucifix, 135
  German mass, 114, 140
  interior reconstructed, 134–9

Mary, cult of, 121–3, 138
  organ, 136
  processions to and from, 112, 134
  site of iconoclasm, 115–16, 121–4, 128, 131, 140, 143
  walls whitewashed, 128
  see also cross, gilded great
Charlemagne as donor, 56, 123
Chrisman, Miriam, 104n3, 117, 120–1
Christian, William, 6
Christian epistemology, 36–41
Christoph von Utenheim, Bishop of Basel (1502–27), 161–2
Corpus Christi, 20, 185
  processions, 19
cross, 50, 78
  gilded great (of Strasbourg Cathedral), 123, 135, 137, 138
  object of verbal or physical attack, 113, 118, 123, 138
Crouzet, Denis, 11n30
crucifix, 39, 45, 49, 50, 95–6, 135, 146, 192
  Francis of Assisi's devotion to, 38–9
  object of iconoclasm, 72–80, 85, 150, 190, 191
  replacing an image, 121
  "cult of the image," 51

Dachßman, Hans, iconoclast, 90–2
Dannenföls, Meinolf, one of "Six Burghers," 121
Davis, Natalie Zemon, 1n1, 11n30
Dominican convents, Strasbourg, 107
Duffy, Eamon, 17
dulia (proskinesis), 42–4, 48
Durandus, 39, 45

Eckstein, Utz, Zurich pamphleteer
  Concilium, 66n38
  Dialogus, 78n78